# STUDIES IN THE FORM OF SIRACH 44–50

SOCIETY
OF BIBLICAL
LITERATURE

DISSERTATION SERIES
J. J. M. Roberts, Old Testament Editor
Charles Talbert, New Testament Editor

Number 75
STUDIES IN THE FORM OF SIRACH 44-50
by
Thomas R. Lee

Thomas R. Lee

# STUDIES IN THE FORM
# OF SIRACH 44-50

Scholars Press
Atlanta, Georgia

# STUDIES IN THE FORM OF SIRACH 44–50

## Thomas R. Lee

Ph.D., 1979
University of California, Berkeley

Advisor:
Victor R. Gold

BS
17 65.2
.L44
1986
C.2

© 1986
Society of Biblical Literature

**Library of Congress Cataloging-in-Publication Data**

Lee, Thomas R.
   Studies in the form of Sirach 44–50.

   (Dissertation series / Society of Biblical Literature ;
no. 75)
   Originally presented as the author's thesis (Ph.D.)—
University of California, Berkeley, 1979
   Bibliography: p.
   1. Bible. O.T. Apocrypha. Ecclesiasticus XLIV–L—
Criticism, Form. I. Title. II. Series: Dissertation
series (Society of Biblical Literature) ; no. 75.
BS1765.2.L44   1986      229'.4066      85-26179

ISBN 0-89130-834-2
ISBN 0-89130-835-0 (pbk.)

Printed in the United States of America
on acid-free paper

To Bonnie,
Brigitta,
and
Brittany

# Contents

vii

# Acknowledgments

In the great hymn that is the subject of this study, Jesus Sirach sings the praise of Israel's heroes—from Adam to Simon II. On a far more modest scale I have my own praises to offer to those persons who, during the eleven years between prospectus and publication, have helped me with this examination of Sirach 44-50.

My roll call of persons to be acknowledged begins with Victor R. Gold—teacher, advisor and friend—who first introduced me to the Cairo Geniza and Masada Ben Sira materials and who suggested the topic of this study. A word of appreciation goes as well to the remaining members of my committee at the Graduate Theological Union and University of California—William Fulco, David Winston, John Dillon and Baruch Bokser—for their careful reading of the dissertation and their helpful comments. This study would not have arrived at the point of publication if it were not for the efforts of several people. My thanks go to Robert R. Wilson, editor of the SBL Dissertation Series at the time my manuscript was accepted for publication, and to the staff of the Scriptorium in Denver, not only for their word processing skills, but for their patience with me during the proof-reading process. A special thank you goes to Paula McNutt, a former student of mine at the University of Montana and now a doctoral candidate at Vanderbilt University, for editing the manuscript according to SBL canons, and to Karen Sitte, secretary at our campus ministry center, for preparing the index.

Finally, there are those persons who have offered their encouragement, both while I was writing and while I was arranging for publication. James W. Flanagan, chair of the Religious Studies Department at the University of Montana, a good friend and colleague, has kept after me to bring this project to completion. And as Ben Sira saved his greatest praise for the end—his praise of Simon in chapter 50—I close by thanking most of all my wife, Bonnie, and daughters—Brigitta and Brittany—for their

encouragement, patience, love, and support over these eleven years. It is
to them that I dedicate this volume.

Thomas R. Lee
Missoula, Montana
May 1986

# Abbreviations

| | |
|---|---|
| AcOr | *Acta Orientalia* |
| AnBib | Analecta Biblica |
| APOT | R. H. Charles, ed., *Apocrypha and Pseudepigrapha of the Old Testament* |
| ASNU | Acta seminarii neotestamentici upsaliensis |
| BASOR | *Bulletin of the American Schools of Oriental Research* |
| Bib | *Biblica* |
| BKAT | Biblischer Kommentar: Altes Testament |
| BVC | *Bible et vie chrétienne* |
| BZAW | *Beihefte zur Zeitschrift für die alttestamentliche Wissenschaft* |
| CBQ | *Catholic Biblical Quarterly* |
| ClassPhil | *Classical Philology* |
| DBSup | *Dictionnaire de la Bible, Supplément* |
| DTC | *Dictionnaire de theologie catholique* |
| FHG | Karl Müller, ed., *Fragmenta Historicorum Graecorum* |
| FrGH | Felix Jacoby, ed., *Die Fragmente der griechischen Historiker* |
| HAT | *Handbuch zum Alten Testament* |
| HR | *History of Religions* |
| HSM | Harvard Semitic Monographs |
| HTR | *Harvard Theological Review* |
| HUCA | *Hebrew Union College Annual* |
| IDB | *Interpreter's Dictionary of the Bible* |
| Int | *Interpretation* |
| JBL | *Journal of Biblical Literature* |
| JJS | *The Journal of Jewish Studies* |
| JNES | *Journal of Near Eastern Studies* |

| | |
|---|---|
| *JQR* | *Jewish Quarterly Review* |
| *JSJ* | *Journal for the Study of Judaism* |
| *JTS* | *Journal of Theological Studies* |
| *KAI* | H. Donner and W. Röllig, eds., *Kanaanäische und aramäische Inschriften* |
| *NTS* | *New Testament Studies* |
| OBO | Orbis Biblicus et Orientalis |
| *OTS* | *Oudtestamentische Studiën* |
| *PEQ* | *Palestine Exploration Quarterly* |
| *PW* | Pauly-Wissowa, *Realencyclopädie der classischen Altertumswissenschaft* |
| *RAC* | *Reallexicon für Antike und Christentum* |
| *RevQ* | *Revue de Qumran* |
| *RSR* | *Recherche de science religieuse* |
| SBLDS | SBL Dissertation Series |
| *SPB* | *Studia postbiblica* |
| *TLZ* | *Theologische Literaturzeitung* |
| *TZ* | *Theologische Zeitschrift* |
| *VT* | *Vetus Testamentum* |
| *VTSup* | *Vetus Testamentum, Supplements* |
| *ZAW* | *Zeitschrift für die alttestamentliche Wissenschaft* |
| *ZTK* | *Zeitschrift für Theologie und Kirche* |

# Part I
# Toward Defining the Form
# of Sirach 44-50

## A. INTRODUCTION

As Jesus Sirach chose to share "instruction in understanding and knowledge" (Sir 50:27) in the book that bears his name, he employed a variety of
*Gattungen* beside that of the proverb. Of the other literary types represented in Sirach, the "hymn," as identified by Baumgartner, plays a significant role.[1] Among the pericopes cited as representing this genre are: Sir
1:1-10 and 24:1-34, hymns in which Wisdom is personified and praised;
39:12-35 and 42:15-43:33, hymns in praise of God the creator; and the
great "hymn in praise of the fathers," 44:1-50:24. The lattermost, however, Baumgartner noted "kann nur mit starker Einschränkung als Hymn
gelten, da hier nicht wie im kultischen Hymnus Gott, sondern Menschen
gepriesen werden."[2]

Others, too, have recognized that with chaps. 44-50 we are dealing
with something new and different in Hebrew literature. E. Jacob,[3] H. L.
Jansen,[4] and G. von Rad[5] are among those who view it as differing from
other hymns or hymnic presentations of Israel's past. Although various
form critical suggestions have been made to account for the unique

---

[1] W. Baumgartner, "Die literarischen Gattungen in der Weisheit des
Jesus Sirach," *ZAW* (1914) 169-92.

[2] Ibid., 173.

[3] E. Jacob, "L'histoire d'Israel vue par Ben Sira," *Mélanges Bibliques
rédigés en l'honneur de André Robert* (Travaux de l'institut catholique de
Paris, 4; Paris: Bloud and Gay, 1957), 290.

[4] H. L. Jansen, *Die spätjüdische Psalmendichtung: Ihr Entstehungskreis
und ihr 'Sitz im Leben'* (SNAVO II: Hist.-filos. Klasse, no. 3; Oslo: I kommisjon hos Jacob Dybwad, 1937) 71, 108.

[5] G. von Rad, *Wisdom in Israel* (New York: Abingdon, 1972) 257-58.

quality of the poem, there has not yet been a systematic treatment, the purpose of which would be to evaluate such suggestions. It will be the object of this study to attempt such an evaluation, and to argue for one possibility which might best explain the form of this great hymn in praise of "men, not God." The proposal which will be made is that Sirach 44-50 appears to have been inspired by the ἐγκώμιον, an εἶδος within the division of Greek rhetoric known as epideictic or "display." If this can be sustained, it would add further confirmation to those studies which argue for Sirach's familiarity with, and use of, Hellenistic literature and Greek literary forms.[6]

Before, however, this hypothesis is tested, we must consider a number of form-critical questions raised to date by commentators on the Praise of the Fathers. These questions are five in number. (1) Is there a relationship between chaps. 44-50 and the hymn in praise of the creator, 42:15-43:33? (2) Since some commentators identify the hymn as encompassing only chaps. 44-49, can chap. 50 be regarded at all as a part of the poem? (3) In that biblical parallels, e.g., the so-called "historical psalms," Psalms 78, 105, 106, 135, 136, have been cited as representing a genre the same as or similar to that of Sirach 44-50, do these offer an explanation of the form of our poem? (4) Since the Praise of the Fathers has been spoken of as an example of pre-rabbinic midrash, is there a relationship between its form and this post-biblical development? (5) Inasmuch as the ἐγκώμιον is only one of several Hellenistic models advanced as Sirach's inspiration for these seven chapters, do any of these other models have merit? The above five questions suggest that before the ἐγκώμιον hypothesis is considered, an investigation has to be made into the limit or extent of the hymn, the biblical and post-biblical forms with which it has been compared, and the other Hellenistic genres offered in explanation of its form. It is to such an investigation that our attention will now be directed.

---

[6]The most recent studies in this regard are: Th. Middendorp, *Die Stellung Jesu ben Siras zwischen Judentum und Hellenismus* (Leiden: E. J. Brill, 1973); and Johann Marböck, *Weisheit im Wandel: Untersuchungen zur Weisheitstheologie bei Ben Sira* (BBB 37; Bonn: Peter Hanstein, 1971). Older studies include: L. Bigot, "Ecclésiastique," *DTC* 4 (ed. A. Vacant; Paris: Librairie Letouzey et Ané, 1939) cols. 2046-2048; Israel Lévi, "Sirach," *The Jewish Encyclopedia: Vol. XI* (ed. Isidore Singer; 12 vols., New York: Funk and Wagnalls, 1905) 389-390; and Raymond Pautrel, "Ben Sira et le Stoicisme," *RSR* 51 (1963) 535-49.

## B. THE EXTENT OF THE HYMN

### 1. Sir 42:15-43:33 and 44-50

A number of commentators have sought to interpret chaps. 44-50 as but a part of a larger poetic unit in the book of Sirach. The larger unit is that of 42:15-50:24 which is then described as a hymn in praise of God for his revelation in nature and history.[7] Such a view is attractive in that certain pericopes, with which the Praise of the Fathers is often compared, exhibit such a structure. In Psalm 135, for example, the hymn praises Yahweh first for his deeds in nature (135:5-7), followed immediately by the praise of his actions in history (135:8-12). The same is true of Psalm 136 and Nehemiah 9.[8]

There are clearly some formal elements shared by 42:15-43:33 and 44:1-50:24 which would serve to unite them in a larger unit. Most apparent is the identical construction of the opening hemistich in each wherein the singular cohortative is followed by the particle נא and the object:[9]

---

[7]Cf. I. Fransen, "Cahier de bible: les oeuvres de Dieu, Sirach 42, 1-50, 20," *BVC* 79 (1968) 26-35; V. Hamp, "Das Buch Sirach oder Ecclesiasticus," *Echter-Bibel: Die Heilige Schrift in Deutscher Uebersetzung, Altes Testament, IV* (Wurzburg: Echter, 1959) 685; R. H. Pfeiffer, *A History of New Testament Times with an Introduction to the Apocrypha* (New York: Harper and Bros., 1949) 362; L. A. Schökel, *Proverbios y Eclesiastico* (Madrid: Ediciones Cristiandad, 1968) 299; R. T. Siebeneck, "May Their Bones Return to Life—Sirach's Praise of the Fathers," *CBQ* 21 (1959) 413; and A. van den Born, *Wijsheid van Jesus Sirach (Ecclesiasticus)* (Roermond: J. J. Romen en Zonen, Uitgevers, 1968) 206.

[8]Yahweh's deeds in creation (Ps 136:4-9; Neh 9:6) are joined with a recital of his mighty acts in history (Ps 136:10-22; Neh 9:7-31). On Psalms 135, 136, and Nehemiah 9 as possibly of the same genre as Sirach 44-50, cf. below pp. 23-29.

[9]Citations of the text and versions of Sirach are from the convenient edition of F. Vattioni, *Ecclesiastico: Testo ebraico con apparato critico e versioni greca, latina e siriaca* (Naples: Istituto Orientale di Napoli, 1968). This edition, however, ought to be used in the light of the cautions expressed in the reviews by A. A. di Lella, *CBQ* 31 (1969) 619-22, and P. W. Skehan, *Bib* 51 (1970) 580-82. For the purpose of checking on the readings of the Geniza MSS in Vattioni, reference will be made, as necessary, to the following: A. E. Cowley and A. Neubauer, *The Original Hebrew of a Portion of Ecclesiasticus (xxxix,15 to xlix,11)* (Oxford: Clarendon, 1897); I. Lévi, *The Hebrew Text of the Book of Ecclesiasticus*

אזכר-נא מעשי אל    (Sir 42:15a)
אהללה-נא אנשי חסד    (Sir 44:1a)[10]

Johann Marböck, in his study of 42:15-43:33, regards it as tied to the
Praise of the Fathers through a common theme of the revelation of the
כבוד of God.[11] In 42:16b Sirach exclaims that "the glory of the Lord doth
fill his works" (כבוד אדני מלא מעשיו),[12] and this note of God's glory
manifest in his works of creation is sounded elsewhere in the poem.[13] The

---

("Semitic Study Series, No., III," reprinted from the edition of 1904;
Leiden: E. J. Brill, 1969); M. H. Segal, *Seper ḥokmat ben-Sira' ha-šalem*
(Jerusalem, 1933); R. Smend, *Die Weisheit des Jesus Sirach: Hebräisch und
Deutsch* (Berlin: Georg Reimer, 1906) [hereafter: Smend, *Text*]; and H. L.
Strack, *Die Spruche Jesus', Des Sohnes Sirachs* (Leipzig: Georg Böhme,
1903). Unavailable to the author was the original publication of the
Geniza MSS, *Facsimiles of the Fragments Hitherto Recovered of the Book
of Ecclesiasticus* in Hebrew (Oxford: Cambridge, 1901). The texts of the
versions printed in Vattioni have been checked against the following:
(1) for the Greek, Joseph Ziegler, *Sapientia, Iesu Filii Sirach,* Vol. XII/2 of
*Septuaginta Vetus Testamentum Graecum* (Göttingen: Vandenhoeck und
Ruprecht, 1965); (2) for the Syriac, Paul A. de Lagarde, *Libri veteris
testamenti apocryphi syriace* (Reprinted from the edition of 1861;
Osnabrück: Otto Zeller, 1972) (the edition reproduced in Vattioni), and
*Biblia sacra juxta versionem simplicem quae dicitur Pschitta* (Beirut:
Typis typographiae catholicae, 1951) (the Mosul edition); and (3) for the
Latin, Robert Weber (ed.), *Biblia sacra iuxta vulgatam versionem* (Stuttgart: Württembergische Bibelanstalt, 1969).
    [10]Sir 42:15a in the Masada scroll. Cf. Y. Yadin, *The Ben Sira Scroll
from Masada* (Jerusalem: The Israel Exploration Society and the Shrine of
the Book, 1965) 26. For 44:1 the Greek text uses the first person plural
(αἰνέσωμεν). This appears to be due to the Greek translator's preference
for the plural. On this cf. Sir 43:32 (plural ἑοράκαμεν for singular ראיתי),
and R. Smend, *Die Weisheit des Jesus Sirach* (Berlin: Georg Reimer, 1906)
[hereafter: Smend, *Commentary*], 415.
    [11]Marböck, *Weisheit,* 148.
    [12]Reading with the Masada scroll, cf. Yadin, *Ben Sira Scroll,* 26, 45.
    [13]Cf. 42:17. Marböck, *Weisheit,* 148, claims that כבוד is used at 42:25
and 43:1, 2. But reading with Yadin, *Ben Sira Scroll,* 28, it is הוד, not
כבוד, that was translated δόξαν by the grandson. Marböck's reference to
כבוד at 43:1, 2 is also in error. Although δόξης appears in 43:1, it is in
translation of הדר. Moreover, there is no mention of "glory" at all in 43:2.
Marböck's 43:1, 2 is evidently, then, a misprint for 43:12 where בכבודה is
used. Another error here is the mention of Ps 9:6 as an instance where the
glory of Yahweh in creation is described. The reference should be Ps 96.

revelation of the divine glory in creation then continues, according to Marböck, into chaps. 44-50 where it is seen in the lives of the fathers of old. In support, he mentions the use of כבוד at 44:2, at 45:3, 7, 20; and that the תפארת of Adam (49:16) may not simply be a reference to Adam's fame or honor, but perhaps points to the divine *Herrlichkeit* revealed in Adam.[14]

While a reference to the gift of God's glory to Aaron may be in the ויאשרהו בכבודו of 45:7, "and he blessed him with his glory,"[15] there are questions about the other passages cited by Marböck. If 44:2 is read according to the proposal of Patrick Skehan, the רב כבוד חלק עליון becomes not "Great glory did the Most High allot" (viz., to the pious ancestors), but rather the fathers are described as "Great in glory, the portion of the Most High."[16] Here, then, כבוד has the sense of *Ehre* or reputation instead of divine *Herrlichkeit*. Also, כבוד as *Ehre* appears to be the intent behind the reference to the glory of Aaron in 45:20, where Sirach employs the tradition of the privileged position of Aaron from Numbers 17-18. Further, in view of the use of כבוד in chaps. 44-50 in the sense of honor, fame, or reputation, it would seem that the תפארת of Adam (49:16) ought to be interpreted similarly.[17] Marböck's suggestion, therefore, that תפארת alludes to the divine glory manifest in Adam appears unlikely at the time of Sirach. Finally, in Sirach's Praise of Moses it is probable that 45:3d, "and he showed him his glory," (ויר]אהו את כבודו[), simply recalls the narrative of Exod 33:17-22, and ought not to be

---

[14]Marböck, ibid.

[15]Reading ויאשרהו, with the Greek ἐμακάρισεν and Syriac, ܘܒܪܟܗ, instead of MS B וישרתהו as proposed by Smend, *Commentary*, 429, and N. Peters, *Das Buch Jesus Sirach oder Ecclesiasticus* (Münster: Aschendorff, 1913) 387.

[16]P. W. Skehan, "Staves and Nails and Scribal Slips (Ben Sira 44:2-5)," *BASOR* 200 (1970) 70-71. The suggestion is that Sirach has made use of Deut 32:9, "for the portion (חֵלֶק) of Yahweh is his people," and that in 44:2b the גדלי (MS B)/ גדלה (Masada) is a corruption of an original גרלו ("his share") in parallel to the חֵלֶק of 2a.

[17]Since this reference to the "glory of Adam" is the earliest known in Jewish literature, care should be taken not to read into it the developed Adamic theology of a later period. Cf. G. H. Box and W. O. E. Oesterley, "The Book of Sirach," *The Apocrypha and Pseudepigrapha of the Old Testament in English, Vol. I: Apocrypha* (ed. R. H. Charles; Oxford: Clarendon, 1913) 507, n. 16.

interpreted as part of a conscious attempt to tie these two poems together under the motif of God's glory in creation and history.

In addition to the formal balance of 42:15a and 44:1a cited above, another form-critical feature seen as indicating the unity of the two poems is the parallel between the summons to praise with which each closes: 43:30 and 50:22-23.[18] In other words, they are tied together in the following structure:

What this analysis fails to note, however, is that the summons to praise of 50:22-23 is not only balanced already within the Praise of the Fathers by 45:25-26, but that, unlike the alleged parallel of 43:30, the verbal correspondence is exact:

וְעַתָּה בָּרְכוּ-נָא אֵת ייי . . .
(45:25c-26a) . . . וְיִתֶּן לָכֶם חָכְמַת לֵב

וְעַתָּה בָּרְכוּ-נָא אֵת ייי . . .
(50:22-23a) . . . יִתֵּן לָכֶם חָכְמַת לֵבָב

The parallel between the summons to praise, then, is an argument to be used in support of the unity between chaps. 50 and 44-49, and not for the integrity of 42:15-50:24. This observation, coupled with the difficulties in tracing the motif of the divine כבוד in nature and history, suggests that, despite some similarities, 42:15-43:33 and 44:1-50:24 appear to be distinct units.

Among those who conclude that we are in fact dealing here with two independent poems are Jansen, B. Noack, and G. te Stroete.[19] Noack

_____

[18]Marböck, Weisheit, 147.

[19]Jansen, Die Psalmendichtung, 71; B. Noack, Spätjudentum und Heilsgeschichte (Stuttgart: W. Kohlhammer, 1971) 41; and G. te Stroete, "Van Henoch tot Simon: Israels geschiednis in de 'Lof der vaderen' van

comments that if there was a unity of theme intended, Sirach would have enumerated the historical deeds of God in 44-50 in the same manner as he listed the divine acts in nature in the previous section. But that he does not do. Rather in 44:1 our attention is drawn to the Fathers of old and not to the actions of the Most High.[20]

Besides the difference in subject matter, there are a number of form-critical and rhetorical features which serve to distinguish 42:15-43:33 from the Praise of the Fathers. According to Baumgartner's analysis, the former is a complete (*Vollständige*) unit, in which all the elements of the hymn *Gattung* appear.[21] The structure is as follows:[22]

A.  Call to Praise ("I will recall the works of God," 42:15) (On the use of the singular cohortative as an introductory formula in the hymn, cf. e.g., Pss 89:2, 108:2-4, 145:1-2.)

B.  Account of Yahweh's Deeds or Qualities (here a description of his works in creation, 42:16-43:26)

C.  Conclusion (Renewed call to praise with added note of how impossible it is to give God his due, 43:27-32)

The concluding section is especially noteworthy in that it returns to elements of the introduction, a feature common to the hymn form (e.g., Pss 104:33, 145:21).[23] Specifically, the conclusion, Sir 43:27-32, can be said to take the form of an "expanded introduction" (*erweiterte Einführung*) like that with which vv 19-21 close Psalm 135.[24] That these verses come at the hymn's close is further indicated by the rhetorical

---

Sirach 44,1-50,24," *Vruchten van de Uithof* (ed. A. R. Hulst; Utrecht: Theologisch Instituut, 1974) 123.

[20] Noack, *Spätjudentum*, 41.

[21] Baumgartner, "Die literarischen Gattungen," 169-71. Also cf. H. Gunkel and J. Begrich, *Einleitung in die Psalmen* (Göttingen: Vandenhoeck und Ruprecht, 1933) 33.

[22] The analysis here is that of Baumgartner, "Die literarischen Gattungen," 169-71, although the terminology chosen is that of E. Gerstenberger, "Psalms," *Old Testament Form Criticism* (ed. John H. Hayes; San Antonio: Trinity University, 1974) 209.

[23] Gunkel and Begrich, *Einleitung*, 57.

[24] Ibid.

device of inclusion whereby certain words in this section balance elements
of the introduction:

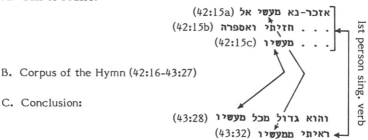

A. Call to Praise:

אזכר-נא מעשי אל (42:15a)

. . . חזיתי ואספרה (42:15b)

. . . מעשי (42:15c)

B. Corpus of the Hymn (42:16-43:27)

C. Conclusion:

והוא גדול מכל מעשיו (43:28)

ראיתי ממעשיו (43:32)

1st person sing. verb

    In view of the foregoing comments on form and content, then, the
Hymn in Praise of the Creator was composed independently of the Praise
of the Fathers. Nonetheless, there remains the view cited earlier, that the
two hymns seem to belong together in some way. But this now must be
thought of as a result of the redactional process through which Sirach
assembled his material into book-form. At 43:33 we seem to have an
example of the author's attempt to link these two hymns:[25]

> "For the Lord has made all things (πάντα, אה-הכל) and to the
> godly (εὐσεβέσιν) he has granted wisdom."

In the Hebrew text of v 33b (MS B), there is a lacuna which, on the basis
of the Greek's εὐσεβέσιν, commentators propose to restore either לאנשי
הסד[26] or לחסידים.[27] In either case the intent seems to be to anticipate
here the "pious men" (אנשי הסד) (44:1) who will be praised in what will
follow. Thus 33a looks back to the works of creation, while 33b points
ahead to the Hymn in Praise of the Fathers. Not only in his redaction of
these pericopes, but in other contexts as well, Sirach has chosen to bring
together the motifs of "wisdom in nature" and "wisdom in history." For
example,

---

    [25]Marböck, *Weisheit*, 33, speaks of 43:33 as a "redaktionelle
Verbindung des Schöpfungsgedichtes mit dem 'Lob der Väter.'"

    [26]Cf. Smend, *Commentary*, 412; and Smend, *Text*, 47. The Masada text
is of no help here in that, with the exception of 2 or 3 letters in vv 29-30,
the closing verses of chap. 43 have not been preserved.

    [27]Cf., e.g., Lévi, *The Hebrew Text*, 58; Strack, *Die Sprüche*, 43.

".. . he poured her (wisdom) out upon all his works (ἐπὶ πάντα τὰ ἔργα αὐτοῦ). She dwells with all flesh (μετὰ πάσης σαρκὸς) according to his gift." (Sir 1:9b-10a)[28]

Thus subsequent to the composition of the two poems in question, he may have chosen to juxtapose them to illustrate, in a general sense, a "wisdom in nature and history" schema.

Another factor in Sirach's placement of chaps. 44-50 after 42:15-43:33 may very well be the imitation of a presumed relationship between Psalms 104 and 105.[29] Psalm 104, like Sir 42:15-43:33, is a hymn in praise of Yahweh the creator, while Psalm 105—a psalm with which Sirach 44-50 is often compared—is a hymn reciting the acts of God in the history of Israel. It appears probable that Psalms 104 and 105 were in their present canonical order by Sirach's time,[30] and moreover, given that order, there is a sense in which Psalm 105 can be interpreted as carrying over the praise of the creator (Psalm 104) into a note of praise for the divine acts in history. For example, Psalm 105 opens with a summons to proclaim "his deeds" (עלילותיו)/"his wonderful works" (נפלאותיו) (vv 1-2), which in the immediate context points to the covenant with Abraham, the Exodus, etc. Yet there are other contexts in the Psalter wherein נפלאות is used to describe Yahweh's creative acts (e.g., Pss 96:3, 136:4), such that subsequent readers of Psalm 105 may have seen here in נפלאות not only the historical deeds of Yahweh, but also the works of creation celebrated in the previous psalm. Thus, given the apposition of Psalms 104 and 105, and the possibility of interpreting the term נפלאות as a thematic link between them, Sirach could have brought the originally independent 42:15-43:32

---

[28]On the similarity between 1:9b-10a and 43:33, see Marböck, *Weisheit*, 33, and Peters, *Das Buch*, 372. Also, compare 16:26-30 with 17:1-4, and 24:7 with 24:12.

[29]Peters, *Das Buch*, 358.

[30]It is known that in one of the psalm fragments from Qumran cave 4 (4QPs[e]) Psalms 104 and 105 appear in order, and that in another fragment (4QPs[a]), dating from the second century B.C., the canonical order of the Psalter was already fixed at least for Books 1 and 2. Cf. F. M. Cross, Jr., *The Ancient Library of Qumran* (rev. ed.; Garden City: Doubleday and Co., 1961) 165; and J. A. Sanders, *The Dead Sea Psalms Scroll* (Ithaca: Cornell University, 1967) 12-13. Although Sanders believes the order may have been more flexible in Book 4, where Psalms 104 and 105 are found, Skehan is of the opinion that the canonical order was fixed prior to the variations seen in 11QPs[a]. Cf. P. W. Skehan, "A Liturgical Complex in 11QPs[a]," *CBQ* 35 (1973) 195-205.

and 44:1-50:24 together in imitation of the Psalm 104-Psalm 105 relationship, with 43:33 serving a redactional function.

## 2. Sir 44-49 and 50

A second issue in delimiting the Hymn in Praise of the Fathers is the
question of the relationship between chaps. 44-49, wherein the focus is on
the heroes of Israel's past, and chap. 50 in which Sirach's attention turns
to his contemporary, the high priest Simon II. A number of commentators,
among them Jacob,[31] V. Hamp,[32] H.Lamparter,[33] T. Maertens,[34] and R.
Smend,[35] are of the opinion that 44-49 form a unit, with chap. 50 as an
appendix and not integral to the hymn. Box and Oesterley summarize it
this way:

> Chapters 44-49 form a well-knit and distinct division of the
> book, having for their theme the praise of the fathers of old.
> . . . An appendix (50:1-24) sets forth the praise of the high-
> priest Simon, who can hardly be reckoned, . . . with the
> fathers of old.[36]

Although they may be reluctant to view Simon II in the same light as
the אנשי הסד of previous generations, the principal reason for marking a
break between chaps. 49 and 50 is the content and construction of 49:14-
16. This subsection, in the form of a recapitulation[37] or Rückblick,[38]
returns to the figure of Enoch, with whom the Praise of the Fathers began

---

[31] Jacob, "L'histoire," 290.

[32] Hamp, "Das Buch Sirach," 708.

[33] H. Lamparter, Die Apokryphen I: Das Buch Jesus Sirach ("Die
Botschaft des Alten Testaments," 25:1; Stuttgart: Calwer, 1972) 211.

[34] T. Maertens, L'éloge des pères (Ecclésiastique XLIV-L) (Collection
lumière et vie, No. 5; Bruges: Editions de l'abbaye de Saint-André, 1956)
195-196. Although Maertens' title indicates that he believes the hymn to
extend through chap. 50, his text ends with a discussion of 49:14-16, which
he labels the "Conclusion."

[35] Smend, Commentary, 412: "Mit dem hier folgenden Lobe der
frommen Väter Israels hängen . . . 50,1-24 eng zusammen, es steht aber
auf sich selbst."

[36] Box and Oesterley, "Book of Sirach," 479.

[37] H. Duesberg and P. Auvray, Le livre de l'Ecclésiastique (La Saint
Bible; 2d ed.; Paris: Les éditions du Cerf, 1958) 218.

[38] Lamparter, Die Apokryphen, 208.

(44:16), and then—with the exception of the mention of Joseph (49:15), who was not covered earlier in the hymn—the recital moves back to cover the antediluvian figures of Shem, Seth (plus Enosh in the Hebrew of 49:16), and Adam. With the list of the Fathers traced back to the first man, then, the hymn appears to have come to a close, and is thereby demarcated from the appendix with its praise of Simon the Just.[39]

There are other ways, however, of interpreting 49:14-16. Kurt Galling regards it as secondary, interrupting an otherwise direct link between the rebuilding activities of Nehemiah (49:13) and those of Simon (50:1-4).[40] Also, Middendorp sees it as a subsequent addition, apparently on the same grounds that cause him to dismiss the originality of the prayer of 36:1-17 and to view the eschatological references to Elijah in 48:10-11 as a later expansion.[41] These passages, he claims, witness to an eschatology more in keeping with the Maccabean era than with the first two decades of the second century B.C.E. It is in the context of his discussion of these "Maccabean" additions to Sirach that he suggests 49:14-16 to be of a later provenance.

Eschatology, moreover, is J. G. Snaith's reason for proposing 49:14-16 to be later. He comments, "These verses were probably added to do justice to certain early heroes whose reputations grew in later teaching outside the Bible: none but Enoch has been mentioned before."[42] But, as noted above,[43] and as will be discussed later in our study, the mention, for example, of Adam in 49:16 does not necessarily imply that we are dealing with the Adamic eschatology of a later time. It will be our contention that 49:14-16 is integral to the hymn and that it appears where it does for the reason suggested by Peters, viz., that it is an *Überleitung* to the Praise of Simon.[44] Sirach's juxtaposition of Adam and Simon will be seen as intentional.[45]

---

[39]Box and Oesterley, "Book of Sirach," 506.

[40]K. Galling, *Studien zur Geschichte Israels im persischen Zeitalter* (Tübingen: J. C. B. Mohr [Paul Siebeck], 1964) 129 n. 3.

[41]Middendorp, *Die Stellung*, 135. On his argument that Sir 36:1-17 and 48:10-11 are of Maccabean provenance, cf. pp. 125-132 and pp. 134-135 respectively.

[42]J. G. Snaith, *Ecclesiasticus* (The Cambridge Bible Commentary on the New English Bible; eds. P. R. Ackroyd et al.; London: Cambridge University, 1974) 248.

[43]Cf. above, p. 5.

[44]Peters, *Das Buch*, 422.

[45]Cf. also A. Eberharter, *Das Buch Jesus Sirach oder Ecclesiasticus*

That chap. 50, together with 49:14-16, properly belongs to the Praise of the Fathers has been advanced recently by Noack[46] and Janssen[47] who, in turn, have been followed by Lang[48] and te Stroete.[49] It is their opinion that the Praise of Simon comes as the climax of the entire hymn.

> In dem Hohenpriester Simon laufen alle Linien des Lobpreises der Väter zusammen. Was immer von einzelnen Israeliten Positives gesagt wurde, das findet bei Simon seine Erfüllung und Verkörperung.[50]

Seen as fulfilled and embodied in Simon, then, are deeds and characteristics introduced in Sirach's enumeration in 44-49 of Israel's cultic and political heroes. Within that list the one figure to whom more attention is given than any other is Aaron (45:6-22),[51] and when this is coupled with the reference to Phinehas (45:23-25), we have a span of twenty verses devoted to a description of the office of the high priest. The parallels with Simon are unmistakable:

---

(Die heilige Schrift des Alten Testaments, VI:5; Bonn: Peter Hanstein, 1925) 157: "Der Sirazide verbindet den Anfang und das Ende der religiösen Entwicklung, daher stellt er Adam und den Hohenpriester Simon nebeneinander."

[46]Noack, Spätjudentum, 42-43.

[47]E. Janssen, Das Gottesvolk und seine Geschichte: Geschichtsbild und Selbstverständnis im palästinensischen Schrifttum von Jesus Sirach bis Jehuda ha-Nasi (Neukirchen-Vluyn: Neukirchener, 1971) 16-33.

[48]B. Lang, Anweisungen gegen die Torheit: Sprichwörter-Jesus Sirach (Stuttgarter Kleiner Kommentar, AT 19; Stuttgart: KBW, 1973) 84, 87.

[49]te Stroete, "Van Henoch," 120-33. Others who regard chap. 50 as the climax of the Hymn of Praise of the Fathers are: Snaith, Ecclesiasticus, 251; and O. Schilling, Das Buch Jesus Sirach (Herders Bibelkommentar VII/2; Freiburg: Herder, 1956) 208. Neither Snaith nor Schilling, however, present an argument in support of their view on the relationship between 44-49 and 50.

[50]E. Janssen, Das Gottesvolk, 28.

[51]Note that Aaron (45:6-22) rates three times more space than Moses (45:1-5), and that the description of Moses climaxes with the consecration of Aaron (45:6). Cf. te Stroete, "Van Henoch," 127: "Mozes wordt als het ware een voorloper wiens belangrijkste taak was Aäron tot priester aan te stellen."

## A. The Covenant with the Priests

| With Aaron | With Simon |
|---|---|

(45:7)    וישימהו לחק עולם

(45:15)    ותהי לו ברית עולם
ולזרעו כימי שמים

(50:24) ויקם לו ברית פינחס

### With Phinehas

52לכן גם לו הקים חק
(45:24)    ברית שלום לכלכל מקדש

## B. Vestments of the Priest

| Aaron | Simon |
|---|---|

"He girded him in vestments
of splendid appearance
(45:7)53"(בתועפות תואר)

"How glorious (מה נהדר) was he
when he came out of the tent"
(50:5)

"He clothed him
(וילבישהו)
completely with splendor
(תפארת)" (45:8)

"When he clothed himself
(התלבשו) in garments
(בגדי) of splendor
(תפארת)" (50:11)

The breastpiece and
Ephod are described as:54

---

52Cf. Num 25:12-13.

53Reading תואר ("of splendid appearance") with MS Bmarg and Gk δόξης against the ראם of B text. On תועפות as vestments ("stoles"?), cf. F. Rundgren, "Zum Lexicon des Alten Testaments," *Acta Orientalia* (Copenhagen) 21 (1953) 325. The ראם is an apparent attempt by MS B to make תועפות ראם conform with the תועפות ראם ("horns of the wild ox") of Num 23:22, 24:8.

54The list of vestments (45:8-12) echoes the description given in Exodus 28. Cf. J. G. Snaith, "Ben Sira's Supposed Love of Liturgy," *VT* 25 (1975) 172-173; and Snaith, *Ecclesiasticus*, p. 224, where he calls attention

בגדי קדש (45:10)                     (50:11) בגדי כבוד

And in the Ephod/                    In a series of similes describing
breastpiece are set:                 Simon's appearance he is compared
                                     to a gold vessel in which are set:
אבני חפץ (45:11)                      (50:9) אבני חפץ

## C. Priestly Functions

Aaron                                        Simon

". . . to minister and to be
a priest for him . . ." (45:15)
                                     Cf. portrayal of Simon's
                                     service at the altar (50:11-15)[55]
". . . to offer sacrifice . . .
incense and a pleasing odor"
(45:16)

## D. Day of Atonement

Aaron                                        Simon

                                     "Blessing of the Lord
"And to bless (לברך)                  (ברכת ייי) on his
the people in his Name               lips, and in the Name
(בשמו)" (45:15)                       of the Lord (בשם ייי)[56]
                                     he boasted (התפאר)" (50:20)
". . . made atonement
(לכפר) for Israel" (45:16)

---

as well to the list of high-priestly vestments in the Mishnah (*Yoma* 7:5).
Another list, similar to that of Sir 45:8-12, is the description of Eleazar's
vesture in *Aristeas* 97-98.

[55]Snaith, "Ben Sira's . . . ," 173-74, notes that the picture in vv 11b-16
seems to be that of the regular daily offering of Tamid, while vv 5-11a
and 2-21 portray the Day of Atonement.

[56]According to the Mishnah (*Yoma* 6:2), the Divine Name was
pronounced by the high priest only on the Day of Atonement. Cf. Snaith,
*Ecclesiasticus*, 224, and Box-Oesterley, "Book of Sirach," 510.

"When he came out from behind
the veil (מבית הפרכת)"[58] (50:5)

". . . made atonement
(ויכפר) for Israel"
(45:23)[57]

It appears, moreover, that Sirach's selection of stories about other figures portrayed in 44-49 was done to suggest a parallel with the office and function of the high priest. Of the thirty-six half-lines that make up his report on Joshua (46:1-10), fifteen or almost half are devoted to the incident involving Joshua and Caleb after the return of the spies from Canaan (Num 13:30-14:38). In this incident Caleb and Joshua champion the minority view that Israel ought to continue on into Canaan. "If Yahweh delights in us, he will bring us into the land and give it to us, a land which flows with milk and honey" (Num 14:8). Their advocacy of such action is interpreted by Sirach, then, as one that "turned the anger [of the Lord] from the congregation" (להשיב חרון מעדה) (46:7).[59] The phrase here is almost the same as that of Num 25:11, "Phinehas the son of Eleazar, son of Aaron the priest, has turned back my wrath from the people of Israel, . . . (השיב את-חמתי מעל בני ישראל). Thus as Janssen expresses it, "Kalebs und Josuas Tat erschienen als Sühnehandlung."[60]

The same theme is repeated in the report on Samuel (46:13-20). Sirach concludes his praise of Samuel by referring in v 20 to the story of Saul and the Witch of Endor (1 Sam 28:3-25). Although the fourth hemistich of the verse is missing in the Hebrew of MS B,[61] it is preserved in both the

---

[57]Cf. Num 25:13.

[58]Cf. מבית לפרכת in the description of the Day of Atonement ritual (Lev 16:2, 12, 15).

[59]The Greek, "to hinder the people from sin" (κωλῦσαι λαὸν ἀπὸ ἁμαρτίας), and the Syriac, "to turn away the congregation" (ܟܢܘܫܬܐ ) seem to be attempts to avoid the reference in MS B to the "anger" (חרון) of the Lord. Smend, Commentary, 442, remarks that the Syriac "den Zorn Gottes gern bei Seite schiebt." חרון in the MT is always the "anger" of Yahweh. Cf. W. Baumgartner and L. Koehler, Hebräisches und Aramäisches Lexicon zum Alten Testament (3d ed.; Leiden: E. J. Brill, 1967) 338.

[60]E. Janssen, Das Gottesvolk, 23.

[61]Smend, Commentary, 447-48, and Peters, Das Buch, 400, suggest that the Geniza Hebrew lacks 46:20d in that in the Vorlage of MS B the 4 half-lines of the verse were evidently compressed into a single line of the text. The only part of 20d that survived was בנבואה, and the remainder,

Greek and Syriac versions, and on the basis of their readings, it may be restored to something on the order of

בנבואה להשחית עון פשע

or בנבואה למחות עון פשע

or (Smend) בנבואה להשבית חטאת/המס.[62]

Sirach, then, has made Samuel's prophetic role in this incident a priestly one as well. As Samuel announces the coming defeat of Israel and death of Saul on Mt. Gilboa, his death is said to have atoned for the sin of the people.[63]

This cultic dimension to Samuel's office is emphasized further in Sirach's version of the Philistine attack on Israel at Mizpah (46:16-18; cf. 1 Sam 7:3-11). While the Deuteronomistic historian opens the Mizpah incident with the prophetic summons by Samuel for Israel to gather and repent at Mizpah, Ben Sira mentions only Samuel's mediatorial role in offering a sacrifice on Israel's behalf.[64] It is worth noting that the description of Samuel's offering is framed between the lines, "He called to

---

from there to the left margin, had been torn away from the *Vorlage* of Geniza B.

[62]In the Greek of 46:20d, ἐξαλεῖψαι presumably translates either an infinitive of שחת (cf. 44:18) or of מחה (cf. 44:13b [Masada] and the LXX of Ps 50:11 and Isa 43:25). ἀνομία is used to translate both פשע (41:18; Isa 43:25) and עון (cf. LXX Ps 50:11). With Smend, *Commentary*, 448, the presence of λαοῦ in the Greek half-line is an addition. The Syriac's ܠܚܛܝܬܐ ܠܡܫܒܝ may represent לשבית חטאת. Cf. the use of ܫܒܐ for שבה in 49:2, and the listing in D. Barthélemy and O. Rickenbacher, *Konkordanz zum hebräischen Sirach mit syrisch-hebräischem Index* (Göttingen: Vandenhoeck und Ruprecht, 1973), 9*. Smend's proposal of המס is on the basis of the use of ܠܚܛܝܬܐ and ἀνομίαν in the translation of 49:3b.

[63]V. Ryssel, "Die Sprüche Jesus', des Sohnes Sirachs," *Die Apokryphen und Pseudepigraphen des Alten Testaments: I* (ed. E. Kautzsch; reprint of the 1921 edition; Darmstadt: Wissenschaftliche Buchgesellschaft, 1962) 459, interprets the death of Saul as atonement for the sin of the people in their demand for a king (1 Samuel 8). More likely the sin meant here is that of Saul in his failure to put all the Amalekites under the ban (1 Sam 15:9-10 and 28:18-19). His sin, in turn, encumbered the people. Cf. Smend, *Commentary*, 448, and Peters, *Das Buch*, 400.

[64]E. Janssen, *Das Gottesvolk*, 23, "Samuel Tätigkeit dabei ist vor allem die eines Mittlers."

God, when his enemies (צרים) pressed him on every side," and "Then the Lord thundered from the heavens . . ." (46:16ab, 17a). The motif of a pious ancestor calling on Yahweh for deliverance when beset by enemies is repeated at 46:5 (Joshua), 47:5 (David), 48:20 (Hezekiah and Isaiah),[65] and may possibly, then, be seen in the description of Simon II. At 50:4 Simon is said to have "strengthened his city from the enemy (מצר)," a reference which comes at Sirach's transition to a portrayal of Simon's mediatorial or cultic role (50:5-15).

The above selection principle is evident as well in Ben Sira's treatment of David. He begins with a cultic analogy to describe David's rise to preeminence, "As the fat is selected from the offering, so (was) David from Israel" (47:2). For vv 8-10 Sirach employs the Chronicler in whose account David was made responsible for the Jerusalem cultus, the appointments, and personnel of the temple (1 Chr 15-16, 21:18-26:28, 28:1-29:22). With the fusion of both cultic and political elements into the Chronicler's David, Sirach sees here a *Vorbild* of the high priest.[66]

In like manner subsequent kings are singled out for their cultic piety or activity. Understandably Sirach extols Solomon's wisdom (47:14-17), but he is also remembered for his construction of the temple (47:13), and all references to his cultic impiety (1 Kgs 11:4-8) are—as in the case of the Chronicler—omitted. Solomon's fault is that he married foreign women (47:19-20), not that he went after other gods. Josiah is another whose cultic piety is celebrated.

כי נחלה על משובתינו
וישבת תועבות הבל

"For he grieved over our apostasy
and put an end to vain abominations" (49:2).[67]

---

[65]The plural subject in the Hebrew and Greek of 46:20ab presumably refers to both Hezekiah and Isaiah who, according to the Chronicler (2 Chr 32:20), prayed together when Sennacherib laid siege to Jerusalem. In 2 Kgs 19:15-19, however, Hezekiah prays alone. The Syriac has dropped 20a and has made Hezekiah the sole subject of 20b.

[66]E. Janssen, *Das Gottesvolk*, 25, and te Stroete, "Van Henoch," 128.

[67]The emendation נחלה (niphal of חלה) instead of the נחל in MS B is made on the basis of Amos 6:6. Cf. Smend, *Commentary*, 468-69, and Ryssel, "Die Sprüche," 465. Behind the Greek translator's κατευθύνθη ("was led aright") may be his reading of נחל as נהל ("to lead, guide"). With his ἐπιστροφή he seems to have shifted the emphasis from Judah's apostasy to its repentance. On this cf. Smend, *Commentary*.

Of significance to Sirach are those leaders who, like Simon, have been
zealous as well for the physical well-being of the temple and Jerusalem.
Solomon's activity in building the temple has already been noted. But
Sirach also calls attention to the construction undertaken by Hezekiah,
Zerubbabel, Joshua, and Nehemiah. The parallel between these figures and
Simon II may be illustrated as follows:

## A. The Temple

|                | Solomon | Simon II |
|----------------|---------|----------|

*Solomon*

*Simon II*

אשר הכין בית לשמו

(50:1b) אשר בדורו

(47:13)            ויצב לעד מקדש

נבדק הבית[68]

*Zerubbabel and Joshua*

*Simon II*

בימיהם הכינו מזבח

(50:1c) בימיו חזק היכל

(49:12)            וירימו היכל קדש

פנות מעון בהיכל מלך

## B. The City

*Hezekiah*

*Simon II*

(48:17a)    יחזקיהו חזק עירו

(50:4b) ומחזק עירו מצר

## C. The Water Supply

*Hezekiah*

*Simon II*

בהטות אל תוכה מים

אשר בדורו נכרה

---

[68]S. Schechter and C. Taylor, *The Wisdom of Ben Sira* (Cambridge: The
University Press, 1899), 63, propose נבדק instead of the נפקד of MS B.
Both the Greek ὑπέρραψεν ("he patched up") and the Syriac ܐܬܒܢܝ
("was built") presuppose a description of Simon's temple repairs. On בדק as
"repair," cf. 1 Chr 34:10. Smend, *Commentary*, 479, suggests that נפקד
appears here in error under the influence of נפקדה and נפקדו in the preceding two verses.

⁶⁹ויחצב בנחשת צורים          מקוה אשיח⁷⁰

(48:17b) ויחסום הרים מקוה     (50:3) כים בהמונו

## D. Repairs to the Walls⁷¹

*Nehemiah*                                    *Simon II*

המקים את חרבתינו          (50:2a) אשר בימיו

וירפא את הריסתינו          נבנה קיר

(49:13) ויצב דלתים ובריח

In addition to the above engineering and cultic parallels between Simon and the Fathers, there is a formal element which serves to unify the whole of 44:1-50:24. Mentioned earlier, this is the doxology which is inserted at the end of chap. 45 and again at 50:22.⁷² There is, as was noted, a correspondence between the two:

---

⁶⁹בנחשת is to be read here, instead of כנחשת, with the Greek ἐν. Cf. Smend, *Commentary,* 465. Note that while the Hebrew portrays the tunnel as having been bored with bronze tools, the Greek makes them tools of iron (ἐν σιδήρῳ). The Siloam tunnel inscription (*KAI* 189), which recounts the completion of this engineering feat of Hezekiah, makes use of חצב (ll. 1, 4, 6) to describe the masons as they cut through the צור (ll. 3, 6).

⁷⁰The בם of MS B is a scribal error for כים. Cf. the Greek ὡσεὶ θαλάσσης and Box-Oesterley, "Book of Sirach," 507, and Smend, *Commentary,* 480. The Syriac is of little help here in that it condenses v 3 into "And he dug the spring." אשיח is used by the author of the Copper Scroll (3Q15) to mention four different reservoirs known to him: at Qumran (V, l. 6), at Jericho (VII, l. 4), at Bethhakkerem (possibly identified with Ramat Rahel) (X, l. 5) and the pool of Bethesda (XI, l. 12). Cf. M. Baillet J. T. Milik, and R. de Vaux, *Discoveries in the Judaean Desert III: Les 'petites grottes' de Qumran: Texts* (Cambridge: University Press, 1965) 244, C 70. The term, written אשוח, also appears in the inscription of King Mesha of Moab. Cf. *KAI* 181:9, 23.

⁷¹The context and the term קיר clearly indicate that Simon rebuilt the temple wall. Nehemiah, however, is remembered for restoring the city wall (חומה), cf. Neh 2:17, 12:27. Despite this difference, it would seem that Sirach intends a comparison to be made between the two.

⁷²Cf. above, 5. Baumgartner, "Die literarischen Gattungen," 174, describes each of these as "Eine Doxologie, ein kleiner kultischer Hymnus mit hymnischer Aufforderung, . . ."

"And now bless the Lord who . . ." (45:25c)
"Now bless the Lord God of Israel who . . ." (50:22a)

"And (who) gave you wisdom of heart . . ." (47:26a)
"May he give you wisdom of heart . . ." (50:23a)

Otto Rickenbacher, however, interprets the doxologies as marking the close of two distinct units within Sirach: viz., 44:16-45:26 and 46:1-50:24. Both units, he maintains, exhibit a structure, "Bittgebet, actio Gottes, Lobpreis," which he has identified elsewhere in Ben Sira.[73] For example, this construction is evident in Sir 51:10-12:

> Bittgebet        51:10
> Actio Gottes    51:11
> Lobpreis        51:12

And it appears again, according to Rickenbacher, twice in the Praise of the Fathers:

> 44:16-45:26:     Bittgebet        45:26
>                  Actio Gottes    44:16-45:25cd
>                  Lobpreis        45:25ef
>
> 46:1-50:24       Bittgebet        50:23-24
>                  Actio Gottes    46:1-50:21
>                  Lobpreis        50:22

Two objections must be made to such an analysis. First of all, in contrast to Sir 51:10-12, the doxologies in chaps. 45 and 50 have to be divided up, transferring one part to the beginning of each unit, in order to fit the outline. Such maneuvering seems to be an attempt to force the Praise of the Fathers into a structure that is alien to it.

A second objection is that in Rickenbacher's schema, the prayer (*Bittgebet*) is followed by an *actio Gottes*, which becomes the ground for the doxology proper. "Dabei ist 44,16-45,25cd praktisch eine einzige grosse actio Gottes, die Menschen stehen ganz in Schatten."[74] Quite on the contrary, the uniqueness of the Praise of the Fathers is that men do not stand "in the shadows," but that they and their deeds are the objects of

---

[73]O. Rickenbacher, *Weisheits Perikopen bei Ben Sira* (Orbis Biblicus et Orientalis, 1; Freiburg: Universitätsverlag, 1973) 194-95.
[74]Ibid., 195.

praise.[75] Rickenbacher's statement ought to be inverted: in 44:16-45:25 (and 46:1-50:21) it is God who moves into the background, not men.

The form-critical role of the doxologies has been recognized by Baumgartner, who notes that they are appended to the two great sections extolling Aaron-Phinehas and Simon II.[76] Moreover, the second doxology closes, at 50:24b (Hebrew), with a reference back to the covenant with Phinehas. This can only be a conscious attempt to link the praise of Simon with the praise of the priests in 45:6-25. The two doxologies, then, are seen as a device which serves to unite chaps. 44-49 with chap. 50, and which stresses the parallel between Simon and Aaron-Phinehas.

This form-critical connection, together with the priestly emphasis in the praise of various ancestors and the parallels between the engineering feats of Simon and Hezekiah, Nehemiah, et al., support the conclusion that the hymn under consideration extends through 50:24.

## C. CURRENT DISCUSSIONS OF GENRE

### 1. The Proposals

Commentators have approached the question of the literary form or genre of Sirach 44-50 from three directions. First of all, there are those who view the Praise of the Fathers as similar to, or in continuity with, certain biblical texts. The texts cited are from the Hebrew canon, from intertestamental works, and from the New Testament. Cognate passages in the Hebrew canon are believed to be Psalms 78, 105, 106, 135, 136, Ezekiel 20, and Nehemiah 9.[77] Intertestamental pericopes advanced as representing the same genre are: 1 Macc 2:51-60; 3 Macc 6:4-8; 4 Macc 16:15-23, 18:9-19; Jdt 16:1-17; Wisdom 10; and CD 2:17-3:12.[78] From the

---

[75]Cf. above, 1.

[76]Baumgartner, "Die literarischen Gattungen," 174.

[77]Among those who compare Sirach 44-50 with the Psalms listed, as well as with Ezekiel 20 and Nehemiah 9 are: Box and Oesterley, "Book of Sirach," 479; Hamp, Das Buch Sirach, 690; Peters, Das Buch, 372; Ryssel, "Die Sprüche," 449; and van den Born, Wijsheid, 213. While they do not mention the passages in Ezekiel and Nehemiah, Fransen, "Cahier de Bible," 31; Pfeiffer, History, 404; and Snaith, Ecclesiasticus, 216, cite the parallel of the historical psalms.

[78]The similarity between chaps. 44-50, 1 Maccabees 2, and Wisdom 10 is noted by Box and Oesterley, Hamp, Peters, and van den Born in the places cited above. On the resemblance of 3 Maccabees 6, cf. Peters, Das

New Testament, Hebrew 11 and Acts 7 are brought into the discussion.[79]
Other students of Sirach, however, note that Ben Sira has employed the
traditions concerning the Fathers as if those traditions were scripture. As
a consequence, then, some choose to interpret Sirach 44-50 as an example
of pre-rabbinic midrash.[80] That is, in chaps. 44-50 Sirach begins with the
"scriptural" remembrances of Israel's heroes and seeks to adapt and apply
them to the contemporary situation.

The third approach to the discussion is taken by those who attribute the
uniqueness of the hymn to its having been inspired by a hellenistic model.
Specifically, Maertens, Hengel, and others suggest the biographical genre
of *De viris illustribus* known from Cornelius Nepos (first century B.C.E.),
Suetonius Tranquillus (first century C.E.), and the church father
Jerome.[81] Hengel goes on to describe the Praise of the Fathers as representing hellenistic biography in general; he draws a parallel between it
and the biographical accounts of the peripatetic school which flourished

---

*Buch*, and for the parallel with 4 Maccabees 16, cf. A. Lumpe, "Exemplum," *RAC* 4 (ed. Theodor Klauser; Stuttgart: Anton Hiersemann, 1966)
1241. In addition to Fransen, "Cahier de Bible," and Peters, *Das Buch*,
both von Rad, *Wisdom*, 258, n. 24, and Lamparter, *Die Apokryphen*, 190,
suggest that Jdt 16:1-17 ought to be compared with the Praise of the
Fathers. For CD 2:17-3:12 as of the same genre, cf. Lumpe, "Exemplum,"
and A. G. Wright, *The Literary Genre Midrash* (Staten Island, NY: Alba
House, 1967) 99-100.

[79] Most of the above commentators call attention to the similarity of
Hebrews 11 to Sirach 44-50. Cf., e.g., Box and Oesterley, Fransen, Hamp,
Peters, and van den Born as cited. Only Fransen, "Cahier de Bible,"
Lumpe, "Exemplum," 1244-45, and Wright, *Literary Genre*, 100, include
Acts 7 in the same category.

[80] Already in 1913 Peters, *Das Buch*, 372, wrote that Sirach 44-50 ". . .
ist sicherlich in der Entwicklung zum haggadischen Midrasch begriffen,
wenn man den Abschnitt nicht schon direkt als solchen bezeichnen will."
More recently the hymn has been identified as a biblical example of
midrash by R. Bloch, "Midrash," *DBSup* V (eds. L. Pirot, A. Robert, and H.
Cazelles; Paris: Letouzey et Ané, 1957) 1274. Following Peters and Bloch
are R. Siebeneck, "May their Bones Return to Life!—Sirach's Praise of the
Fathers," *CBQ* 21 (1959) 416, and G. Maier, *Mensch und freier Wille nach
den jüdischen Religionsparteien zwischen Ben Sira und Paulus* (WUNT 12;
Tübingen: J. C. B. Mohr, 1971) 50.

[81] Maertens, *L'éloge*, 11; Pautrel, "Stoicisme," 541; Siebeneck, "May
their Bones . . . ," 414, n. 8; and M. Hengel, *Judaism and Hellenism: I*
(Philadelphia: Fortress Press, 1974) 136.

from the fourth to the second centuries B.C.E.[82] In such works as the βίοι of Hermippus and Satyrus, the περὶ ἐνδόξον ἀνδρῶν of Neanthes of Cyzicus, and Sotion's διαδοχὴ τῶν φιλοσόφων are to be found the impetus behind the manner in which Sirach has described Israel's אנשי חסד.[83]

Beyond the general proposal that Sirach 44-50 was inspired by peripatetic biography or that it represents to some degree the genre De viris illustribus, there occasionally have been descriptions of it as a panygeric, a eulogy, or as an encomium.[84] But it appears that these terms have been applied to the hymn in only the most general sense, and do not represent the results of any form-critical analysis. The task at hand, then, is to evaluate the above proposals, attempting to survey their applicability to the form of Sirach 44-50, before proceeding to investigate how suitable the term encomium might be. This will be done in the following order: (1) by considering the Jewish models that have been advanced, viz., prototypes from the Hebrew Bible which antedate Ben Sira, the pericopes from the intertestamental period which appear to be similar, and finally, the midrashic model; and then, (2) our attention will be directed to the hellenistic genres De viris illustribus and those cited from peripatetic biography.

## 2. Sirach 44-50 and Forms Known
## in the Hebrew Canon

Although the alleged canonical parallels to Sirach 44-50 share the pattern of a historical retrospect or survey of events from Israel's past, they appear to represent two different types of literature. It will be seen that Psalms 105, 135, and 136 are examples of the hymn Gattung, while Psalms 78, 106, Nehemiah 9, and Ezekiel 20 exhibit a distinct form of their own.

---

[82]Hengel, Judaism and Hellenism, II, 90, n. 209.

[83]Others who comment in general terms on the hellenistic quality of Sirach 44-50 are Maier, Mensch, 50, and Marböck, Weisheit, 16.

[84]As panegyric, cf. Bigot, "Ecclésiastique," 2048; Lévi, "Sirach," 329; Pfeiffer, History, 404; and Siebeneck, "May Their Bones," 425. Wright, Literary Genre, 99-100, mentions that the hymn has been called a eulogy. The term encomium is employed by Ben Zion Wacholder, Eupolemus: A Study of Judaeo-Greek Literature (Monographs of the Hebrew Union College, III; Cincinnati: Hebrew Union College, 1974) 12; and A. Momigliano, Alien Wisdom: The Limits of Hellenization (New York: Cambridge University, 1975) 98. Both Wacholder and Momigliano, however, use the designation only in regard to chap. 50, the Praise of Simon II.

Psalms 105, 135, and 136 each open with an introductory summons to render praise (105:1-6; 135:1-3; 136:1-3), followed by the main body of the poem which supplies the reasons for giving praise. Such is the basic shape of the hymn as recognized by Gunkel.[85] According to Gunkel's description, the subject of the main unit of the hymn is Yahweh, spoken of in the third person, whose attributes and deeds become the grounds for the summons to praise. The transition from the summons to the body of the hymn is accomplished either through the use of the particle כי, a relative clause, a participial phrase, or by setting the attributives of Yahweh in apposition to him as the object of praise in the summons. That these three psalms are of this form may be seen from the following:

| Psalm 105: | Summons | "O give thanks to the Lord, call on his name . . . Remember the wonderful works (נפלאותיו) that he has done . . ." (vv 1, 5) |
|---|---|---|
| | Body (in apposition) | "He is the Lord . . . He is mindful of his covenant . . . the covenant which he made with Abraham . . ." (vv 7, 8) |
| Psalm 135: | Summons | "Praise the Lord . . ." (vv. 1-3) |
| | Body (with כי) | "For (כי) the Lord has chosen Jacob . . . (v 4) He it was who smote the first-born . . ." (vv 4, 8) |
| Psalm 136: | Summons | "O give thanks to the Lord . . ." (vv 1-3) |
| | Body (with participle) | "*to him who does* (לעשה) greatwonders (נפלאות) . . ." (v 4) |

---

[85]Cf. Gunkel and Begrich, *Einleitung*, 33-34, 43-49; H. Gunkel, *The Psalms: A Form-Critical Introduction* (Facet Books: Biblical Series, 19; Philadelphia: Fortress, 1967) 10-13; Gerstenberger, "Psalms," 207-9.

Consequently, then, commentators have not hesitated to identify these psalms as belong to the hymn *Gattung*.[86] As such they share in this characterization of the hymn:

> The predominant mood in all the Hymns is the enthusiastic but reverent adoration of the glorious and awe-inspiring God. To a certain extent, it might be said that the purpose of the Hymns was to give pleasure to Yahweh, whom they extol with such exuberance.[87]

But when we attempt to compare Sirach 44-50 to this hymn genre it is apparent that we are dealing with something different. For rather than praising God, as does the hymn, Sir 44-50 is in praise of the <u>Fathers</u>. Note the contrast between the hymnic structure of "Praise Yahweh, who did X," and, for example:

Sir 48:1-11    "How glorious <u>you were</u>, O Elijah
               in your wonderous deeds . . .
               <u>You who</u> raised a corpse from death . . .
                    <u>who</u> brought kings down to destruction . . .
                    <u>who</u> heard rebuke at Sinai . . ."

Sir 46:1-7     "<u>Joshua</u> the son of Nun was mighty in war, . . .
               <u>He</u> became . . . a great savior . . .
               How glorious <u>he was</u> . . .
                    <u>He</u> called on the Most High . . .
                    <u>He</u> hurled down war upon that nation . . .
               And in the days of Moses, <u>he</u> did a loyal deed . . ."

Thus, as was noted earlier, Baumgartner commented that Sirach 44-50 can only be called a hymn in an extremely restricted sense, "da hier nicht wie im kultischen Hymnus Gott, sondern Menschen gepriesen werden."[88]

This fundamental difference between the hymn, as represented by

---

[86]Cf. Gunkel and Begrich, *Einleitung*, 21; H. J. Kraus, *Psalmen: II* (Biblischer Kommentar: Altes Testament, XV/2; Neukirchen: Neukirchener, 1960) 718-19 [ Psalm 105], 895 [ Psalm 135], 900 [Psalm 136]; S. Mowinckel, *Psalmstudien: V* (Amsterdam: P. Schippers, 1961) 123-24, n. 2 [Psalm 105]; S. Mowinckel, *The Psalms in Israel's Worship: I* (Oxford: Basil Blackwell, 1962) 85 [Psalm 136].

[87]Gunkel, *The Psalms*, 13.

[88]Baumgartner, "Die literarischen Gattungen," 173. Cf. above, 1, and also the comments of Noack, *Spätjudentum*, 41.

Psalms 105, 135, and 136, and the Praise of the Fathers, applies as well to
the other set of canonical pericopes with which Sirach 44-50 has been
compared, viz., Psalms 78, 106, Ezekiel 20 and Nehemiah 9. Here too it is
the deeds of Yahweh that are remembered.

Psalm 78:

"We will . . . tell to the coming generation the glorious deeds
of the Lord and the wonders which he has wrought. He established a testimony in Jacob, . . . He divided the sea . . . He
cleft the rocks in the wilderness. . . ." (vv 4-5, 13, 15)

Ezekiel 20:

"Thus says the Lord God: 'On the day when I chose Israel, . . .
On that day I swore to them that I would bring them out of
the land of Egypt. . . . So I led them out of the land of Egypt
. . . I gave them my statutes and showed them my ordinances,
. . .'" (vv 5, 6, 10, 11)

Nehemiah 9:

"(And Ezra said:) 'Thou art the Lord, the God who didst
choose Abram . . . and thou didst see the affliction of our
fathers in Egypt . . . and thou didst divide the sea before
them . . .'" (vv 6, 7, 11)

Rather than presenting a straightforward recitation of Yahweh's acts in
the history of Israel, these particular texts portray that history according
to a deuteronomistic or prophetic understanding: Israel has responded to
Yahweh's grace with rebellion and is therefore threatened with punishment. Israel, then, either repents, or Yahweh relents, and his grace is
manifested in yet another event in Israel's history. That schema may be
illustrated in the case of Psalm 106:

*In the Exodus:*
        Yahweh's act (7a)
        Israel's rebellion (7b)
        Yet Yahweh's grace (8-11)
            ("for his Name's sake," v 8)
        Israel's response—
            Belief (12)

Rebellion (13-14)
Yahweh punishes (15)

*In the Wilderness:*

| Rebellion | 16 | 19-22 | 24-25 | 28-29 | 32a |
|---|---|---|---|---|---|
| Punishment | 17-18 | — | 16-27 | — | 32b-33 |
| *or* Intended Punishment Avoided | — | 23 | — | 30-31 | |

*In the Land:*

| Rebellion | 34-39 |
|---|---|
| Punishment | 40-43 |
| Yet Yahweh's Grace | 44-46 |

This pattern dominates Psalms 78 and 106, leading commentators to differentiate between these and the purely hymnic recitations of Israel's history.[89] The same pattern is evident in Ezekiel 20 and Nehemiah 9 as well.[90] All four pericopes recount that although Israel spurned Yahweh's affection, his grace continued to be revealed in history, and therefore there are grounds for the conviction that Yahweh will continue to act graciously in the future (cf. Ps 106:44-47; Neh 9:31; Ezek 20:33-44).

While a deuteronomistic theology of reward and punishment is characteristic of Ben Sira, both in the book as a whole and in chaps. 44-50,[91]

---

[89]On Psalm 78, cf. H. J. Kraus, *Psalmen: I* (Biblischer Kommentar: Altes Testament, XV/1; Neukirchen: Neukirchener, 1960) 539: "Man müsste von einer Geschichtslehre sprechen;" Mowinckel, *The Psalms in Israel's Worship: II* (Oxford: Basil Blackwell, 1962) 112: "A kind of didactic hymn." For Psalm 106, cf. Kraus, *Psalmen: II,* 727: "Die formgeschichtliche Analyse des Rahmens ergibt demnach, dass vor allem zwei Gattungselemente zu beachten sind: der hymnische Introitus und die Worte der Busse und Bitte."

[90]On Nehemiah 9, cf. J. M. Myers, *Ezra-Nehemiah* (AB 14; Garden City: Doubleday, 1965) 166: "(Nehemiah 9) . . . reflects a deep feeling for the nation's historical experiences, as illustrated by the conceptions of the Deuteronomist," and 167: "This prayer psalm is a marvelous expression of God's continued faithfulness to his covenant despite the nation's equally continued apostasy."

[91]Cf., e.g., Sirach 2:10-11; 12:2-3, 6; 16:12-14; and in the Praise of the Fathers note the punishment of Dathan, Abiram, and Korah (45:18-19), and the judgments on Solomon (47:19-21), Rehoboam, and Jeroboam

there is a difference between its use in the latter and in the canonical texts examined above. In all of these pericopes it is Israel's rebellion or disobedience which is the basis for Yahweh's intention to punish:

"They did not keep God's covenant,
but refused to walk according to his law." (Ps 78:10)

"They murmured in their tents,
and did not obey the voice of the Lord." (Ps 106:25)

"But the house of Israel rebelled against me in the wilderness;
they did not walk in my statutes . . ." (Ezek 20:13)

"Nevertheless they were disobedient and rebelled against thee
and cast thy law behind their back . . ." (Neh 9:26)

In Sirach 44-50, however, the emphasis is not on Israel's obedience or disobedience, but on that of specific individuals:

"He (Abraham) kept the law of the Most High and was taken
into covenant with him . . ." (44:19)

"Phinehas . . . zealous in the fear of the Lord, and
stood fast, when the people turned away. . . . Therefore
a covenant of peace was established with him. . . ." (45:23)

"Rehoboam . . . Jeroboam . . . Their sins became exceedingly
many, so as to remove them from their land." (47:23-24)

"For Hezekiah did what was pleasing to the Lord, and he
held strongly to the ways of David his father, . . ." (48:22)

Thus, just as Sirach 44-50 is distinct from the hymn form of Psalms 105, 135, and 136 in that it celebrates particular men rather than the deeds of Yahweh, so too it is differentiated from Psalms 78 and 106,

---

(47:23-25). On Sirach and the deuteronomistic theology of retribution, cf. A. A. di Lella, "Conservative and Progressive Theology: Sirach and Wisdom," *CBQ* 28 (1966) 143-146; W. Dommershausen, "Zum Vergeltungs-denken des Ben Sira," *Alter Orient und Altes Testament: Wort und Geschichte* (eds. H. Gese and H. P. Rüger; Neukirchen-Vluyn: Neukirch-ener, 1973) 37-43; and J. L. Crenshaw, "The Problem of Theodicy in Sirach: On Human Bondage," *JBL* 94 (1975) 47-64, esp. 59-60.

Ezekiel 20 and Nehemiah 9 by its description of the obedience and disobedience of individuals. Karlheinz Müller, therefore, suggests that with
Sirach 44-50 we have before us a form with a new attitude toward past
history:

> All das steht jedoch nicht in Dienst einer zusammenhang-
> enden Darbeitung der Geschichte Gottes mit dem Volk seiner
> Zuneigung, sondern gilt der Würdigung der herausragenden
> Männer der Vergangenheit von Henoch bis Nehemiah.[92]

Noack, as well, recognizes that the form of the Praise of the Fathers
must be differentiated from the historical summaries of the Hebrew
canon. He makes the distinction, then, between that of a *Rückverweis*,
the last of which would be Nehemiah 9, and that of a *Geschichtsüberlick*,
the most complete of which is Sirach 44-50.[93] Both Noack and Müller are
of the opinion that the Praise of the Fathers, with its review of a series of
individuals from Israel's past, is far closer in form to those intertestamental and NT texts in which persons are offered as examples or para-
digms of piety or conduct. It is to these that we shall now turn.

### 3. Sirach 44-50 and Biblical Forms
### outside the Hebrew Canon

Of the several intertestamental and NT passages with which Sirach 44-
50 has been compared, three of them, Jdt 5:5-21, 16:1-17, and Acts 7:2-
53, appear to represent genres which we have already considered. Judith
16, which von Rad and Lamparter find to be "entirely in the same key" as
the Praise of the Fathers,[94] is upon examination, clearly a hymn of praise

---

[92]K. Müller, "Geschichte, Heilsgeschichte und Gesetz," *Literatur und
Religion des Frühjudentums* (eds. J. Maier and J. Schreiner; Würzburg:
Echter, 1973) 75.

[93]Noack, *Spätjudentum*, 29. H. Thyen, *Der Stil der Jüdisch-
Hellenistischen Homilie* (Göttingen: Vandenhoeck und Ruprecht, 1955)
111-12, does not discriminate as sharply between Psalms 78, 106, Nehemiah 9, and Sirach 44-50, yet he notes the new quality apparent in the
latter: "Jetzt steht nicht mehr die Volksgeschichte, sondern die
Geschichte der einzelnen Frommen in Vordergrund des Interesses."

[94]The comment is that of von Rad, *Wisdom*, 258, n. 4. Cf. also
Lamparter, *Die Apokryphen*, 190.

to God. It shares all the formal characteristics of the Hymn *Gattung* discussed above, viz.

I. Call to Praise (Jdt 16:1 v 2 EV )
    "Begin a song (ἐξάρχετε) to my God . . .
        Sing (ᾄσατε) to the Lord . . .
        Raise to him a new psalm (ψαλμὸν καινόν);[95]
        Exalt him, and call upon his name."

II. Corpus of the Hymn (Jdt 16:2-12 vv 3-12 EV )
    "For (ὅτι)[96] God is the Lord who crushes wars;[97]
        for he has delivered me
        . . . . . . . . . . . . . . . . . .
        The Lord almighty has foiled them by the hand of a woman,
        . . . . . . . . . . . . . . . . . .
        . . . they perished before the army of my Lord."

III. Conclusion (Jdt 16:13-17)
    "I will sing to my God a new song (ὕμνον καινόν) . . .
        Let all thy creatures serve thee,
        for thou didst speak, and they were made
        Thou didst send forth thy spirit,
        and it formed them;
        . . . . . . . . . . . . . . . . . .
        Woe to the nations that rise up against my people!
        The Lord almighty will take vengeance on them."[98]

---

[95] Reading ψαλμὸν καινόν, with Codex A, thus forming an inclusion with the ὕμνον καινόν of 16:13.

[96] Cf. above, p. 24, on the use of כי to effect the transition between the Call to Praise and the Corpus of the Hymn.

[97] Cf. the κύριος συντρίβων πολέμους of Exod 15:3 (LXX). Besides the use of LXX diction here, the whole of Judith 16 seems to reflect the style and mood of the ancient Yahwistic hymns of Exodus 15 and Judges 5.

[98] The reference to God's creative activity, with which Judith 16 closes, is a common theme of the hymn. Cf. Gunkel, *The Psalms*, 12-13; Mowinckel, *The Psalms in Israel's Worship: I*, 84; and Pss 33:6-9, 104:30. The invective (v 17) is reminiscent of the close of the Song of Deborah (Judg 5:31).

Thus in form, Judith 16 is as distinct from Sirach 44-50 as we found the hymns of Psalms 105, 135, and 136 to be. Moreover, it is further set apart by its content; it celebrates only one event—Judith's deliverance of her people—rather than enumerating a series of events from Israel's past.

Norbert Peters, in his commentary on Sirach, advances Jdt 5:5-21, the speech of Achior to Holofernes in which he narrates a summary of Jewish history, as a parallel to the Praise of the Fathers.[99] But it appears to correspond to the type of historical retrospect seen earlier in Psalms 78 and 106, Ezekiel 20, and Nehemiah 9. As in the case of these pericopes, Judith 5 enumerates not a series of individuals from Israel's past, but presents a deuteronomistic interpretation of the history of a people: when Israel gave its obedient response to specific acts of Yahweh's grace in history, the nation prospered; but when it failed to do so, the consequence was Exile in Babylon.

I. The Patriarchs

> "Then their God commanded them to leave the place where they were living and go to the land of Canaan. There they settled, and prospered, with much gold and silver and very many cattle." (Jdt 5:9)

II. Exodus/Wilderness

> "Then they cried out to their God, and he afflicted the whole land of Egypt with incurable plagues; . . . Then God dried up the Red Sea before them, and he led them by the way of Sinai. . . ." (5:12-14)

III. Period of the Monarchy

> "As long as they did not sin against their God, they prospered, . . ." (5:17)

IV. Exile

> "But when they departed from the way which he had appointed for them, they were utterly defeated . . . and were led away captive to a foreign country; the temple of their God was razed to the ground, . . ." (5:18)

---

[99]Peters, *Das Buch*, 372.

A similar deuteronomistic schema appears in the Speech of Stephen, Acts 7:2-53. Here Yahweh's saving action toward Israel is recalled in events from the lives of Abraham (7:2-8), Joseph (7:9-16), Moses (7:17-38), and David (7:45-46). Israel's response to these saving acts is characterized as idolatry (7:39-43a), with that idolatry resulting in the punishment of the Exile (7:43b). Thus, even though Acts 7 is often classified with Sirach 44-50,[100] it, like Judith 5, stands far closer to the genre of what Noack calls a *Rückverweis*, viz., Psalms 78 and 106, Ezekiel 20 and Nehemiah 9.[101]

Unlike the passages above, the majority of intertestamental pericopes to which discussions of Sirach 44-50 make reference do not present a coherent theology of history, but rather are collections of examples drawn from history. Such *Beispielreihen*, as well as individual *Beispiele*, "entweder der blossen Belehrung und Verdeutlichung oder wollen auf den Hörer bzw. Leser moralisch einwirken, indem sie ihn zur Tugend ermahnen oder vor Lastern warnen."[102] 1 Macc 2:51-60 and 4 Macc 16:15-23, and 18:9-19 offer illustrations of the basic form of the *Beispielreihe*, while 3 Macc 2:3-8, 6:2-8, Wisdom 10, CD 2:17-3:12, and from the NT, Hebrews 11, offer variations on the form.[103]

The transition from the canonical type of historical summary to that of the *Beispielreihe* is believed by H. Thyen to have taken place first in the Diaspora.

> In der Diaspora, die sie zunächst wohl einfach übernommen hat, erfahren sie aber alsbald eine charakteristische Änderung. Jetzt steht nicht die Volksgeschichte, sondern die Geschichte der einzelnen Frommen im Vordergrund des Interesses.[104]

---

[100]Cf. above, n. 79 for those who compare Sirach 44-50 with Acts 7.

[101]On *Rückverweis*, cf. Noack, *Spätjudentum*, and above, 29. W. Eichrodt, *Ezekiel* (Philadelphia: Westminster, 1970) 263, observes that "There is only one parallel in the Bible to this declaration of judgment [viz., Ezekiel 20], Stephen's Speech in Acts 7."

[102]Lumpe, "Exemplum," 1230.

[103]For the names of those who point to a similarity between these passages and Sirach 44-50, cf. above 21, n. 78. For 3 Macc 2:3-8, cf. Lumpe, "Exemplum," 1241.

[104]Thyen, *Der Stil*, 112.

This change presumably came about under hellenistic influence,[105] for the use of historical examples (παραδείγματα, ὑποδείγματα, exempla) was a common feature in hellenistic literature and rhetoric. In the rhetorical treatises of the time considerable space is devoted to the use of the historical example. Among these treatments are: Aristotle, *Rhetoric* (1.2 [1357b], 2.20 [1393ab-1394] ),[106] the first century B.C.E. *Rhetorica ad Herennium* (2.29.46; 4.1.1-6.10; 4.44.62),[107] and Quintilian's *Institutio Oratoria* (5.11.6-21).[108] Anaximenes, moreover, in the fourth century B.C.E. *Rhetorica ad Alexandrum*, employs a *Beispielreihe* to illustrate his discussion of examples which are contrary to probability.[109] His series of examples, arranged chronologically—as is the case in the intertestamental

---

[105]Cf. Lumpe, "Exemplum," 1241: "Im Spätjudentum nimmt die Vorliebe für E(xempla) durch der Einfluss der Popularphilosophie auf die jüdisch-hellenistische Homilie und dadurch auf die spätjüd. Literatur überhaupt stark zu."

[106]References to the *Rhetoric* of Aristotle are to the Loeb volume: J. H. Freese (trans.), *Aristotle: The 'Art' of Rhetoric* (Loeb Classical Library; New York: G. P. Putnam's Sons, 1926).

[107]The text used is that of Harry Caplan (trans.), [*Cicero*] *ad C. Herennium: De Ratione Dicendi (Rhetorica ad Herennium)* (Loeb Classical Library; Cambridge: Harvard University, 1954).

[108]In H. E. Butler (trans.), *The Institutio Oratoria of Quintilian: II* (Loeb Classical Library; Cambridge: Harvard University, 1953). Treatments dealing with the use of παραδείγμα and *exemplum* in classical literature may be found in H. Kornhardt, *Exemplum: Eine bedeutungsgeschichte Studie* (Göttingen: Robert Noske, 1936); H. Lausberg, *Elemente der literarischen Rhetorik* (3d ed.; Munich: Max Hueber, 1967) 134; Lumpe, "Exemplum"; M. McCall, *Ancient Rhetorical Theories of Simile and Comparison* (Cambridge: Harvard University, 1969); S. Perlman, "The Historical Example, Its Use and Importance as Political Propaganda in the Attic Orators," *Scripta Hierosolymitana: VII* (Jerusalem: Magnes, 1961) 150-66; and R. Volkmann, *Die Rhetorik der Griechen und Römer in systematischer Uebersicht* (2d ed.; Leipzig: B. G. Teubner, 1885) 233-38.

[109]*Rhetorica ad Alexandrum* 8 (1429b) 5-25, in W. S. Hett and H. Rackham (trans.), *Aristotle: Problems: II and Rhetorica ad Alexandrum* (Loeb Classical Library; Cambridge: Harvard University, 1957). On the date of the *Rhet. ad Alex.* and on Anaximenes of Lampsacus as the probable author, cf. the introductory comments by Rackham, 259-62; D. C. Bryant, *Ancient Greek and Roman Rhetoricians: A Biographical Dictionary* (Columbia, MO: Artcraft, 1968) 3; and McCall, *Ancient Rhetorical Theories*, 20-21.

type of *Beispielreihe*—enumerate cases where outnumbered military forces were able to gain victories. The four examples, in order, are: the defeat of the forces of the Thirty Tyrants by Thrasyboulos and his followers at Phyle (403 B.C.E.); the infiltration of Spartan-held Thebes by Theban exiles which, in turn, led to the liberation of the city (379 B.C.E.); the defeat of Dionysius II of Syracuse by Dion (357 B.C.E.); and how Timoleon and his small force of Corinthians were victors over the Carthaginians who held Syracuse (341 B.C.E.).[110]

Other *Beispielreihen* in classical texts include the series of examples employed by the nymph Calypso (*The Odyssey*, 5) in her reply to the request, brought by Hermes from Zeus, that she release Odysseus and send him on his way. Regarding the request as an expression of divine jealousy, she cites two illustrations of similar past behavior on the part of the gods: (1) when Dawn fell in love with Orion, Artemis slew him; and (2) when Demeter loved Iasion, Zeus struck the latter dead with a thunderbolt.[111] At the close of the series, Calypso returns to the present moment with the words, "And even so again do ye begrudge me, O ye Gods, that a mortal man should abide with me" (5:129).

The speech of the fourth century Attic orator Lycurgus, *Against Leocrates*, lists a series of individuals who exemplify patriotism and who thus provide a standard against which the traitorous conduct of Leocrates is to be judged. The *Beispielreihe* opens with the introduction:

> Let me remind you of a few past episodes; and if you take them as examples (παραδείγμασι) you will reach a better verdict in the present case and in others also. The greatest virtue of your city is that she has set the Greeks an example (παράδειγμα) of noble conduct (83).[112]

Then the following examples are cited: the reign of King Codrus whose

---

[110]For brief descriptions of the events which Anaximenes employs as examples, cf. A. R. Burn, *The Pelican History of Greece* (Baltimore: Penguin Books, 1966) 303, 318-19; and N. G. L. Hammond and H. H. Scullard (eds.), *The Oxford Classical Dictionary* (2d ed.; Oxford: Clarendon, 1970) 349-50, 1076-77.

[111]*The Odyssey*, 5.121-128. Cf. A. T. Murray, *Homer: The Odyssey: I* (Loeb Classical Library; Cambridge: Harvard University, 1950), 179.

[112]Lycurgus, *Against Leocrates*, in J. O. Burtt, *Minor Attic Orators: II* (Loeb Classical Library; Cambridge: Harvard University, 1962).

patriotism, to the point of death, is contrasted with Leocrates' flight from Athens; Callistratus whom, like Leocrates, fled and returned to Athens providentially for punishment; the sacrifice Erechtheus made of his daughter to guarantee victory over Eumolpus and the Thracians (100); Homer in whose poetry are described the "noblest actions," and who "through argument and demonstration convert(s) men's hearts" (102-104); and Tyrtaeus whose verses portray "what sort of conduct brought men fame among the Spartans" (106-108). The series continues, but rather than with examples of patriotic conduct, Lycurgus now lists illustrations of the punishment that was awarded in prior cases of treason: Phrynichus (111-115) whose punishment was to have his bones removed from Attica following his posthumous conviction on charges of treason. Having shared this example, Lycurgus pauses momentarily to contrast it with the present situation, ". . . will you, then, who have the very person (Leocrates) who has betrayed the city alive and at the mercy of your vote, let him go unpunished?" (115). He then resumes the series of examples: Hipparchus, the deserters who fled to Decelea (121), the man executed in Salamis (122), and finally, examples of Spartan punishment (128-130):

> Your city was not alone in dealing thus with traitors. The Spartans were the same . . . we shall be well advised to take examples (παραδείγματα) of just conduct from a city which has good laws . . . (128).

That such a use of *Beispielreihen* in speeches and treatises was known over a period of several centuries, and elsewhere in the ancient world, may be inferred from the works of Philo. For example, in his *Quod omnis probus liber sit*, Philo includes a catalogue of those who exemplify the point that it is the wise man or virtuous man who enjoys liberty (62-130). The examples are drawn from all over the ancient world: Greek heroes and sages, Persian Magi, Indian Gymnosophists, and the Essenes of Jewish Palestine.[113]

Two centuries before Philo, and two centuries after Lycurgus' *Against Leocrates*, the author of 1 Maccabees employs a *Beispielreihe* in the speech of Mattathias to his sons. He begins with an exhortation: "Remember the deeds of the fathers, which they did in their generations; and receive great honor and an everlasting name" (1 Macc 2:51). Next comes a list of those

---

[113]The text and translation of *Quod omnis probus liber sit* is that of F. H. Colson, *Philo: IX* (Loeb Classical Library; Cambridge: Harvard University, 1967).

fathers whose piety was rewarded: Abraham, Joseph, Phinehas, Joshua, Caleb, David, Elijah, Hananiah, Azariah, Mishael, and Daniel (2:52-60). The catalogue of heroes in this late second century B.C.E. composition closes with a final appeal of Mattathias,[114] "And so observe, from generation to generation, that none who put their trust in him will lack strength" (2:61).

The same technique of using a series of examples from Israel's history in order to illustrate steadfastness in the face of persecution is employed by the author of 4 Maccabees. The Alexandrian author, writing either in the late first century B.C.E. or just after the beginning of the Common Era,[115] includes two *Beispielreihen,* at 16:15-23 and 18:9-19. Both are employed in the story of the mother and her seven sons, and represent the mother's exhortation to the seven to remain faithful despite the torture ordered by Antiochus. The mother introduces the first catalogue:

> My sons, noble is the fight; and do ye, being called thereto to bear witness for our nation, fight therein zealously on behalf of the Law of our fathers. . . . Therefore ye owe it to God to endure all pain for his sake; for whom also our father Abraham made haste to sacrifice his son Isaac, . . . (4 Macc 16:16, 19-20).[116]

The examples continue with Isaac, who "seeing his father's hand lifting his knife against him, did not shrink"; Daniel amidst the lions; and Ananias, Azarias, and Mishael in the fiery furnace (16:20-22).

In the second series the mother comments on how her late husband had laid the foundation for the sons' present fidelity:

> He read to us of Abel who was slain by Cain, and of Isaac who was offered as a burnt-offering, and of Joseph in the prison. And he spake to us of Phinehas, the zealous priest, and he taught you the song of Ananias, Azarias and Mishael in the fire (18:11-12).

The list concludes with a reference to Daniel which is followed in turn by

---

[114]Composition of 1 Maccabees is believed to have taken place in Palestine late in the reign of, or shortly after the death of, John Hyrcanus I (134-104 B.C.E.). Cf., e.g., R. H. Pfeiffer, *History,* 491.

[115]Cf. Thyen, *Der Stil,* 12, R. B. Townshend, "IV Maccabees," *APOT* 2 (R. H. Charles, ed.; Oxford: Clarendon, 1913) 657.

[116]The translation is that of Townshend, "IV Maccabees."

quotations from Isaiah, a psalm of David, a proverb of Solomon, Ezekiel, and finally a quotation from Moses taken from Deut 32:39.

Hartwig Thyen, in his discussion of *exempla,* classifies the catalogues of heroes in 1 and 4 Maccabees as "Historische Exempla für die Rettung Gerechter," which he titles *exemplum* type 'a'.[117] Corresponding to this type of *Beispielreihe* would appear to be Ben Sira's treatment of figures from Israel's past in chaps. 44-49. Although there are textual difficulties with MS B at 44:16—to which we will have occasion to return later— Enoch's being taken up into heaven was judged a consequence of his being found blameless (נמצא תמים).[118] Moreover, in the Greek translation of the grandson, Enoch is thereby advanced as an example (ὑπόδειγμα) to the generations. That he is said to exemplify repentance (μετάνοια) brings to mind that Philo treated Enoch in the same terms in the series of examples employed in *De Praemiis et Poenis.*[119] There Enoch's repentance led to his reward of "a new home and a life of solitude" (*De Praem. et Poen.* 16).[120]

Noah the righteous (צדיק) (44:17) was also found blameless (תמים) and therefore become a continuator (תחליף). Abraham is likewise presented by Sirach as an example. He "kept the commandments of the Most High (שמר מצות עליון), . . . was found faithful in a time of testing (בניסוי נמצא נאמן) . . ." (44:20), and "therefore (על-כן) he (God) made an oath to him to bless the nations in his seed: (44:21). The fact that Phinehas was given a "covenant of peace" (ברית שלום) wherein he had the privilege of managing (לכלכל) the sanctuary (45:24) is seen by Sirach as the reward which comes to one who is zealous for "the God of All" and is steadfast in a time of religious crisis (45:23). In like manner the Judges are offered as

---

[117] Thyen, *Der Stil,* 112-14.

[118] 44:16 is omitted in both the Masada Scroll and in the Syriac. This leads Yadin, *Ben Sira Scroll,* 38, to suggest that it was not original. At some early time, therefore, an attempt was made to transfer Ben Sira's observations on Enoch from 49:14 to create 44:16 so that a reference to Enoch would appear in chronological order, viz., before Noah. We will return to a discussion of 44:16 and 49:14 in Part II, 230-33.

[119] Philo's use of two sets of three examples each—Enosh, Enoch, and Noah (13-23), and Abraham, Isaac, and Jacob (24-51) in *De Praemiis et Poenis* suggests that these would also represent Thyen's type 'a' "Exempla für Rettung Gerechter."

[120] The text and translation are from the edition of F. H. Colson, *Philo: VIII* (Loeb Classical Library; Cambridge: Harvard University, 1960).

further illustrations of those who were faithful; for this "May their memory be blessed" (46:11). The concluding premonarchical example of piety is Samuel, who "by his faithfulness (באמונתו?, cf. Gk. ἐν πίστει αὐτοῦ)[121] was found to be a prophet" (46:15).

Ben Sira's catalogue of παραδείγματα continues into the kings with references to David (47:5) and Hezekiah, who "did the good and clung to the ways of David" (48:22ab, MS B). Although vv 22cd-23 are missing in Hebrew, they presumably added that the ways of David to which Hezekiah clung were those—to judge from the Greek and Syriac—"which Isaiah the prophet commanded, (Isaiah) who was great and faithful (πιστός) in his vision" (48:22cd).[122] Not surprising is that the final monarch offered as a model of piety is Josiah, who "set his heart on the Lord and in violent days (בימי חמס) did חסד" (49:3).

In contrast to the above kings whose conduct is praised, Sirach includes mention as well of rulers who set a bad example: Solomon, who is remembered for his foreign wives (47:19-21) plus Rehoboam and Jeroboam who led their nations to sin (47:23-25). The force of the negative examples is amplified by the inclusion of two summary statements. In 48:15-16 the people of the Northern Kingdom are offered as an illustration of those who failed to respond to the ministry of Elijah or Elisha (cf. 48:1-14) and who, as a consequence, are punished by exile. And then in 49:4-5 all the kings of Judah—save David, Hezekiah, and Josiah—are remembered as those "who abandoned the law of the Most High (ויעזבו תורת עליון)." Such an interweaving of negative examples with illustrations of those whose piety Sirach commends is reminiscent of the Beispielreihe referred to above in Lycurgus' Against Leocrates.[123] There Lycurgus has combined examples of patriotic conduct (Codrus, Erechtheus, and the quotations from Homer and Tyrtaeus) and those of treasonable behavior (Callistratus, Phrynichus, and Hipparchus.)

Such a mixture of examples is a feature recognized by Thyen in a number of hellenistic Jewish texts in addition to Sirach.[124] Thus, several texts are a mixture of Thyen's type 'a' exempla, discussed above, and what he calls type 'b', "Historische Exempla für die Bestrafung von Frevlern."

---

[121]Smend, Text, 52, and Commentary, 445, proposes באמונת פיו instead of the באמונתו of Lévi and Vattioni.

[122]Smend, Commentary, 467, assumes the Hebrew of vv 22cd-23 was destroyed.

[123]Cf. above, 34-35.

[124]Thyen, Der Stil, 114-15.

Among these he includes 3 Macc 2:3-8, 6:2-8; and Philo's *De Praem. et Poen*. In the two passages from 3 Maccabees the interweaving of positive and negative examples is seen in the prayers offered respectively by the high priest Simon II and Eleazar of Alexandria. Each prayer for deliverance from Ptolemy IV Philopator is based upon the examples of how in past times God saved those who were faithful and destroyed those who persecuted his people. Thus the Alexandrian author of this first century B.C.E. legend has Simon pray:[125]

> Thou didst destroy those who aforetime did iniquity, among whom were giants . . . bringing upon them a boundless flood of water. Thou didst burn up with fire and brimstone the men of Sodom, workers of arrogance, . . . and didst make them an example (παράδειγμα) to those who should come after. (3 Macc 2:4-5)[126]

The prayer continues with the example of the punishment inflicted on the Pharaoh of the Exodus (2:6-7a) and concludes with the contrasting example of the deliverance granted to "those who trusted in thee, the ruler of all creation, . . ." (2:7b-8).

In Eleazar's prayer the *Beispielreihe* begins with the example of the punishment experienced by Pharaoh and Sennacherib (6:4-5). The transition, then, from these two negative examples to those whose piety was rewarded is supplied by the story of the three young men:

> Thou, when the three friends in Babylon freely gave their life to the flames that they should not serve vain things, didst make as dew the fiery furnace, and deliver them unharmed even to the hair of their head, turning the flame upon all their adversaries. (3 Macc 6:6)

Following this transition two positive examples are cited, Daniel (6:7) and

---

[125]Dates for 3 Maccabees range from the early first century B.C.E., cf. e.g., C. W. Emmet in Charles, *Apocrypha*, 156-58, to the last quarter of that century, cf. O. Eissfeldt, *The Old Testament: An Introduction* (New York: Harper & Row, 1965) 582; and L. Rost, *Judaism Outside the Hebrew Canon* (Nashville: Abingdon, 1976) 107.

[126]The translation of 3 Maccabees is that of C. W. Emmet in Charles, *Apocrypha*, 164.

Jonah (6:8), which stand in contrast with the opening illustrations of Pharoah and Sennacherib.

This mixture of *exempla* is evident in *De Praem. et Poen.* Mention was made already of Philo's use of type 'a' examples grouped into "trinities": the rewards given to Enosh, Enoch, and Noah; and to Abraham, Isaac, and Jacob.[127] At this point Philo turns to include type 'b' *exempla:*

> We have discussed typical examples of the rewards assigned in the past to the good both individually and in common with others. . . . We have next to consider in their turn the punishments appointed for the wicked. . . . (*De Praem. et Poen.* 67)

The examples listed are those of Cain (68-73) and Korah's rebellion (74-78). At 78 there is a lacuna in the text which led Colson to suggest that other *exempla* of this same type were included.

> Possibly he (Philo) may have cited also the disasters which befell the Egyptians through the plagues and at the Red Sea to cover (the categories) of "nations and countries."[128]

The final section of Philo's *De Virtutibus* is similar.[129] This section, "On Nobleness of Birth" (περὶ εὐγενείας), is composed, first, of negative or type 'b' examples illustrating the point that nobility of birth does not make one noble, and then, second, this is followed by a series of positive (type 'a') examples offered in proof of the assertion that those born of ignoble parents can be virtuous. The first series consists of *exempla* common to all men: Cain, who certainly was of high birth, but who murdered his brother (199); Ham, though born to Noah, "ventured to pour reproach upon the author of his preservation" (202); and Adam, whose "Father was no mortal but the eternal God" (204), chose "the false, the base and the evil" (205). Philo continues with the example of those sons who, although born to the Patriarchs, "profited nothing by the virtues of their ancestors" (206): viz., the sons of Abraham other than Isaac (207) and Esau (208-210). Thereupon comes the transition to the contrasting class of examples:

---

[127]Cf. above, 37, n. 119.

[128]F. H. Colson, *Philo: VIII*, 455.

[129]The text and translation of *De Virtutibus* are from Colson, *Philo: VIII.*

> Now these belong to the erring class, evil children of good
> parents, . . . But I can cite others of the opposite and better
> class, whose ancestors were men of guilt, but their own lives
> were worthy of emulation and full of good report (211).

Cited, therefore, as illustrations of the thesis that virtue can be acquired
apart from the character of one's forefathers are Abraham, who was "the
son of an astrologer" (212); Tamar, while "bred in a house and city which
acknowledged a multitude of gods," became "the servant and suppliant of
the one great Cause" (221); and finally Jacob's concubines, Zilpah and
Bilhah, "women born beyond the Euphrates" who passed from "mere con-
cubinage to the name and position of wedded wives" (223). At this point
the *Beispielreihe* concludes with a restatement of the thesis (226-227).

The texts we have discussed thus far witness to the use of *Beispielreihen* in the ancient Mediterranean world from the fourth century Athens
of Lycurgus down to the second and first century Jewish communities,
Egyptian and Palestinian, which produced 1, 3, and 4 Maccabees. Use of
the form in Judaism, moreover, extends into the Common Era as indicated
in the examples from Philo. The forms of the *Beilspielreihe* which have
been examined here have been of the type wherein individuals are
selected who will provide positive examples of virtue or conduct and
where these examples are often linked with a series of individuals who
illustrate the contrary. Given the similarity between these *Beispielreihen*
and the form of Sirach 44-50, it would seem that Ben Sira has cast his
presentation of the heroes of Israel through the use of this classical
form.[130]

Before we leave our consideration of the proof from example form, we
ought to recall that earlier mention was made of three additional texts
which are similar to the above and have been compared with Sirach 44-50:
viz., Wisdom 10, CD 2:17-3:12, and Hebrews 11.[131] Wisdom 10, of
Alexandrian provenance from the first century B.C.E., a full century after
Ben Sira, presents a series of examples of how Dame Wisdom preserved

---

[130]Thyen, *Der Stil*, 114, points out that negative or type 'b' *exempla*
may appear in texts apart from type 'a', and that in Sir 16:6-14 there is an
example of this. In this *Beispielreihe*, designed to prove that God will certainly punish the wicked, the following examples are offered: the
Nephilim (16:7), the Sodomites (16:8), the Canaanites (16:9), and the
Israelites who murmured in the wilderness (16:10). The section then concludes with a series of sayings on reward and punishment (16:11-14).

[131]Cf. above, 32.

the righteous in Israel of old.[132] Curiously, Thyen classifies Wisdom 10 as belonging to his type 'b': "Historische Exempla für die Bestrafung von Frevlern."[133] On the contrary, much of Wisdom 10 is given over to listing the positive example of those righteous ones whom Wisdom preserved: Adam (10:1-2), Noah (τὸν δίκαιον, 10:4), Abraham (τὸν δίκαιον, 10:5), Lot (δίκαιον, 10:6), all those who served Wisdom (τοὺς θεραπεύοντες αὐτήν, 10:9), Jacob (δίκαιον, 10:10), Joseph (δίκαιον, 10:13), and Israel, "a holy people and blameless race" (λαὸν ὅσιον καὶ σπέρμα ἄμεμπτον, 10:15). At the same time, however, the author does include the negative examples of Cain (ἄδικος, 10:3) and the wicked citizens of the Five Cities who "passed wisdom by" (παροδεύσαντες σοφίαν, 10:8).[134] Thus Wisdom 10 would seem to represent a mixture of Thyen's types 'a' and 'b', similar to the Beispielreihen of Sirach 44-50, 3 Maccabees, and the passage from Lycurgus.

What sets Wisdom 10 apart from the exempla considered thus far is, first of all, in the focus on the role of Wisdom in the lives of each example. Consequently, chap. 10 has been called a poem "celebrating Wisdom,"[135] and "practically an aretalogy of Wisdom."[136] The use of the term aretalogy here can be misleading. Perhaps the term could be applied to Wisdom 10 if we understand aretalogy "to be a helpful descriptive term for correlating a variety of . . . traditions in which the ἀρεταί of a god or

---

[132]Opinions differ as to when in the first century Wisdom was composed. Among those who would place it in the first half of the century are R. H. Pfeiffer, History, 328: ". . . extremely improbable that Wisdom was written later than 50 B.C."; and E. G. Clarke, The Wisdom of Solomon (Cambridge: The University Press, 1973) 2. Others date it as coming from the last half of the century: cf. J. M. Reese, Hellenistic Influence on the Book of Wisdom and its Consequences (Analecta Biblica 41; Rome: Biblical Institute, 1970) 146; and S. Holmes, "The Wisdom of Solomon," in R. H. Charles, Apocrypha, 521. Reese dates it prior to the accession of Augustus (27 B.C.E.), while Holmes considers Wisdom 10 to be within that part of the book composed between 50 and 30 B.C.E.

[133]Thyen, Der Stil, 114. See, however, 115 where he modifies this classification by noting that Wisdom 10 is built of both 'a' and 'b' exempla.

[134]Citations of the Greek text of Wisdom are from the edition of J. Ziegler, Sapientia Salomonis (Septuaginta Vetus Testamentum Graecum, XII/1; Göttingen: Vandenhoeck und Ruprecht, 1962).

[135]S. Holmes, p. 518.

[136]W. L. Knox, Some Hellenistic Elements in Primitive Christianity (London: Oxford University, 1944) 38, n. 1.

illustrious man are recounted."[137] Yet aretalogy, as the term is used in current discussions, does not appear to describe a well-defined literary genre.[138]

The only "pure" form of aretalogy is the self-praise of Isis known from inscriptions,[139] and with which J. Marböck has compared the self-praise of Wisdom in Sirach 24.[140] The form of the Isis aretalogy is marked by the repetition of the first person pronoun ἐγώ (or ἐγώ εἰμι), the predicates of which are grouped into categories of the deity's φύσις, δύναμις, and ἔργα καὶ εὑρήματα.[141] In contrast to the Isis aretalogy, the description of Dame Wisdom in Wisdom 10 is in the third person and neither her φύσις nor δύναμις is portrayed, but only her ἔργα in the lives of Israel's patriarchs. In the strict sense, then, Wisdom 10 is not an aretalogy. This, however, does not prevent using the term in a less formal sense as a way of acknowledging the theme of Wisdom's ἔργα which sets the passage apart from other exempla. At any rate, the term aretalogy when used of Wisdom 10 does not suggest that we're dealing with a different genre; Wisdom 10 is still a Beispielreihe.

A second feature which distinguishes Wisdom 10 from other exempla is its omission of the proper names of the individuals cited as examples. Thus Adam is not mentioned by name, but is only identified as "the first-formed father of the world" (πρωτόπλαστον πατέρα κόσμου, 10:1), Cain is simply "an unrighteous man" (10:3), and the figures of Noah, Abraham, Lot, Jacob, and Joseph are never named as such. Each one is simply referred to by the title δίκαιον (10:4, 5, 6, 10, 13).[142] James Reese comments:

> His omission of the proper names of Israel's heroes . . . is in keeping with the style of the protreptic, which deals with

---

[137]D. L. Tiede, The Charismatic Figure as Miracle Worker (SBLDS 1; Missoula: Scholars Press, 1972) 1.

[138]Tiede, Charismatic Figure; M. Hadas and M. Smith, Heroes and Gods (New York: Harper and Row, 1965) xiii; and M. Smith, "Prolegomena to a Discussion of Aretalogies, Divine Men, the Gospels and Jesus," JBL 60 (1971) 195-96.

[139]Tiede, Charismatic Figure, 2-3.

[140]Marböck, Weisheit, 49-54.

[141]Ibid., 52.

[142]See also the omission of the subjects' names in Philo, De Virt., §§198-205.

persons as types. The use of character types was a favorite practice in Greek writing, . . .[143]

By this, however, Reese does not mean that the genre of Wisdom 10 is that of the προτρεπτικὸς λόγος which was "an exhortation to some general course—philosophy, rhetoric, virtue."[144] Rather he applies the classification to the book as a whole which, in turn, employs subordinate genres such as that of the *Beispielreihe*.[145] Consequently, the protreptic features in Wisdom 10 are due to the nature of the Book of Wisdom; the genre of chap. 10 remains that of the *exemplum*.

In the Damascus Document, known from the Cairo Geniza and from Qumran, there is a passage, CD 2:17-3:12, which appears to be in the form of a *Beispielreihe*. Although this text, like Wisdom 10, dates from the first century B.C.E.,[146] it comes out of the Palestinian Essene community. In this particular section the teacher of the community utilizes a series of examples in the context of his exhortation "to choose that with which (God) is pleased and to reject that which he hates" לבחור את אשר רצה ולמאוס כאשר שנא, CD 2:15).[147] To illustrate those things which God hates—"thoughts of a guilty inclination" (מחשבות יצר אשמה) and "eyes of fornication" (עני זנות) (CD 2:16)—the teacher lists those figures who in the past stumbled on account of their sin:[148] The Heavenly Watchers (CD

---

[143]Reese, *Hellenistic Influence*, 119.

[144]T. C. Burgess, "Epideictic Literature," *University of Chicago Studies in Classical Philology* 3 (1900) 229-31, n. 2. Also H. I. Marrou, *A History of Education in Antiquity* (New York: Sheed and Ward, 1956) 206-7, describes the protreptic as "an inaugural lecture that tried to gain converts and attract young people to the philosophic life."

[145]Reese, *Hellenistic Influence*, 147 and 105.

[146]There does not seem to be a consensus as to what period within the first century the work should be assigned. G. Vermes, *The Dead Sea Scrolls in English* (Baltimore: Penguin Books, 1965) 95, prefers an earlier date, ca. 100 B.C.E., since the Romans (Kittim) are not mentioned. O. Betz, "Zadokite Fragments," *IDB* 4, 933, interprets "the head of the kings of Javan" (CD 8:11) as a reference to Pompey's intervention of 63 B.C.E. Consequently, he suggests a date during the latter half of the first century. E. Lohse, *Die Texte aus Qumran: Hebräisch und Deutsch* (2d ed.; Munich: Kösel, 1971) 63, is content to leave it as "I. Jahrhundert v. Chr."

[147]The Hebrew text is in the edition of E. Lohse, *Die Texte*, 68.

[148]Cf. O. J. R. Schwarz, *Der Erste Teil der Damaskusschrift und das Alte Testament* (Lichtland: Diest, 1965) 16: ". . . zwei Hauptsünden (schuldiger Trieb und Augen der Unzucht), durch die im Laufe der

2:18), their sons (2:19), all flesh at the time of the flood (2:20-21), Noah's sons (3:1), Jacob's sons (3:4-5), and the people of Israel, both in Egypt and during the wilderness and conquest experiences (3:5-12). On the basis of these examples, Thyen assigns this passage to his 'b' category. "Historische Exempla für die Bestrafung von Frevlern."[149] Yet, as was also true of Wisdom 10, it might be best viewed as of the mixed type ('a'/'b') because of the positive example of Abraham, Isaac, and Jacob:

> Abraham did not walk in it (sin) and was accounted a friend (of God), because he kept the commandments of God and did not choose his own will. And he transmitted (the commandments) to Isaac and to Jacob, who kept them and were recorded friends of God and partners of the covenant forever (CD 3:2-4).[150]

Earlier it was suggested that a feature which makes Wisdom 10 distinct from other *Beispielreihen* is the emphasis on the role Wisdom played in the life of each example. In four of the examples Wisdom is identified by the noun σοφία (10:4, 8, 9, 21). In the remaining examples, however, Wisdom is referred to by means of the f.s. demon. pronoun αὕτη (10:1, 3, 5, 6, 13; 11:1). Now, if we return to CD 2:17-3:12, do we not have something similar in the repeated use of the pronominal suffix on the preposition ב? I would suggest that the recurrent use of this pronominal element is a way by which the conduct of each example is related back to the theme of "thoughts of guilty inclination and eyes of fornication" (CD 2:16). Note the following structure:

I. Theme: Do not go after

מחשבות יצר אשמה ועני זנות (CD 2:16)

II. Examples: Those who did/didn't
   A.   Pre-patriarchal
       1.   Summary: Many men have gone astray
                  through them (בם)

---

Geschichte Israels schon viele 'starke Helden' gestrauchelt und zu Fall gekommen sind. Dieser Fall . . . wird . . . an ganz konkreten Beispielen aus der biblischen Geschichte illustriert. . . ."

[149]Thyen, *Der Stil*, 114.

[150]The translation is mine from the Hebrew text of Lohse, *Die Texte*.

And mighty heroes have stumbled

through them (בם)

(2:17)

2.  Specific Examples of those who walked
    in stubbornness of heart

(בשרירות לבם)

(2:17-18)

a.  The heavenly watchers . . .

they were caught in it (בה)

(2:18)

b.  The sons of Noah went        astray in it (בה)

(3:1)

c.  Their families were cut off        in it (בה)

(3:1)

B.  The Patriarchs (3:2-4)

Abraham did not walk in it(בה)

. . . Isaac and Jacob kept
the commandments

C.  In Israel

1.  Summary: The sons of Jacob

astray through them (בם)

(3:9)

2.  Specific examples of those who
    walked in stubbornness of heart

(בשרירות לבם)

(3:5)

a.  Their sons perished through it        (בו)

(3:9)

b.  Their kings were cut off in it        (בו)

(3:9)

c.  Their mighty men perished through it (בו)

(3:9-10)

d.  Their land was ravaged through it (בו)

(3:10)

D.   Conclusion: Summary Statement:

In it (בו) were guilty those who first entered into the ←
covenant (3:10) . . . those who went after the stubbornness of their hearts (3:11-12)

( שרירות לבם ) ←

That the three-fold mention of the sin of stubbornness of heart is to be
identified with מחשבות יצר אשמה and עני זנות is confirmed by the following passage from the Rule of the Community:

לוא ללכת עוד בשרירות לב אשמה ועיני זנות . . .
(1QS 1:6)

The expressions שרירות לב and מחשבות יצר appear, then, to be inter-
changeable.[151] Thus the examples of all those who either walked or did
not walk in "stubbornness of heart" are all subsumed under the introductory appeal of 2:16 not to go after "thoughts of guilty inclination and
eyes of fornication."

One might question the identification of the fem. pl. מחשבות as the
antecedent of the 3 m. pl. pronominal suffixes on the preposition ב in the
above passage. This, however, does appear in biblical Hebrew: cf. Exod
2:17 and Num 27:7 for examples of where m. pl. pronominal suffixes are
used to refer back to fem. pl. substantives.[152] On the use of the m. s.
suffixes in 3:9-10 for the fem. s. antecedent שרירות, cf. Exod 11:6 and
25:19.

The repetition of the terms "stubbornness of heart" and "thoughts of a
guilty inclination" in CD 2:17-3:12, and of the term "Wisdom" in Wisdom
10, whether by use of the noun or by utilizing the pronominal suffix/
independent pronoun, suggests that these terms have become catch-words

---

[151]On the meaning of יצר in the Zadokite Document and in other
Qumran materials, cf. R. E. Murphy, "Yeser in the Qumran Literature,"
*Bib* 39 (1958) 334-44; and J. Hadot, *Penchant mauvais et volonté libre
dans la sagesse de Ben Sira (l'Ecclésiastique)* (Bruxelles: Universitaires de
Bruxelles, 1970) 50-55.

[152]On this usage, cf. E. Kautzsch, *Gesenius' Hebrew Grammar* (2d
English edition; Oxford: Clarendon, 1910), §135o. That this is the case in
CD 2-3 was noted by R. H. Charles, "The Fragments of a Zadokite Work,"
in Charles, *Pseudepigrapha*, 805; and by Hadot, *Penchant mauvais*, 52 n.
30.

around which each *Beispielreihe* is constructed. As such I would suggest
that the *exempla* of CD 2-3 and Wisdom 10 are of the same form as that
of Hebrews 11 in the NT where the *Stichwort* is "by faith" (πίστει). The
form of Hebrews 11, built around the recurrent use of πίστει, is recognized by Thyen as a distinct type of *Beispielreihe*.[153] To this particular
form, then, may be added the *exempla* of CD 2:17-3:12 and Wisdom 10.
Moreover, since they are fashioned around the use of catch-words, they
are distinct from the *Beispielreihen* of Sirach 44-50, 1 Macc 2, 3 Macc 2
and 6, and 4 Macc 16 and 18.

With a tentative conclusion that the form of the Hymn in Praise of the
Fathers is that of the "proof from example" known from classical texts
and hellenistic Jewish literature, and that it resembles most closely the
*exempla* used in the books of the Maccabees, the next question to address
is how does the *Beispielreihe*—which begins with Enoch at 44:16 and
concludes with Adam at 49:16—relate to the hymn as a whole (44:1-
50:24). Already we have mentioned that *exempla* appear as subordinate
genres in other compositions. Reese observed that the *Beispielreihe* of
Wisdom 10 is a part of the larger structure of a προτρεπτικὸς λόγος.[154]
And in the speech of Lycurgus, *Against Leocrates*, the catalogue of
examples plays a subordinate role. May the same be said of Sir 44:16-
49:16 within Sirach 44-50? Thus we must address the question as to
whether or not there is a *Gattung* in which the *Beispielreihe* is employed
and to which the Hymn in Praise of the Fathers can be compared. Prior to
considering that question, however, I want to take up the two remaining
suggestions that commentators have made as to the form of Sirach 44-50.

### 4. Sirach 44-50 and Pre-Rabbinic Midrash

Another form-critical direction in the study of the Hymn in Praise of
the Fathers has been taken by those who view it as an example of pre-
rabbinic midrash. Norbert Peters, in his commentary of 1913, wrote that
Sirach 44-50 ". . . ist sicherlich in der Entwicklung zum haggadischen
Midrasch begriffen, wenn man den Abschnitt nicht schon direkt als

---

[153] Here Thyen, *Der Stil*, 111, 115, follows R. Bultmann, *Theology of
the New Testament: I* (New York: Charles Scribner's Sons, 1951) 96:
"Series of examples collected from history according to a particular
catch-word. Of this nature is Heb. 11. . . ."
[154] Cf. above, 43-44; Reese, *Hellenistic Influence*, 105.

solchen bezeichnen will."[155] More recently, Mlle. Renée Bloch went so far as identifying the passage as such. It was her claim that it manifests the two principal characteristics of midrash: "l'utilisation des textes scripturaires dans un but d'edification, en fonction des besoins contemporains."[156] These characteristics, coupled with the exhortation in Sir 51:23 that all who are untaught should come and lodge in Ben Sira's בית מדרש, suggested to Mlle. Bloch—and after her, Siebeneck[157] and Maier[158]—that the Hymn is an example of haggadic midrash.

Given her definition, I suppose we could regard it as such. It is clear that Sirach starts with scripture. Studies in recent years by Koole,[159] J. G. Snaith,[160] and Middendorp,[161] as well as work done shortly after the publication of the Cairo Geniza MSS—e.g., that of Schechter and Taylor[162]—have established that Ben Sira did not simply quote, but also offered interpretations of the Hebrew scriptures. Not only do the scriptural examples enumerated in chaps. 44-49 confirm this, but at various points in the Hymn it becomes evident that Sirach had before him the materials which would become those of the Hebrew canon. For example, he refers to "The Twelve" (49:10), he draws upon the Deuteronomistic historian's picture of Solomon (47:12-22), and like the Chronicler, he attributes the establishment of the Jerusalem cultus and the organization of the temple singers to David (47:9-10). And with respect to the second characteristic of midrash as described by Bloch, Sirach certainly is addressing our Hymn to a contemporary need. The care with which we saw him draw the parallel between Aaron and Simon II suggests that he is attempting to apply the examples from scripture to his own day.

The question is, however, whether or not the "midrashic" elements in Sirach 44-50 define a particular literary genre. The problem, it seems to me, is in the use of the term genre with respect to midrash. In the article

---

[155]Peters, *Das Buch,* 372.

[156]R. Bloch, "Midrash," 1274.

[157]Siebeneck, "May Their Bones," 416, n. 14.

[158]Maier, *Mensch,* 50.

[159]J. L. Koole, "Die Bibel des Ben-Sira," *OTS* 14 (1965) 374-396.

[160]J. G. Snaith, "Biblical Quotations in the Hebrew of Ecclesiasticus," *JTS* (new series) 18 (1967) 1-12.

[161]Middendorp, *Die Stellung.* See esp. chap. 2, "Ben Sira und das Alte Testament."

[162]Schechter and Taylor, *Wisdom of Ben Sira,* 12-38; A. Eberharter, *Der Kanon des alten Testaments zur Zeit des Ben Sira* (Münster: Aschendorff, 1911) 6-52.

in which she classified Sirach 44-50 as midrash, Mlle. Bloch chose to describe midrash as a *genre litteraire*.[163] If, however, we are thinking in terms of the methodology of biblical form criticism—which would understand genre to be synonymous with *Gattung* or literary type—Bloch's terminology becomes confusing. For instance, in addition to Sirach 44-50 as an example of pre-rabbinic midrash, she includes two texts which we examined earlier, Psalms 78 and 105.[164] Yet these two psalms, form-critically understood, are not only distinct from Sirach 44-50, but from each other as well: Psalm 105 is a "hymn," while Psalm 78 is a "didactic hymn."[165] Thus texts which are disparate in form, or represent diverse types, are brought together as examples of a midrashic genre by Bloch.

This inconsistency in the use of the term genre led Addison G. Wright to undertake an investigation of midrash as a literary form.[166] In so doing he affirmed Bloch's definition of midrash as the use of scripture in a way that makes it relevant for a later generation.[167] Wright, however, goes on to add that the new composition—midrash—has no value apart from the earlier composition—the biblical text—with which it begins.[168] As such, he distinguishes midrash from the mere quotation or citation of a biblical passage. In the case of a citation or quotation, the biblical text is being used to serve the purpose of a new composition. But then this new composition, Wright claims, would not be midrash. Rather for a composition to be midrashic, it must exist for the sake of the biblical text and not the other way around. With this attempt to define midrash more precisely as a literary genre, Wright proceeds to examine those pieces of pre-rabbinic midrash proposed by Bloch. Of concern to us, then, are his comments on Psalms 78 and 105 and Sirach 44-50:

> . . . it seems clear that it is the events and personages themselves and not some specific biblical narration of them which are the object of interest. The works are not a literature about a literature.[169]

In other words, Sirach 44-50 exists not for the purpose of interpreting

---

[163]Bloch, "Midrash," 1265. Also *genre midrashique*, 1280.
[164]Ibid., 1275.
[165]Above, 23-29, and on Psalm 78, cf. 27, n. 89.
[166]Cf. A. G. Wright, *Literary Genre*.
[167]Ibid., 74, 143.
[168]Ibid., 114.
[169]Ibid., 100.

particular biblical texts about the fathers of old, but it is a new composition that just happens to employ material from scripture. It is in scripture that Ben Sira found the particular examples he needed for his *Beispiel-reihe*.[170] Because the biblical material serves the purpose of the Hymn, then, and not vice versa, Wright concludes that Sirach 44-50 does not belong to the genre midrash.

Wright's contention—that a new composition which uses scripture can only be called midrash when it exists for the sake of scripture—has been criticized in subsequent discussions. Roger le Déaut is of the opinion that Wright's distinction does not do justice to the tension in midrash between the text and the adaptation of that text.[171] That is, as midrash seeks to actualize a text, it does so in the form of a new composition which may well use scripture in a different manner and with different meanings than it originally had. He suggests:

> Even the adaptation of ancient texts in their midrashic re-elaboration seems to serve the purpose of new compositions. . . . The Targum itself is *midrashic* precisely to the extent that it suggests new meanings, often very far from the texts in which they originated.[172]

Similar criticism of Wright's one-sided description of midrash has come

---

[170]Similar things, Wright contends, may be said about other pieces of literature which retell or re-present biblical accounts. For example, in books 1-10 of the *Jewish Antiquities,* Josephus makes use of biblical material. Wright, however, says that the *Antiquities* at this point is not midrashic. For Josephus is consciously writing a history that is modeled after the *Roman Antiquities* of Dionysius of Halicarnassus (93). Thus the *Jewish Antiquities,* even where biblical material is used, does not exist for the sake of the biblical text. The same, Wright adds, can be said of the Chronicler's use of Samuel-Kings; in contrast to Bloch, he believes 1-2 Chronicles is not a midrash on the Deuteronomic History (95-99). On the idea that Chronicles is Midrash, cf. Bloch, "Midrash," 1271.

[171]R. le Déaut, "Apropos a Definition of Midrash," *Int* 25 (1971) 274-75.

[172]Ibid., 275. It is for this reason that le Déaut criticizes Wright's denial of a midrashic character to the Chronicler's and Josephus' use of scripture.

from Brevard Childs[173] and Merrill Miller.[174] They prefer to speak of a reciprocity between the text and the new situation to which it is directed:

> . . . the interpretation moves from the biblical text to seek a connection with a new situation. But then again, the reverse direction is equally important; namely, the interpretation comes from the situation and moves back to the text.[175]

Thus, although they do not comment specifically on Sirach 44-50, the fact that Ben Sira's selection of examples from scripture is guided by the manner in which he seeks to portray Simon II would be considered by them as perhaps a midrashic type of activity.

Moreover, Ben Sira's focus on persons, rather than on a specific biblical narration about those persons, does not trouble le Déaut. One need not expect explicit citation or quotation of particular biblical texts about a person or event. "An implicit citation as well as a historical allusion is therefore sufficient to reveal a midrash."[176]

Having begun with our own criticism of Bloch's attempt to view Sirach 44-50 as representative of a midrashic literary genre, and then having observed that Wright's attempt to define genre more precisely has not met with acceptance, we're still left with the question as to whether or not midrash can be understood as a form-critical category. Perhaps we are dealing here with an exegetical method rather than a specific literary form.[177] Rather than being itself a particular *Gattung*, in the sense that a *Beispielreihe* is, midrash is a method or a process which made use of a variety of literary forms.[178] If so, that would seem to raise a new question: is Ben Sira engaged in creating a midrash as he employs *exempla* in chaps. 44-49?

It is known that rabbinic midrash made use of classical, Greco-Roman

---

[173]B. S. Childs, "Midrash and the Old Testament," *Understanding the Sacred Text* (ed. John Reumann; Valley Forge: Judson, 1972) 52.

[174]M. P. Miller, "Targum, Midrash and the Use of the Old Testament in the New Testament," *JSJ* 2 (1971) 44.

[175]Childs, "Midrash," 52.

[176]le Déaut, "Apropos," 274.

[177]Ibid., 273. Cf. also G. Vermes, "Bible and Midrash:  Early Old Testament Exegesis," *The Cambridge History of the Bible, I: From the Beginnings to Jerome* (P. R. Ackroyd and C. F. Evans, eds.; Cambridge: The University Press, 1970) 199, who speaks of midrash as a "process."

[178]le Déaut, "Apropos," 282; Miller, "Targum," 43.

literary forms. That such was the case has been demonstrated by the work of Henry Fischel,[179] Saul Liebermann,[180] and Siegfried Stein.[181] For example, Fischel has detected the presence in midrashim of the classical anecdote form known as χρεῖαι which was common in Greco-Roman rhetoric.[182] Also, he has drawn a parallel between a midrash of Ben Zoma (ca. 110 C.E.) and classical treatments of the history and evaluation of civilization (e.g., that of Plato's *Republic*).[183] Stein, besides providing a catalogue of parallels between the table customs of Greek *symposia* and those of the Passover Seder, analyzes the Seder liturgy in terms of the various literary forms incorporated in the *symposia* literature. In so doing he concludes that in the midrash on Deut 26:5-8 are traces of common rhetorical procedures associated with the *genos epideiktikon*. Thus, for example, the technique of *auxesis,* amplification or embellishment, is seen in the augmentation of the number of plagues in Egypt from 10 to 50 to 250.[184]

If, then, rabbinic midrash made use of classical *Gattungen,* could not pre-rabbinic Jewish materials of the hellenistic period, engaged in a similar exegetical method, make use of them as well? If so, could we not

---

[179]H. Fischel, "The Transformation of Wisdom in the World of Midrash," *Aspects of Wisdom in Judaism and Early Christianity* (Robert L. Wilken, ed.; Notre Dame: University of Notre Dame, 1975) 67-101; and H. Fischel, *Rabbinic Literature and Greco-Roman Philosophy* (Studia Post-Biblica 21; Leiden: E. J. Brill, 1973).

[180]In S. Liebermann, *Greek in Jewish Palestine* (New York: The Jewish Theological Seminary, 1942), cf. esp. the essays "The Greek of the Synagogue," 29-67; and "Greek and Latin Proverbs in Rabbinic Literature," 144-60. "The Rabbis elucidated the verses of the Bible not only by means of quoting from Jewish sources but sometimes also from Greek law and literature as well as proverbs" (37). Also cf. his later volume, *Hellenism in Jewish Palestine* (New York: The Jewish Theological Seminary, 1950).

[181]S. Stein, "The Influence of Symposia Literature on the Literary Form of the Pesaḥ Haggadah," *JJS* 8 (1957) 13-44. Greek rhetorical influence can be traced in Rabbinic materials other than midrash. In the case of Rabbinic jurisprudence cf. David Daube, "Rabbinic Methods of Interpretation and Hellenistic Rhetoric," *HUCA* 22 (1949) 239-264.

[182]Cf., e.g., "A Chria on Absent-Mindedness," Genesis Rabba II.4 on Gen. 1:7, in Fischel, *Rabbinic Literature,* 78ff.

[183]Ibid., 51-61.

[184]Stein, "Influence," 39. The role of *auxesis* in Greek epideictic will be discussed in chap. 2 when we consider Sirach 44-50 as an example of the encomium.

say that Ben Sira is engaged in a kind of midrashic activity that, while
looking back to the scriptural narration of Israel's patriarchs, prophets,
and kings, he cites these figures according to the pattern of the classical
*exempla* or *Beispielreihe?* Thus, in accord with the broad, non-form-
critical definition of midrash held by le Déaut, Childs, Miller, and Vermes,
we may still consider Sirach 44-50 as an example of pre-rabbinic midrash.
Yet at the same time the form-critical question remains unanswered: viz.,
what is the larger literary structure in which the *exempla* of Sirach 44-49
are employed?

### 5. Sirach 44-50 and Hellenistic Biography

In addition to the genre proposals which have been considered thus far,
there remains one area yet to be examined: the suggestion that the Hymn
in Praise of the Fathers is reminiscent of a type of biographical writing
that came to expression in the Hellenistic Age. Thierry Maertens, for
example, was the first among recent commentators to compare Sirach 44-
50 with the genre *De Viris Illustribus.* Concerning Ben Sira he wrote:

> . . . il introduit un nouveau genre littéraire dans la littérature
> vétero-testamentaire, qui ne trouvera d'égal dans la littéra-
> ture païenne, quelques rares témoignages stoicens mis à part,
> qu'un siècle après notre auteur: Cornelius Nepos, . . . d'un *De*
> *Viris Illustribus*, . . .[185]

Subsequent to Maertens, Siebeneck,[186] Pautrel,[187] and Hengel[188] have
suggested the same. Hengel, however, has added to this a note on the type
of Greek biography which was being written in Ben Sira's time:

> Greek biography reached a climax in the third century B.C.
> under Peripatetic influence, with Hermippus, Satyrus and
> Sotion. From the latter, between 200 and 170 B.C., come the
> διαδοχαὶ τῶν φιλοσόφων. . .[189]

We have before us, then, two proposals as to types of literature with

---

[185]Maertens, *L'éloge*, 11.
[186]Siebeneck, "May Their Bones," 414.
[187]Pautrel, "Stoicisme," 541.
[188]Hengel, *Judaism*, 136.
[189]Hengel, *Judaism*, II, 90, n. 209.

which Sirach 44-50 may have some affinities: the genre *De Viris Illustribus* and Peripatetic biography. In addition we have the names of several authors we will want to consider, ranging from Hermippus to Cornelius Nepos. Before passing on the merits of these proposals, it may be helpful to survey the materials and authors involved.

Although only Cornelius Nepos was cited by Maertens, et al. in conjunction with the genre *De Viris Illustribus*, biographies of this type are known to have been written by several Roman authors. The church father Jerome names, in order, Varro (116-27 B.C.E.), Santra, Cornelius Nepos (99-24 B.C.E.), Hyginus, and Suetonius Tranquillus (69-121 C.E.).[190] Moreover, Jerome patterned his own *De Viris Illustribus*, a series of notices on 135 Christian writers, on the model of Suetonius' work of the same name.[191] Of the works of this genre known to have been written by these four Romans, we have extant selections of only Cornelius Nepos and Suetonius; those of Varro, Santra, and Hyginus have been lost.

As the name suggests, Peripatetic biography had its origins among Aristotle's students at the Academy. The creator of this type of literature is believed to have been Aristoxenus (b. 375/360 B.C.E.),[192] and other students of Aristotle—e.g., Phaenias of Eresus (ca. 320 B.C.E.) and Dicaearchus of Messana (326-296 B.C.E.)—as well as those of Theophrastus, e.g. Duris of Samos (340-260 B.C.E.), followed his lead. From the Academy Peripatetic biography was carried to Alexandria where it was represented in the third century *Successions of the Philosophers* of Sotion. The biographies of the Peripatetics, however, are no longer available to us. With the exception of a second century C.E. papyrus fragment of Satyrus' *Life of Euripides*, our knowledge of the Peripatetics is only in terms of quotations from them in later works, especially in Athenaeus' *The Deipnosophists* (ca. 192 C.E.) and Diogenes Laertius' *Lives of Eminent Philosophers* (third century C.E.).[193]

Peripatetic biography and the genre *De Viris Illustribus*, though, do not represent two distinct bodies of literature. Rather it is generally held that

---

[190]F. Leo, *Die Griechisch-römische Biographie* (Leipzig: Druck und Verlag von B. G. Teubner, 1901) 136.

[191]H. Lietzmann, "Hieronymos," *PW: VIII,2*, 1580-81.

[192]Leo, *Die Griechisch-römische*, 102; A. Momigliano, *The Development of Greek Biography* (Cambridge: Harvard University, 1971) 74-77.

[193]Citations or quotations of the Peripatetics in the works of Athenaeus and Diogenes Laertius were located by the use of K. Müller, *Fragmenta Historicorum Graecorum: II-III* (Paris: Editore Ambrosio Firmin Didot, 1928).

the latter, as known in the works of Varro, Santra, Hyginus, Cornelius Nepos, and Suetonius, is but a Roman development of the former. Jerome again, in the introduction to his *De Viris Illustribus*, made the comment—which he evidently took from Suetonius—that the Roman biographers considered themselves heirs of Hermippus, Antigonus of Carystus, Satyrus, and Aristoxenus.[194] And on the basis of analyzing the content of Peripatetic biography and that of the Roman *De Viris Illustribus*, the relationship between the two is apparent in terms of their common use of anecdotes, gossip, and attention to the personal lives of the subjects involved.[195]

> As in the *Lives of the Caesars*, Suetonius' sources for the *Lives of Illustrious Men* were in the main literary, in particular Varro, the previous writers of books of the same title (Nepos, Santra and Hyginus), . . . In part through these writers, and perhaps in part directly, his work goes back to the Greek authors Antigonus of Carystos, Aristoxenus, Satyros and Hermippus.[196]

This relationship between the two I believe will be illustrated in the examples which will follow. Consequently, since we are dealing not with two completely different types of literature, it may be advantageous to drop the use of the term *De Viris Illustribus* in discussions pertaining to Sirach 44-50. Inasmuch as it describes a genre that does not appear until the first century B.C.E., our concern should be with the form hellenistic biography took in Sirach's time.[197] Thus, the question we want to ask is

---

[194]D. R. Stuart, *Epochs of Greek and Roman Biography* (Berkeley: University of California, 1928) 193. Momigliano, *The Development*, 74, places Antigonus of Carystus outside the Peripatetic school.

[195]Cf. Leo, *Die Griechisch-römische;* and H. J. Rose, *A Handbook of Greek Literature* (4th ed.; London: Methuen and Co., Ltd., 1951) 357.

[196]J. C. Rolfe, *Suetonius: II* (Loeb Classical Library; Cambridge: Harvard University, 1959) 392.

[197]The situation here is similar to that encountered above in our discussion of Sirach 44-50 as an example of pre-rabbinic midrash. Part of the confusion in applying the title midrash to the manner in which later biblical material uses earlier traditions (e.g., Sirach's use of biblical traditions in chaps. 44-50) is the borrowing of terminology from the rabbinic period. With respect to rabbinic literature, the term midrash refers to a genre, while in terms of biblical material the term refers to a process.

whether or not Sirach 44-50 can be compared with the "Lives" of Hermippus, Satyrus, Sotion, and their predecessors, rather than with the biographies of Nepos and Suetonius.

For the purpose of studying Sirach 44-50 in the light of Peripatetic biography, we will want, first of all, to gain an idea of the content of these works, or of the manner in which the biographers treated their subjects. In so doing it ought to suggest something of their intention and of the audience for which they wrote. Secondly, we will want to determine, as best we can, the form in which this literature appeared. It is to the first of these that we now turn by means of an examination of fragments from these authors in roughly chronological order from Aristoxenus to Sotion. And to illustrate that the Roman *De Viris Illustribus* continues the same type of biographical treatment, we will append some quotations from Cornelius Nepos and Suetonius.

## a. The Content of Peripatetic Biography

Aristoxenus, who, as has already been noted,[198] is considered the founder of Peripatetic biography, portrayed his subjects in terms of material which can be described as (1) anecdote, (2) personal touches, viz., the use or invention of details about the subject's personal life, and (3) gossip or slander. As we will see, these seem to be features which appear not only throughout the Peripatetics, but which also extend into the work of Suetonius.[199] In part, their fascination with this type of material may have been in that their biographies were intended for a popular audience,[200] and that the characterization of, and attacks on, certain individuals through the use of gossip and anecdote were often designed to discredit the philosophical school or tradition to which the subject belonged.[201] An example of this may be seen in Aristoxenus' reference to Socrates having been a student of the physicist Archelaus (Diog. Laert. 2:19), which apparently was intended to be an attack on the notion that Socrates was intellectually independent of any teacher.

---

[198]Above, n. 192.

[199]Those who have commented on the use of anecdotes, gossip, and personal touches through the various Peripatetic *Lives* include: Leo, *Die Griechisch-römische,* 102; Rose, *Handbook,* 357; and Momigliano, *The Development,* 71-73.

[200]Cf. Stuart, *Epochs,* 168.

[201]Momigliano, *The Development,* 71.

. . . er (Aristoxenus) zum ersten Mal Sokrates einen Lehrer gibt, den Physiker Archelaos. In den Augen der Sokratiker war Sokrates reiner Autodidakt; Aristoxenos hat diese idealisierende Anschauung der Sokrates-Schüler angegriffen und dem Sokrates eine recht anrüchige Lehrzeit bei Archelaos nachgesagt.[202]

Moreover, Aristoxenus wrote that Socrates' income came from loaning money out at interest: ". . . he would at all events invest sums, collect the interest accruing, and then, when this was expended, put out the principal again" (Diog. Laert. 2:20).[203] But, as Momigliano notes, ". . . ancient philosophers were not supposed to get angry or lend money; and it is difficult to escape the conclusion that Aristoxenus brought an element of malice into his picture of the Socratic schools."[204] The mention or invention of such gossip is also evident in Aristoxenus' depiction of Plato as a plagiarist: ". . . the *Republic* itself Aristoxenus declared to have been nearly all of it included in the *Controversies* of Protagoras" (Diog. Laert. 3:37).

In contrast to the negative picture he paints of Socrates, Plato, and Aristotle—the leadership of whose Academy was given not to Aristoxenus, much to his dismay, but to Theophrastus—he revealed his Pythagorean sympathies in the type of anecdote and personal touches employed with respect to the members of that school.

Aristoxenus says that our Pythagorean (viz., Archytas) was never defeated during his whole generalship, though he once resigned it owing to bad feeling against him, whereupon the army at once fell into the hands of the enemy (Diog. Laert. 8:82).

A contemporary of Aristoxenus, Phaenias of Eresus, shared the former's fascination for personal details. Along the line of the discrediting notes known in Aristoxenus is Phaenias' report on Aristippus:

---

[202]W. von Kienle, *Die Berichte über die Sukzessionen der Philosophen in der hellenistischen und spätantiken Literatur* (Berlin: Philosophischen Fakultät der freien Universität, 1961) 76.

[203]The translation of Diog. Laert., here as well as below, is that of R. D. Hicks, *Diogenes Laertius: Lives of Eminent Philosophers: I-II* (Loeb Classical Library; Cambridge: Harvard University, 1970, 1972).

[204]Momigliano, *The Development*, 75.

. . . as Phaenias of Eresus, the Peripatetic, informs us, he (Aristippus) was the first of the followers of Socrates to charge fees and to send money to his master (Diog. Laert. 2:65).

And an example of a pure anecdote is one from Phaenias' *On the Tyrants of Sicily* regarding Philoxenus and Dionysius I:

Phaenias says that Philoxenus, the poet of Cythera, who was devoted to dainty food, was once dining with Dionysius, and when he saw that a large mullet had been set before Dionysius, while a small one had been served to himself, he took it up in his hands and placed it to his ear. When Dionysius asked him why he did that, Philoxenus answered that he was writing a poem on Galatea and desired to ask the mullet some questions about Nereus and his daughters. And the creature, on being asked, had answered that she had been caught when too young, and therefore had not joined Nereus' company; but her sister, the one set before Dionysius, was older, and knew accurately all that he wished to learn. So Dionysius, with a laugh, sent him the mullet that had been served to himself (Ath. 1:6ef).[205]

The blend of anecdote, gossip, and report of idiosyncrasies, seen in Aristoxenus and Phaenias, is also apparent in the biography of Plato from the hand of a third student of Aristotle, Dicaearchus of Messana:

Others again affirm that he (Plato) wrestled in the Isthmian Games—this is stated by Dicaearchus in his first book *On Lives*—and that he applied himself to painting and wrote poems, first dithyrambs, afterward lyric poems and tragedies (Diog. Laert. 3:4-5).

There is a story that the *Phaedrus* was his first dialogue. For the subject has about it something of the freshness of youth. Dicaearchus, however, censures its whole style as vulgar (Diog. Laert. 3:38).

---

[205]The translation of Athenaeus, here as well as below, is that of C. B. Gulick, *Athenaeus: Deipnosophists: I-VII* (Loeb Classical Library; Cambridge: Harvard University, 1928-51).

(Among Plato's students were) two women, Lastheneia of
Mantinea and Axiothea of Philus, who is reported by Dicaearchus to have worn men's clothes (Diog. Laert. 3:46).

While the subjects portrayed in the above manner by the first generation of Peripatetics tended to be fellow-philosophers, or in the case of
Phaenias political leaders as well, by the time we come to the next generation the range of subject-matter has broadened. Thus Duris of Samos,
who was not an artist, writes about artists:

> Lysippus of Sicyon is said by Duris . . . to have been originally
> a copper-smith and to have first got the idea of venturing on
> sculpture from the reply given by the painter Eupompus when
> asked which of his predecessors he took for his model; he
> pointed to a crowd of people and said it was Nature herself,
> not an artist, whom one ought to imitate (Pliny, *Nat. Hist.*,
> 34:61).[206]

And besides the above anecdote about artists, he also invents or emphasizes the artistic qualities of philosophers:

> Duris makes him (Socrates) out to have been a slave and to
> have been employed on stonework, and the draped figures of
> the Graces on the Acropolis have by some been attributed to
> him (Diog. Laert. 2:19).

This new breadth of biographical subjects is seen in other Peripatetics
of the early third century. The title of Neanthes of Cyzicus' work, περὶ
ἐνδόξων ἀνδρῶν, implies that the biographer's interest extended to men
from various walks of life. As we would expect, philosophers continue to
be discussed. Neanthes, along with the other Peripatetics, thought that
the circumstances surrounding the death of philosophers would have a
special appeal to his audience. Thus the following anecdote concerning the
death of Heraclitus is attributed to him:

> Neanthes of Cyzicus states that, being unable to tear off the
> dung (with which the servants of Heraclitus had covered him
> thinking that the warmth of the manure would draw off the

---

[206]The translation of Pliny is that of H. Rackham, *Pliny: Natural
History: IX* (Loeb Classical Library; Cambridge:   Harvard University,
1952).

fluids of the dropsy he suffered), he remained as he was and, being unrecognizable when so transformed, he was devoured by dogs (Diog. Laert. 9:4).[207]

But poets, such as the comic poet Epicharmus of Sicily, were topics for Neanthes as well. In a fragment in the 'Εθνίκα of Stephanus of Byzantium (ca. 500 C.E.) where, under his discussion of the Sicilian city Κραστός, he reports that in it lived "Epicharmus and his companion Lais, ὡς Νεάνθης ἐν τῶι Περὶ ἐνδόξων ἀνδρῶν (FrGH 84 F13).[208] And from philosophers and poets, Neanthes' interests ranged to a treatment of the semi-legendary Timon of Athens, the Misanthrope.[209] Although we remain uncertain as to whether or not the notices in Neanthes are truly biographies or merely a collection of anecdotes,[210] the emergence of a blanket title such as περὶ ἐνδόξων ἀνδρῶν marked a stage in the development of biography as an independent, objective art.[211] This breadth of interest on the part of the Peripatetics is represented not simply by Neanthes, but by Idomeneus of Lampsacus (325-270 B.C.E.), who treated the Socratic philosophers under the heading περὶ τῶν Σωκρατικῶν, but rulers and statesmen under the title περὶ δημαγωγῶν. "At all events the epoch was at hand at which the noteworthy career in any walk of life was to furnish the biographer sufficient excuse."[212]

Peripatetic biography had experienced the foregoing development by the time we come to the third and second century Alexandrian biographers with whom Hengel has sought to compare Ben Sira in his Praise of the Fathers: viz., Hermippus, Satyrus, and Sotion. As Leo commented, these three authors "gründete sich durchaus auf die peripatetische Arbeit, benutzte und ergänzte deren Material, befolgte und vervollkommnete ihre Methoden."[213]

---

[207]Other anecdotes in Neanthes concerning various philosophers include Diog. Laert. 3.4, where he writes that Plato received his name from the "breadth" (πλατύς) of his forehead; and Diog. Laert. 6.13, where Neanthes is said to have reported that Antisthenes was the first to practice the custom of "doubling his mantle" (διπλῶσαι θοιμάτιον).

[208]Neanthes is no. 84 in F. Jacoby, *Die Fragmente der Griechischen Historiker: Zweiter Teil: A* (Berlin: Weidmannsche, 1926) 194.

[209]Stuart, *Epochs*, 162.

[210]Momigliano, *The Development*, 71.

[211]Stuart, *Epochs*, 161.

[212]Ibid., 162.

[213]Leo, *Die Griechisch-römische*, 118. Stuart, *Epochs*, 155-88, stresses

Hermippus, the earliest of the three, lived and wrote in Alexandria ca. 200 B.C.E.[214] A description of Hermippus' method and style, which suggests its connection with the earlier Peripatetics, is that of Momigliano:

> He used Callimachus' files for his biographies, including archaic legislators, the Seven Wise Men, Pythagoras, Gorgias, Isocrates, Aristotle, and their respective pupils. His interest in the frivolous, the morbid (death scenes), the paradoxical is well established: he went all out to captivate his readers by learned sensationalism. . . . He continued the Peripatetic practice of grouping men of the same profession in the same book.[215]

Witness these concerns in the following citations from Hermippus:

(1) Anecdote:

> Hermippus gives another anecdote. (lit., "and Hermippus tells another one concerning Pythagoras.") Pythagoras, on coming to Italy, made a subterranean dwelling and enjoined his mother to mark and record all that passed, and at what hour, and to send her notes down to him until he should ascend. She did so. Pythagoras some time afterwards came up withered and looking like a skeleton, then went into the assembly and declared he had been down to Hades, and even read out his experiences to them. They were so affected that they wept and wailed and looked upon him as divine, going so far as to send their wives to him in hopes that they would learn some

---

the relationship between the biographies of the earlier Peripatetics and those of the Alexandrians when he discusses Hermippus et al. under the heading "Alexandrian Continuators." For additional treatments of the Alexandrian biographers, over and above that of Leo and Stuart, cf. F. Susemihl, *Geschichte der Griechischen Literatur in der Alexandrinerzeit: I* (Leipzig: B. G. Teubner, 1891) 491-99.

[214]Momigliano, *The Development*, 79. Susemihl, *Geschichte*, 495, notes that Hermippus' *Lives* included a report concerning the death of the Stoic Chrysippus (207 B.C.E.) (cf. Diog. Laert 8.184), and suggests that the appearance of Hermippus' work probably appeared not long after this event. A convenient summary of scholarship on Hermippus is that of Pfuhl, "Hermippos," *PW: VIII, 1*, 845-852.

[215]Momigliano, *The Development*, p. 79.

of his doctrines; and so they were called Pythagorean women. Thus far Hermippus. (Diog. Laert. 8:41)

(2) Gossip/Scandal:

> Hermippus, in his work *On Isocrates*, says that Isocrates, when considerably advanced in years, took the courtesan Lagisca into his house and from her there was born to him a daughter (Ath. 8:592d).[216]

(3) Personal Touches/Idiosyncracies:

> And Hermippus, in the third book of his work *On the Disciples of Isocrates* says that Hypereides always took walks in the fish-market at early dawn (Ath. 8:342c).

> Hermippus says that Theophrastus used to appear at the school at the regular hour glistening with oil and exquisitely dressed, and after seating himself he gave free play to every emotion and gesture in delivering his discourse. On one occasion, while portraying an epicure, he thrust forth his tongue and licked his lips (Ath. 1:21a).

The same type of material appears in the works of Hermippus' younger Alexandrian colleagues: the βίοι of Satyrus and the διαδοχαὶ τῶν φιλοσόφων of Sotion. Of particular interest in the case of Satyrus, whose biographical writings—coming between the reigns of Ptolemy IV Philopator (d. 205 B.C.E.) and Ptolemy VI Philometer (180 B.C.E.)—were contemporary with Ben Sira,[217] is the fact that the fragment discovered of his *Life of Euripides* is in dialogue form. To this fragment we will return below. But in terms of Satyrus' use of anecdote and gossip, note the combination of the two in his description of the marital relationships of Philip of Macedon:

> . . . Philip always married a new wife with each new war he undertook. 'In the twenty-two years of his reign, at any rate,'

[216]The translation of Athenaeus is that of C. B. Gulick, *Athenaeus: The Deipnosophists: VI* (Loeb Classical Library; Cambridge: Harvard University, 1930).
[217]On the dates for Satyrus, cf. Momigliano, *The Development*, 80. For general discussions of Satyrus, cf. that of Kind, "Satyros," *PW: IIA, 1*, 228-235; and Leo, *Die Griechisch-römische*, 118-124.

as Satyrus says in his *Life* of him, 'he married Andata of
Illyria, . . . he also married Phila, . . . Wishing to put a claim
on the Thessalian nation, . . . he begot children by two women
of Thessaly, . . .' (Ath. 8:577c)

The quote from Satyrus continues with mention of Philip's marriage to
Olympias and Meda, and concludes with an anecdote from the story of his
marriage to one Cleopatra, niece of Attalus (not to be confused with
Attalus I or II of Pergamum):

> . . . by bringing her (Cleopatra) home to supplant Olympias,
> he (Philip II) threw the entire course of his life into utter
> confusion. For immediately, during the celebration of the
> wedding itself, Attalus remarked, 'But now, I warn you,
> princes will be born who will be legitimate, and not bastards.'
> Alexander, on hearing that, threw the goblet which he held in
> his hands at Attalus, and he retaliated upon Alexander with
> his own cup (Ath. 8:557de).

Not only the love-life of a ruler, but that of a philosopher was
believed by Satyrus to be worth discussing. He may have invented the
following report about Socrates' wives:

> . . . some writers, including Satyrus and Hieronymus of
> Rhodes, affirm that they (Xanthippe and Myrto) were both his
> wives at the same time. For they say that the Athenians were
> short of men and, wishing to increase the population, passed a
> decree permitting a citizen to marry one Athenian woman
> and have children by another; and that Socrates accordingly
> did so (Diog. Laert. 2:26).

And Satyrus shared the Peripatetic interest in the financial affairs of
their subjects; Satyrus believed Plato to be a rich man:

> Some authorities, amongst them Satyrus, say that he (Plato)
> wrote to Dion in Sicily instructing him to purchase three
> Pythagorean books from Philolaus for 100 minae. For they say
> he was well off, having received from Dionysius over eighty
> talents (Diog. Laert. 3:9).

In the διαδοχαί of Sotion, whose date, 200-170 B.C.E., is comparable
to that of Satyrus, the same Peripatetic concerns appear even though

technically he was not a member of the school.[218] Examples of anecdote
in Sotion include these two regarding Aristippus:

> He (Aristippus) enjoyed the favors of Lais, as Sotion states in
> the second book of his *Successions of Philosophers.* To those
> who censured him his defence was, 'I have Lais, not she me;
> and it is not abstinence from pleasures that is best, but
> mastery over them without ever being worsted' (Diog. Laert.
> 2:74-75).

> . . . Aristippus the Socratic was a fish-eater, and when re-
> proached on one occasion by Plato for his love of dainties, as
> Sotion and Hegesander say—but here is what the Delphian
> writes (viz., Hegesander; but presumably Sotion's notice
> included the same anecdote): 'when Plato criticized Aristip-
> pus for buying so many fish, he replied that he had bought
> them for only fourpence. To this Plato said that he could have
> bought them himself at that price, whereupon Aristippus said:
> 'You see Plato! It isn't I who am a fish-lover but you who are
> a money-lover' (Ath. 8:343d).

All of the various types of material which went into Peripatetic biography, and which we have illustrated above, show up as well in the Roman
genre *De Viris Illustribus.* The continuity between the Peripatetics and the
Roman biographers has already been noted. But at the same time it needs
to be mentioned that the continuity between them does not mean that the
Roman biographers had no distinctiveness of their own.[219] Thus, even
though Cornelius Nepos employed anecdotes and personal touches in the
extant *Great Generals of Foreign Nations* ( *Liber de excellentibus ducibus
exterarum Genitum)* of his *De Viris Illustribus,* he used them not for the
amusement of his audience, but for a commemorative purpose:[220]

---

[218]Momigliano, *The Development,* 81, comments that Sotion "did not
belong to the Peripatos," while Münzer, "Sotion," *PW: IIIA, 1,* 1235, calls
him a "Peripatetiker."

[219]Stuart, *Epochs,* 221-22, criticizes those who tend to regard Roman
literature as but "a servile imitation of Greek."

[220]J. C. Rolfe comments that Cornelius Nepos employed a number of
different forms of biography—Peripatetic, Alexandrian, and encomiastic-
-as he eulogized the great generals of foreign nations, cf. Rolfe and E. S.
Forster, *Lucius Annaeus Florus:  Epitome of Roman History; Cornelius
Nepos* (Loeb Classical Library; New York: G. P. Putnam's Sons, 1929) 360.

He (Iphicrates, the Athenian general) left a son Mnestheus, the offspring of a Thracian woman, the daughter of King Cotus. When Mnestheus was once asked whether he thought more of his father or of his mother, he answered: 'My mother.' When everyone expressed surprise at this reply, he added: 'I have good reason for that; for my father did everything in his power to make me a Thracian; my mother, on the contrary, made me an Athenian'. (Nep. 11. Iphicrates 3:4)[221]

And in his commemoration of Aristides, nicknamed "The Just," there is this anecdote concerning the vote taken to exile him on account of his rivalry with Themistocles:

Aristides himself, when he realized that the excited populace could not be quieted, and, as he was withdrawing, saw a man in the act of voting that he should be banished, is said to have asked him why he did so, and what Aristides had done to be thought deserving of such a punishment. To which the man replied that he did not know Aristides, but that he was displeased because he had worked so hard to be distinguished from other men by the surname 'The Just.' (Nep. 3. Aristides 1:3-4)

A personal touch is the report Nepos includes on the frugality of his friend Atticus:

I shall not pass over the fact, although I suppose that some will regard it as trivial, that although he (Atticus) was one of the richest of the Roman knights, and with no little generosity invited to his house men of all ranks, we know from the entries in his day-book that he consistently limited his expenses to not more than three thousand sesterces each month. And this I state not from hearsay, but from actual knowledge; for because of our intimacy I was often familiar with the details of his domestic life. (Nep. 25. Atticus, 13:6-7)

A century later, the same fascination with the details of a person's finances is seen in Suetonius. This time, however, the information is to

---

[221]The translation of Nepos is that of Rolfe, *Lucius*.

the subject's discredit rather than to his praise. Suetonius, commenting on the grammarian Quintus Remmius Palaemon, wrote:

> He was so given to luxurious living that he went to the bath several times a day, and could not live within his income, although he received four hundred thousand sesterces a year from his school.[222]

Two additional examples which illustrate the continuation of the Peripatetic biographical style in Suetonius are the following:

> He (Crates of Mallos, grammarian) was sent to the senate by King Attalus between the second and third Punic wars, at about the time when Ennius died; and having fallen into the opening of a sewer in the Palatine quarter and broken his leg, he held numerous and frequent conferences during the whole time both of his embassy and of his convalescence, . . .[223]

> While he (Quintus Caecilius Epirota) was teaching his patron's daughter, who was the wife of Marcus Agrippa, he was suspected of improper conduct towards her and dismissed; whereupon he attached himself to Cornelius Gallus and lived with him on most intimate terms, . . .[224]

Thus far our concern has been to survey the content of hellenistic biography from Aristoxenus down through the Alexandrians and on to Suetonius' *De Viris Illustribus*. The question is, then, whether or not the reports Ben Sira includes on the fathers of old in Sirach 44-50 evidence the same or a similar kind of biographical interest to that reflected in the above Peripatetic selections. I think the answer is no. What the above quotations illustrate is that the concern of these biographers was primarily that of entertainment. After acknowledging that Peripatetic biography was sometimes used in the battles between rival philosophical schools, Momigliano goes on to comment:

> But more often biography provided entertainment for educated people who liked to know something about the lives of poets, philosophers and kings. . . . The basic interest in

---

[222]J. C. Rolfe, *Suetonius: II*, 429.
[223]Ibid., 397.
[224]Ibid., 421.

discovering a variety of human characters had a philosophic
root, but the wealth of strange details, of piquant anecdotes,
was ultimately meant to satisfy the curiosity of the common
reader.[225]

Quite in contrast, however, is the description of persons in Sirach 44-
50. Ben Sira does not employ anecdotes, gossip, or slander in depicting
Abraham, Moses, et al. Rather than seeking to entertain, his purpose is to
offer examples of piety. Thus, he may summarize the piety of some
("Noah was found perfect and righteous," 44:17), or when he narrates or
alludes to particular incidents, they serve to illustrate the faithfulness of
the individual:

> And in the days of Moses he (Joshua) did a loyal deed, he and
> Caleb the son of Jephunneh: they with-stood the congrega-
> tion, restrained the people from sin, . . . And the Lord gave
> Caleb strength, . . . so that he went up to the hill country,
> and all his children obtained it for an inheritance; so that all
> the sons of Israel might see that it is good to follow the Lord
> (46:7, 9-10).

As was established earlier,[226] Sir 44:16-49:16 has the form of a *Beispielreihe* wherein the persons offered as examples are, in Lumpe's words,
"zur Tugend ermahnen oder vor Lastern warnen."[227] With that intention
in mind, I do not think that Ben Sira would have found inspiration in the
biographical collection of Hermippus, Satyrus, and Sotion.

### b. The Form of Peripatetic Biography

Although the citations which appear in Athenaeus and Diogenes
Laertius inform us as to the content of Peripatetic biography, they do not
provide us with any understanding of the form in which the βίοι were
written. In the case of two early Peripatetics, however, the citations of
them make reference to various titles under which their biographies
appeared and from which we may infer something about how their works
were structured. We have already mentioned some of the works of

---

[225]Momigliano, *The Development,* 84.
[226]Above, 37-38.
[227]Lumpe, "Exemplum," 1230; cf. above, 32.

Phaenias, his *On the Tyrants of Sicily* (περὶ τῶν ἐν Σικελίᾳ τυράννων, Ath. 4:232c). But Phaenias also included among his βίοι works entitled *On the Socratics* (περὶ τῶν Σωκρατικῶν, Diog. Laert. 6:8) and *On Poets* (περὶ ποιητῶν).[228]

It would seem, then, that Phaenias has arranged his biographies according to the various walks of life of his subjects: political leaders were treated separately from poets and philosophers. The same organizational principle was evidently employed by Idomeneus who had his own *On the Socratics* (Diog. Laert. 2:20) as well as one with the title *On Civic Leaders* (περὶ δημαγωγῶν).[229] Moreover, such grouping of lives according to categories of statesmen, philosophers, poets, etc. is supposed to have been true of Neanthes and Hermippus.[230] Hermippus is cited on several occasions by reference to his works *On Lawgivers* (περὶ νομοθετῶν, cf., Ath. 4:154d, 13:555c) and *On the Seven Sages* (περὶ τῶν ἑπτὰ σοφῶν, cf., Ath. 10:443a; Diog. Laert. 8:88).

We would not be in a position to say any more than this about the structure of Peripatetic biography had it not been for the discovery and publication (in 1912) of papyrus fragments of one of the *Lives* of Satyrus. The fragments, dating from the second century C.E., are from those found at Oxyrhynchus, and are of the *Life of Euripides*.[231] In frg. 39, col. 23, we are provided with not only a reference to the subject, Euripides, but identified for us as well are the author, Satyrus, the title of the work as a whole (Βίων Ἀναγραφῆς), the information that this biography of Euripides has been included in Book Six (ζ′) with the biographies of Aeschylus (Αἰσχύλου) and Sophocles (Σοφοκλέους), and that within the book the treatments of the three poets are arranged in chronological order.[232] Moreover, we know that Book Four was composed of the biographies of

---

[228]On Phaenias, περὶ ποιητῶν, cf. Leo, *Die Griechisch-römische*, 105, 110.

[229]For explicit mention of the title περὶ δημαγωγῶν, cf. Idomeneus, frg. 17, in Müller, *FHG I*, 493. Also, cf. Leo, *Die Griechisch-römische*, 111.

[230]Stuart, *Epochs*, 162-63.

[231]The papyrus is no. 1176. It was published in A. S. Hunt, *The Oxyrhynchus Papyri: IX* (London: Oxford University for the Egypt Exploration Fund, 1912) 124-182.

[232]For the text of frg. 39.23, cf. ibid., 168 and for Hunt's comments, 124.

philosophers.[233] Thus, Satyrus, by grouping poets together in one book and philosophers in another, was evidently following the pattern of the other Peripatetics—Phaenias, Idomeneus, and Hermippus.

The most striking piece of information gained from the papyrus about the form of Satyrus' *Lives* is that they were cast in the pattern of a dialogue.[234] Hunt believes the fact to be beyond question, even though the copyist failed to employ the double dots which were normally used to distinguish the various parts of the speakers in a dialogue or drama.[235] In the transcription of the text, however, Hunt has reproduced the raised dot or Greek colon which seems to mark off the words of one participant from that of another (cf., e.g., frgs. 39.13,22; 39.14,27; 39.15,34,38). The characters participating are three in number: the principal part, whose name is not given, is presumably that of Satyrus; and the two lesser parts are those of Diodorus (ὦ Διόδωρε, frg. 39.3,19; 39.15,13) and of a woman, Eucleia (Εὔκλεια, frg. 39.14,31).[236]

Although the opening portion of the dialogue is extremely fragmentary, it seems that the biography of Euripides began with a rehearsal of the main events of his life. This in turn was followed by a topical arrangement of the poet's views on philosophical, religious, political, and ethical matters.[237] For example, in frg. 38.2,14-30 Satyrus quotes Euripides as a way of illustrating the latter's attitude toward wealth:

> Why, mortals as you are, have you acquired great wealth for nought, why think you to produce by means of riches? What though you possessed Etna's mount or the marbles of Paros wrought in gold in your ancestral halls? Not then, unless you

---

[233]Ibid., 126.

[234]Ibid. For additional discussion of the dialogue form in Satyrus, cf. Stuart, *Epochs*, 178-88; F. Leo, "Satyros ΒΙΟΣ ΕΥΡΙΠΙΔΟΥ," *Ausgewählte Kleine Schriften: II* (Reprint of the original article of 1912; E. Fraenkel, ed.; Rome: Edizioni di storia e letteratura, 1960) 366-68; and Rose, *Handbook*, 177, no. 1.

[235]Hunt, *Oxyrhynchus Papyri*, 126.

[236]On Satyrus as the chief interlocutor in the dialogue, cf. Stuart, *Epochs*, 180, n. 48.

[237]For discussion of Satyrus' outline, cf. Stuart, *Epochs*, 182-83; and Hunt, *Oxyrhynchus Papyri*, 127. For an example of rubrics which served to divide one topic off from another, cf. frg. 8.2,9-12, "Such were the man's artistic qualities." (The translation is Hunt's, 171.)

are good of heart are you deserving of honour , but you sit
unblessed in the midst of wealth.[238]

From describing his opinions on such subjects and outlining the characteristics of his poetry, the dialogue then turns to portray Euripides' preference for the *vita solitaria*. "He was the owner of a large cave there (on
Salamis) with the mouth toward the sea, and here he passed the day by
himself engaged in constant thought or writing, despising everything that
was not great and elevated" (frg. 39.9,4-19).[239] Stuart notes that from
this picture of "lonely, brooding genius the biographer passed by an easy
step to the popular disfavor likely to be visited on a man who holds himself aloof from his fellows and wields an iconoclastic and radical pen."[240]
Thus Satyrus notes that "Everyone disliked him, the men because of his
unsociableness, the women because of the censures in his poems" (frg.
39.10,1-10). Mention of the latter serves to introduce a lengthy discussion
of Euripides' views on women. Extending from col. 10 to col. 15, it closes
as the narrator (Satyrus) responds to a line of Diodorus with the phrase:
"Perhaps, Diodorus. But let this be the defence of women and let us return
to Euripides" (frg. 39.15,13-20). The remaining columns continue to provide material to Euripides' discredit, and as was the Peripatetic custom,
the biography ends with a description of his old age and death. One passage from col. 18 illustrates not only the dialogue form, but provides an
example of the type of transitional phrase used to introduce an anecdote
about his old age:

> . . . began the songs. Or do you not know that it is this that he
> says? (Diodorus:) How then? (A:) In saying "to mingle my
> flight with Zeus" he metaphorically designates the monarch
> and also magnifies the man's power. (Diodorus:) What you say
> seems to me to be more subtle than true. (A:) Take it as you
> like. Anyhow, he migrated and spent his old age in Macedonia,
> being held in much honor by the sovereign; and in particular
> the story is told that . . . (καὶ δὴ καὶ μν[η]μονεύε[ται ὅ]τι
> . . .) (frg. 39.18,1-34).

Although the contents of this particular anecdote are lost to us in that

---

[238]The translation is that of Hunt, 173, who calls attention to the fact
that the quote from Euripides is found, in condensed form, in Plutarch.
[239]Ibid., 176.
[240]Stuart, *Epochs,* 183.

the lower portion of the column is no longer extant, other anecdotes do appear in the text (cf. frg. 3, cols. 19, 21, 22). The use of anecdotes, as was noted already, served to make Peripatetic biography readable and appealing. The same could be said of the dialogue form in which this *Life* is cast. Leo believes that Satyrus wrote not in a learned style, but in the style of a dialogue for the pleasure of the reader.[241] Moreover, he advances the idea that the dialogue in Satyrus is not an isolated form; it was common, rather, to all Peripatetic biography. Beginning with Aristotles' περὶ ποιητῶν, biography in dialogue form may be traced through the Peripatetics down to Cicero's *Brutus* and beyond.[242] Besides our papyrus fragment of Satyrus, it is known that Clearchus of Soli (ca. 340-250 B.C.E.) wrote βίοι in the style of a dialogue.[243] Thus both Leo and Stuart conclude that Satyrus did not set a literary precedent, but chose to employ an established biographical *Gattungsform.*[244]

From the foregoing, then, we may infer that the type of Peripatetic biography with which Hengel seeks to compare Sirach 44-50 had the following characteristics: (1) the overall pattern was to divide the subjects into categories according to whether they were poets, philosophers, or statesmen; (2) within each category individual biographies were arranged in chronological order; (3) the contents of each biography were structured according to a topical scheme wherein a rehearsal of the subject's life might be followed by discussion of his religious, political, and ethical views, and would conclude with a description of his last days and death; and (4) the biography itself was composed in the form of a dialogue between two or more characters in order to make the life-story enjoyable reading.

If we examine the structure of Sirach 44-50 in the light of the formal characteristics of Peripatetic biography, I believe that we must conclude that there is little to commend the suggestion that Ben Sira found his inspiration in the βίοι of Hermippus and Satyrus. As was the case with respect to the content of biography, so it is with the form. With the use of anecdote, gossip, and the dialogue-form, Peripatetic biography sought to entertain. Sirach 44-50, however, is commemorative. And to this end the *exempla* are structured not as a part of a dialogue or of a narrative, but

---

[241]Leo, "Satyros," 366. Also Hunt, *Oxyrhynchus Papyri,* 126.

[242]Leo, "Satyros," 366. Momigliano, *The Development,* 80, while acknowledging the dialogue form in Peripatetic biography, does not see Aristotle's περὶ ποιητῶν nor Cicero's *Brutus* as comparable examples.

[243]Leo, "Satyrus," 367, 376, n. 3.

[244]Stuart, *Epochs,* 179.

are given a "hymnic" character. Although we have dismissed the proposal that Sirach 44-50 is a hymn in a strict, form-critical sense,[245] there
is a laudatory quality to the manner in which the various heroes of Israel
are recalled. For example, note the hymnic phrases, "How glorious he
was . . ." (מה נהדר ב-) in the praise of Joshua (46:2) and Simon II (50:5).
"How wise you were in your youth") (מה חכמת בנעריך) addressed to
Solomon (47:14), and "How glorious you were. O Elijah" (מה נורא אתה
אליהו (48:4). The latter praise of Elijah continues in hymnic fashion with a
recitation of Elijah's deeds. Each deed is introduced by the definite
article, functioning as a relative particle, followed by a participle: "(You)
who raised a corpse . . ." (המקים גוע) (48:5), "Who brought kings down . . ."
(המוריד מלכים) (48:6), etc.[246] The eulogistic quality of these passages,
coupled with the use of rhetorical questions designed to express the
incomparability of the fathers (46:3; 49:11), and the lengthy descriptions
of the beauty and majesty of Aaron and Simon II (45:8-13; 50:6-13), all
suggest that Ben Sira wrote not to entertain his audience with
remembrances of the personal lives of his subjects, but that he wrote to
praise and commemorate and to offer them as examples to be emulated.

Moreover, apart from the question of a commemorative versus an
entertaining style, there seems to be little resemblance between Peripatetic biography and Sirach 44-50 in terms of the arrangement of material
within each. From Satyrus we infer that the presentation of the events in
a person's life was followed by a topical discussion of his opinions and
attitudes. Ben Sira, however, limits his portrayal of each patriarch, king,
or prophet to the citation of only those specific events—known from the
biblical narrative—through which the subject demonstrated his piety or
fidelity to the law. The only point at which there exists some kind of
topical arrangement is in the praise of Simon II where there is first a
remembrance of Simon's accomplishments as a political leader (50:1-4),
followed by a description of his cultic role (50:5-21). But even here the
emphasis is on what Simon did, not on what he thought nor the details of
his personal life.

---

[245]Cf. above, 24.

[246]On the use of the relative and a participle to introduce the deeds
for which the subject is praised in a hymn, cf. above, 23. On the definite
article serving as a relative particle, cf. Kautzsch, *Gesenius' Hebrew
Grammar*, sec. 138i; or R. Meyer, *Hebräisches Grammatik: II* (Berlin:
Walter de Gruyter, 1969) 16.

c. Sotion's διαδοχαί τῶν φιλοσόφων

There remains yet one item to be considered in our discussion of Sirach 44-50 and Peripatetic biography: Martin Hengel's comparison of the Praise of the Fathers with the form of Sotion's *Successions of the Philosophers*. We have already indicated that in terms of content, Sotion's work made use of scandal and anecdote.[247] The question remains, though, if there is anything to the suggestion that Ben Sira employed a principle of succession such as that around which Sotion organized his biographies of the philosophers.

Sotion's διαδοχαί, which appeared in thirteen books sometime between the years 200 and 170 B.C.E., made the succession of teachers to students within a given philosophical school its guiding principle.[248] Such a concern to trace a philosophical heritage, however, was not new with Sotion. Aristoxenus, for example, made Socrates a student of Archelaus.[249] Later in the fourth century, Phaenias, in his περὶ τῶν Σωκρατικῶν, appears to have dealt with the succession of philosophers within that school.[250] And in the third century, the same may be said of Callimachus, Ariston of Ceos, Hermippus, and Hippobotus, whose φιλοσόφων ἀναγραφή, it is said, must have been similar to the διαδοχαί of Sotion.[251]

Since our knowledge of Sotion's *Successions of the Philosophers*—like that of the other Peripatetics, save Satyrus—is only through excerpts which appear in later authors, we do not know its original form. It has been argued that even Diogenes Laertius, on whom we are dependent for much of what we have of Sotion, did not have a copy of the διαδοχαί itself or even of the *Epitome* of it by Heraclides Lembus (ca. 170 B.C.E.).[252] He knew of it and used it only indirectly. Yet it is believed

---

[247]Cf. above, 64-65.

[248]Münzer, "Sotion," *PW: IIIA*, 1, 1235-36.

[249]von Kienle, *Die Berichte*, 76.

[250]Leo, *Die Griechisch-römische*, 110.

[251]von Kienle, *Die Berichte*, 76-78.

[252]Ibid., 80-82. Here von Kienle argues on the basis of three passages in Diogenes Laertius where information is attributed to Sotion of which he could have had no knowledge given the date of 200-170 B.C.E. for his work. Thus in Diog. Laert. 1.1 Sotion is cited as an authority for the view that the study of philosophy began with the Barbarians, of whom the Celtic Druids were offered as an example. But, according to von Kienle, Sotion could not have written this. The earliest references to the Druids in ancient literature date from the first century B.C.E. Cf. also Münzer, "Sotion," who believes Diog. Laert. could not have used Sotion directly.

that the general plan of Sotion's work can be reconstructed from references in Diogenes Laertius, despite the latter's indirect usage of it.[253]
Whenever Diogenes cited Sotion, he listed the particular number of the
book from which the material about a philosopher was taken. Thus
Aristippus and his teacher Socrates were described as having been discussed in Book 2 of Sotion (Diog. Laert. 2.75), while Plato we know to
have been the subject of Book 4 (Diog. Laert. 6.26). From the references
in Diogenes, then, the pattern emerges wherein each of the thirteen books
of Sotion was devoted to a particular philosopher and/or philosophical
tradition. Moreover, by the order in which the books appear, Sotion sought
to introduce a relationship or a principle of succession between the various traditions. He began with the Ionian succession, starting with Thales
(Book 1) to Socrates and the Socratics (Books 2-3), where the line divides
into three branches: Plato and the members of the Academy (Books 4-5),
the Peripatetics (Book 6), and the Cynics-Stoics (Books 7-8). The Italian
succession began with Pythagoras (Book 9), and ran through the Eleatics
and Atomists (Book 10), the Pyrrhonian skeptics (Book 11) to the Epicureans (Book 12). Those who fell outside the succession, e.g., the barbarians, were the subject of the final book.[254] The principle of succession,
then, around which Sotion's work is organized, was that of the student-
teacher relationships within each of the schools, and in turn, each school
was described with respect to the earlier and later schools with which it
shared either the Ionian or Italian succession. The question we need to ask
is whether or not there is anything comparable to this succession principle
in Sirach 44-50.

Hengel would see a succession principle at work at six points in the
Hymn of Praise of the Fathers. Three of the six are in terms of Ben Sira's
use of the term תחלף:[255]

> Noah the Righteous was found blameless;
> In a time of destruction he became a continuator
>
>                                           (תחלף; 44:17)

---

[253]von Kienle, *Die Berichte*, 82.

[254]Cf. the table in von Kienle, *Die Berichte*, 83, where he places the
order of the thirteen books of Sotion alongside the order of books in Diog.
Laert. The sequence in which philosophers are discussed is the same in
both works. Cf. also R. D. Hicks, *Diogenes Laertius: I*, p. xx.

[255]Hengel, *Judaism*, 136.

May their (the Judges') bones break out of their grave,
And their name be continued (תחליף) in their sons
                                                    (46:12)[256]

(Elijah) who anointed kings[257] of retribution
And a prophet (to be) a continuator (תחליף) in your place
                                                    (48:8)

In the first and last instances תחליף is understood by the Greek translator to be a noun and is rendered by ἀντάλλαγμα ("exchange") and δια-
δόχους ("successors," N.B. Greek plural against Hebrew singular).[258] The
תחליף of 46:12 evidently is a verb,[259] cf. the Greek ἀντικαταλλασσόμε-
νον.
The remaining three instances of a succession principle in Sirach 44-50
are:

A mighty man of valor was Joshua son of Nun,
A minister (משרת; Greek διάδοχος "successor")
of Moses in prophecy (46:1).

And for his (David's) sake there stood up after him (עמד אחריו)
A wise son who dwelt in safety (47:12).

Elijah was hidden in the whirlwind
And Elisha was filled (with) his spirit (נמלא רוחו)
                                                    (48:12)

These six passages seem to describe four different successions. First,
47:12 is simply Ben Sira's version of the royal succession from David to

---

[256]Sir 46:12a, תהי עצמתם פרחות תחתם, missing in MS B, is restored on
the basis of the Greek, Syriac, and the Hebrew of 49:10. Cf. Smend,
Commentary, 443-44; Peters, Das Buch, 397-98; and Oesterley-Box, "Book
of Sirach," 492.
[257]Reading מלכי in place of MS B מלא. Cf. Greek, Syriac, and Smend,
Commentary, 460.
[258]The Syriac also understands תחליף in 44:17 and 48:8 to be a noun.
Cf. ܚܠܘܦ (44:17) and ܚܠܘܦܗ "his successor" (48:8b).
[259]Cf. Peters, Das Buch, 398. The Syriac is of no help here in that
46:12b is freely translated with "And they will leave their good name to
their sons and to all the people their honor." The last half of the phrase
evidently represents the opening of v 13 in MS B. Cf. Smend, Commentary, 444-45.

Solomon. This succession, however, had long been a part of the tradition received by Sirach, cf., e.g., 2 Sam 7:11-16; 1 Kgs 1:32-37, 2:1-4. The second reference to succession is in 44:17 where Sirach uses the new term תחליף as a way of expressing Gen 6:9. But the thought expressed here is not that of a succession of one king to another or of teacher to student. Rather the picture is of Noah providing the link between creation and history at a time when that link was in jeopardy.[260]

A third succession is indicated by the use of תחליף as a verb in 46:12 to state that the "name" of the Judges would be continued in their sons. Although there appears to be no consistent presentation of a judge-son succession in the Deuteronomistic history, there are a few passages from which Ben Sira may have fashioned his summary. A closing note to the story of Gideon is that he had seventy sons (Judg 8:30) as well as Abimelech, whom he had had by his Shechemite concubine (8:31). The latter is reported to have put the question to the people of Shechem, following the death of Gideon/Jerubbaal, "which is better for you, that all seventy of the sons of Jerubbaal rule over you, or that one (viz., Abimelech) rule over you (Judg 9:2)?" In the narrative that follows, Jotham—the sole survivor of the seventy whom Abimelech murdered—denounces Abimelech for his crime against his "father's house" by slaying Gideon's sons and making himself king (9:16-21).[261] Can we infer that Gideon's administrative role was somehow to have been continued by his sons, and that by his act of murder and desire to be king rather than judge, Abimelech thwarted that policy? Here the references to the sons of three of the minor judges would seem to be referring to the same idea. Jair has "thirty sons," who in turn had "thirty cities" (Judg 10:4); Ibzan likewise had thirty (12:9); and Abdon is said to have had "forty sons and thirty grandsons" (12:14). The mention of the sons in each of these cases apparently indi-

---

[260]If the basic theme of the Priestly writer is expressed at Gen 1:28, and the P narrative witnesses to how this way played out in Israel's history, then the *toledoth* of Noah at Gen 6:9 serves to bridge the antediluvian promise with its realization in history. Cf. W. Brueggemann and H. W. Wolff, *The Vitality of Old Testament Traditions* (Atlanta: John Knox, 1975) 102, n. 9.

[261]Cf. also the historian's note that Abimelech's crime was against Gideon through the murder of his sons (Judg 9:56); and that Israel did not live up to a covenant obligation it had with respect to Gideon's household (Judg 8:35).

cates that we are dealing with groups of elders (sons, brothers, or kin of some type) who had responsibility in the administration of justice.[262] Moreover, the historian also wrote that Samuel was a judge (1 Sam 7:15-17) who, in turn, made judges of his sons ( 1 Sam 8:1-2). Thus the idea of a succession of judges may not be a creation of Ben Sira, but something he had taken over from his reading of Judges-Samuel.

That the succession principle in 46:12 is described in terms of the judges' names living on in their sons expresses a concept already known from 2 Sam 18:18. Here, since Absalom has "no son" to keep his "name in remembrance," he set up a pillar and gave it his name. Also two passages in Trito-Isaiah witness to the idea that a man's name will live on in his offspring. In Isa 66:22, "name" and "offspring" are in apposition, while the oracle in Isa 56:4-5 speaks of the faithful eunuchs who will leave a name which will be "better than sons and daughters."

The fourth type of succession is that of the prophets: two passages describe Elisha as the heir of Elijah (48:8, 12), which Sirach knew from 1-2 Kings (cf. 1 Kgs 19-21; 2 Kgs 2:1-22). The remaining passage, 46:1, identifies Joshua as the "minister" (משרת) of Moses (cf. Exod 24:13, 33:11; Num 11:28; Josh 1:1), which the Greek translator of Ben Sira—as Smend noted —interprets correctly (richtig erklärend) with the phrase διάδοχος Μωυσῆ.[263] Sirach, then, is simply reporting on two examples of prophetic succession which were already a part of the biblical tradition. Even if Sirach had made use of a more comprehensive principle of prophetic succession than that of these two passages, there would still be biblical precedent for it. Smend commented that the succession of the prophets was an idea already in the Chronicler's time, stemming ultimately from Deut 18:15.[264] I assume that by identifying the principle in the Chronicler, Smend was thinking of Ezra's confession in Nehemiah 9. There the refrain is repeated in vv 20, 26, and 30 that Yahweh continually sent prophets to instruct and warn Israel. The prophets were the agents through which Yahweh's spirit was repeatedly at work (vv 20, 30; cf. Num 11:25 with Neh 9:20), and at four different places in 1-2 Chronicles it is the spirit that

---

[262]Cf. R. Boling, Judges (Anchor Bible 6A; Garden City: Doubleday, 1975) 162, 188, 216; J. Gray, Joshua, Judges and Ruth (Century Bible, New Edition; London: Thomas Nelson and Sons, 1967) 342; and C. F. Burney, The Book of Judges with Introduction and Notes (Library of Biblical Studies; H. M. Orlinsky, ed.; New York: Ktav, 1970) 289.

[263]Smend, Commentary, 439.

[264]Ibid.

comes upon various prophets as, one-by-one, they illustrate the principle described in Nehemiah 9 (1 Chr 12:19; 2 Chr 15:1, 20:14, 24:20).[265]

I am of the opinion, then, that whatever succession motifs are present in Sirach 44-50 are there because they were already a part of the biblical tradition out of which Sirach drew his *exempla*. They do not represent the kind of succession principle developed by the Peripatetics which came to expression in Sotion's *Successions of the Philosophers*. In Sirach we have noted that the successions are of different types—king to king, judge to son, prophet to prophet—while the Peripatetic successions are of teacher to student within a particular philosophical school. If there is any resemblance between Sotion and Jewish literature at this point, it is not in terms of Sirach 44-50. The more likely Jewish parallels would be in the works of two other authors whom Hengel brings into his discussion: Josephus and Eupolemos.[266] Josephus, in his *Against Apion*, wrote of the failure of "the exact succession of the prophets" (τὴν τῶν προφητῶν ἀκριβῆ διαδοχήν) (1:41) as the reason why Jewish literature written after Artaxerxes was not considered "canonical." And Eupolemos, the hellenized Jewish historian and Maccabean envoy to Rome, wrote of an exact succession of prophets and kings in his *On the Prophecy of Elias:* Moses to Jesus (Joshua) to Samuel to Saul and to his son (*sic*) David (FrFG 723 F2b).[267] To this Hengel would add another parallel from Eupolemos, FrGH 723 F5 (Euseb., Praep. Evang. 9:39), where his account of the fall of Jerusalem is included under the title *On the Prophecy of Jeremiah.*[268]

---

[265]Cf. also the editorial comment of 2 Chr 24:19, and Jehoshaphat's exhortation, "Believe his prophets and you will succeed" (2 Chr 20:20).

[266]Hengel, *Judaism*, 136.

[267]Cf. the translation of FrGH 723 F2b (=Eusebius, *Praep. Evang.* 9.30,1) in Ben Zion Wacholder, *Eupolemus*, 129, 308.

[268]Ibid., 227, n. 1,2; 311-12. Mention should be made as well of the principle of succession in the tractate *Aboth* of the Mishnah: Moses to Joshua to the elders to the prophets to the Men of the Great Synagogue and then from Simon the Just down to Rabbi Judah the Prince.

# Part II
# Sirach 44-50:
# An Encomium of Simon II

## A. THE PROPOSAL OF AN ENCOMIASTIC GENRE

This study began with Baumgartner's observation that Sirach 44-50 is a hymn in praise of men and not God.[1] As a consequence, then, some commentators have chosen to refer to the hymn by means of terms which call attention to the fact that Sirach's purpose is to extol Israel's heroes. Addison Wright, for example, notes that the passage has been called a eulogy.[2] Another term that has entered the discussion is that of panegyric.[3]

In the course of Part I we sought to establish that the hymn does not treat each of the fathers equally, but that the focus of the whole is on Simon II, the high priest with whose praise the passage closes.[4] Thus we would not want to call Sirach 44-50 a panegyric of Israel's ancestors, but rather of Simon. This, however, is what I. Lévi has done in his use of the term:

> This form of sacred history, however, is little more than a panegyric on the priests, terminating in an enthusiastic delineation of the high priest Simon ben Onias.[5]

---

[1]Above, p. 1.
[2]Wright, *Literary Genre*, 99-100, n. 52.
[3]Bigot, "Ecclésiastique," 2048; and Siebeneck, "May Their Bones," 425. The use of the term panegyric in discussions of Sirach 44-50 has prompted Tarn and Griffith to deny that it is such; cf. W. Tarn and G. T. Griffith, *Hellenistic Civilisation* (3rd ed.; London: Edward Arnold, Ltd., 1952), 230.
[4]Above, 10-21.
[5]Lévi, "Sirach," 389.

As we will see, Lévi's use of the term is more in keeping with the general meaning panegyric came to have in Greek rhetoric, viz., that a panegyric was a composition in praise of a specific person and was, for all practical purposes, synonymous with the term encomium. Thus, in view of Lévi's comment, we could say that Sirach 44-50 is an encomium of the high priest Simon II. It should be added, though, that recent references to the Praise of the Fathers in the literature have already introduced the term encomium into the discussion. Yet in the cases of both Momigliano and Wacholder, they have employed the term with respect to only chap. 50 of Ben Sira.[6] What we propose to do, however, is to examine the entire hymn—in view of Lévi's suggestion—to see if the whole of chaps. 44-50 may properly be described as an encomium.

Our method will be as follows. First, since we have already seen a number of terms introduced into these preliminary comments, we need to determine whether or not these terms—eulogy, panegyric, encomium and others—are synonymous or if they had distinct meanings in classical rhetoric. Second, since in our discussion of the *Beispielreihe* we concluded that Sirach 44:16-49:16 is of this form and raised the question of how one might describe the larger unit 44:1-50:24, which embraces the series of examples, we will then want to ask if encomia made use of *exempla* as a subordinate genre. And third, following a survey of the history and form of the Greek encomium, we will analyze Sirach 44-50 from this perspective.

## B. TERMINOLOGY

### 1. ἐπιδεικτικός

Inasmuch as rhetorical treatments of the encomium and panegyric are often subsumed under the heading of epideictic literature, and since epideictic is also used to designate a genre,[7] it may be helpful to clarify the use of this category before we consider how these other terms are used.

Technically, epideictic describes a genre of γένος within classical

---

[6]Momigliano, *Alien Wisdom*, 98; Wacholder, *Eupolemus*, 12.

[7]G. Kennedy, *The Art of Persuasion in Greece* (Princeton: Princeton University, 1963) 152: ". . . the genre is called epideictic." W. Schmid, "'Επίδειξις," *PW: VI, 1, 55*, refers to λόγος ἐπιδεικτικός as a *Gattung*.

rhetoric. Aristotle, for example, in his *Rhetoric,* notes that there are
". . . three kinds of rhetorical speeches, deliberative, forensic, and epideictic" (τρία γένη, τῶν λογῶν τῶν ῥητορικῶν, συμβουλευτικόν,
δικανικόν, ἐπιδεικτικόν; *Rh.* 1.3.3). The distinction between genres is
made on the basis of the type of audience for which the speech is intended: viz., the deliberative speech is directed to the legislative assembly, a judge "of things to come" (τῶν μελλόντων); the forensic is addressed
to the dicast, a judge "of things past" (τῶν γεγενημένων); while the epideictic has as its audience the mere spectator (θεωρός) whose interest is
only in the ability (δύναμις) of the orator (*Rh.* 1.3.2). Thus in addition to
the difference in audiences, there is also a difference in purpose. Whereas
forensic and deliberative oratory are to persuade, epideictic serves to
entertain. Hence the name epideictic, from ἐπίδειξις "display" / ἐπι-
δείκνυμι "to exhibit, display."

Aristotle's understanding of epideictic was already present in Isocrates,
and prior to him, Gorgias.[8] Isocrates, for example, writes that there are
speeches for the law-courts (πρὸς τοὺς ἀγῶνας . . .) and speeches for
oratorical display (πρὸς τὰς ἐπιδείξεις) (*Antidosis* 1). And in taking
issue with those critics who complain about elaborate oratory and who
would judge it by the standards of forensic oratory, he writes:

> (They think) both kinds should be alike and should not be
> distinguished, the one by plainness of style (τοὺς μὲν
> ἀσφαλῶς), the other by display (τοὺς δ' ἐπιδεικτικῶς) . . .
> (*Panegyricus* 11).

The above examples, in that they describe epideictic in terms of
audience and style, suggest that we are dealing with a relatively broad
category and not a precise type of speech. Thus Aristotle writes that
epideictic speeches may take the form of either those whose specific
purpose is to offer praise (ἔπαινος) or blame (ψόγος) (*Rh.* 1.3.3). In the
case of Anaximenes, praise and blame are regarded as two species or
subdivisions of the epideictic genre or γένος. In discussing the structure
of epideictic oratory he considers both eulogy (ἐγκωμιαστικόν, ἐγκω-
μιαζομένους), and vituperation (κακολογικόν, ψεγομένους), and then
refers to "speeches of these classes" (τούτων τῶν εἰδῶν) as being

---

[8]Burgess, "Epideictic Literature," 102, n. 1: "Epideictic literature as a
distinct division of oratory may for all practical purposes be said to begin
with Gorgias. The ornaments of language known as the Gorgian figures
belong to the epideictic branch far more fully than any other."

different than those of the forensic type. (*Rhet. ad Alex.* 35.1440b.5, 10).
Moreover, at other points in the same work Aneximenes identifies the
eulogy or encomium as an εἶδος or species within the genre or γένος of
epideictic: τὸ ἐγκωμιαστικὸν εἶδος (3.1425b.35), τοῦ ἐγκωμιαστικοῦ
εἶδους (35.1441a.24).[9] Such a breakdown of epideictic into several species
was pursued by the rhetoricians of the Common Era. The third century
rhetor Menander, for example, in his work *On Epideictic* (περὶ ἐπιδεικτικῶν), presents rules for composing 23 different types of epideictic
speeches. Such speeches include the funeral oration and various speeches
which would be offered on the occasion of the subject's birthday or wed-
ding, as well as the encomium itself, which in Menander went by the title
λόγος βασιλικός.[10]

In summary, then, epideictic appears to be the term used to designate
that class of oratory whose *Sitz im Leben* was neither in the assembly or
the lawcourt. It was applied to those speeches through which the rhetor
sought to impress his audience rather than to persuade them. And within
this category there were a variety of possible forms through which this
goal could be accomplished: the rhetor might offer an oration in praise of
someone or something, or he could choose to compose a vituperative
piece. Thus as we seek to identify a form within classical rhetoric that
may have served as a model for Sirach's Praise of the Fathers, our attention should be restricted to the possible species within the general classification of epideictic whose purpose was that of praise. It is to these
species that we will now turn.

## 2. εὐλογία

As was noted above, Addison Wright has pointed out that some commentators have spoken of Sirach 44-50 as a eulogy. Use of the term could
be taken in any one of three ways: (1) it might be intended in the current
sense of any address or composition in honor of the deceased, (2) it might
be the translator's attempt to render a less familiar technical term, or

---

[9]Aristotle, in contrast, classifies forensic, deliberative and epideictic
speeches as εἴδη rather than γένη (*Rh.* 1.3.1). But by distinguishing
between those epideictic speeches which offer praise and those which
offer blame, the εἶδος of epideictic would be made up of more than just
one type of speech.

[10]For a text of Menander, cf. C. Bursian, *Der Rhetor Menandros und
seine Schriften* (Munich: Verlag der K. Akademie, 1882).

(3) it might simply be a transliteration of εὐλογία in the Greek text of a composition.

Inasmuch as the Hymn in Praise of the Fathers "speaks well" of the now-dead heroes of Israel,[11] it could be called a eulogy in the sense of the first possibility outlined above. Yet the question has to be asked as to whether or not eulogy, with respect to literature of that period, is an acceptable form-critical category.

The second way by which the term may have been introduced as a description of Sirach 44-50 is due to the tendency of some to employ it in translating technical rhetorical terms. For example, translators of classical texts which are clearly ἐγκώμια, or are discussions of encomiastic theory, have referred to these texts in translation as "eulogies." Thus in the Loeb translation of the fragments of Pindar, Sir John Sandys describes the ἐγκώμια as "eulogies."[12] Moreover, in Rackham's edition of the Rhetorica ad Alexandrum, he consistently renders ἐγκωμιάζειν, ἐγκωμιαστικός, and ἐγκώμιον as "to eulogize," "eulogistic," and "eulogy."[13] The same practice was followed in his translation of ἔπαινος "commendation" and ἐπαινεῖν "to praise, commend" by "eulogy"—although the verb at times is literally translated as "praise."[14] Thus our consideration ought to be directed not to the word "eulogy," but to the technical terms which stand behind it in the discussions of the rhetors, viz., ἐγκώμιον and ἔπαινος.

There are, however, some encomiastic texts and rhetorical treatises which do in fact employ the Greek εὐλογία or εὐλογεῖν, which have in turn been translated by "eulogy" or "to eulogize." Yet in each case they appear to be synonymous with ἐγκώμιον/ἔπαινος and ἐγκωμιάζειν/ἐπαινεῖν respectively. A brief survey of the materials will bear this out.

---

[11]It is assumed that by the time of the composition of Sirach 44-50, Simon II was no longer living.

[12]J. E. Sandys, The Odes of Pindar (Loeb Classical Library; New York: G. P. Putnam's Sons, 1930) 510, 578.

[13]For a translation of ἐγκωμιάζειν by "eulogize," cf. Rhet. ad Alex. 35.1440b.20, 30; 35.1441a.10; ἐγκωμιαστικός by "eulogistic/eulogy," cf. 35.1440b.5, 35.1441a.20; and ἐγκώμια by "eulogy," cf. 6.1428a.5, 3.1426a.15, 35.1441b.25. Also, cf. "eulogy of love" for τοῦ ἐγκωμίου τῷ Ἔρωτι and ἐγκωμιαζέτω τὸν Ἔρωτα in Plato, Symposium, 194D and 177E respectively, in the Loeb series translation by W. R. M. Lamb.

[14]For the translation "eulogy" for ἔπαινος, cf. Rhet. ad Alex. 35.1441a.10, 35.1441b.10; "eulogy" for ἐπαινεῖν, 35.1441a.20, 25; and "praise" for ἐπαινεῖν, 35.1441a.5.

In early material εὐλογία/εὐλογεῖν were employed in contexts which later rhetoricians would clearly understand to be encomiastic. The herald in Aeschylus's *Agamemnon*, boasting of the Argive victory over Troy, says "Whoso hears the story of these deeds must need extol (εὐλογεῖν) the city and the leaders of her host; . . ." (*Ag.* 580).[15] In Pindar, a slightly later contemporary of Aeschylus, εὐλογία appears as the term describing the praise due to the victors in his Epinician Odes:

> If any one among men hath good fortune, by the winning of glorious prizes, or by might of wealth, yet in his heart restraineth insatiate insolence, such a man is worthy to be blended with his townsmen's praises (εὐλογίαις) . . . (*Isthm.* 3.1-3)

> And as for you, ye sons of Aeacus with your golden chariots, I deem it my clearest law to shower praises (εὐλογίαις) on you, . . . (*Isthm.* 6.19-21)[16]

It is with these Odes of Pindar—as will be discussed below—that the history of the encomium is believed to have begun. Thus εὐλογία is being used in these texts to describe the type of praise which would be later associated with the rhetorical term ἐγκώμιον. Moreover, Aristophanes in his *Peace* (421 B.C.E.) has the chorus speak encomiastically of the poet: "Our poet is free to acknowledge that he is deserving of high commendation (εὐλογίας μεγάλης) . . ." (*Peace* 738).[17]

In Isocrates—whom we shall see is generally regarded as the originator of the prose encomium—εὐλογία/εὐλογεῖν are synonymous with ἔπαινος/ἐπαινεῖν and ἐγκώμιον/ἐγκωμιάζειν. This may be seen in the following two excerpts from his encomium of Evagoras, king of Cyprus:

> Now other writers should have *praised* (ἐπαινεῖν) those who in their own time had proved themselves good men, in order that
> . . .
> . . . . . . . . . . . . . . . . . . . . . . . . . . . . .
> . . . the younger generation might with greater emulation have

---

[15]The translation is that of H. W. Smyth, *Aeschylus: II* (Loeb Classical Library; Cambridge: Harvard University, 1963).

[16]The translation is that of Sandys, *Odes*. For εὐλογία in other odes, cf. e.g., Olympian 5.24 (εὐλογίαν) and Nemean 4.5 (εὐλογία).

[17]The translation is that of Benjamin Rogers, *Aristophanes: II* (Loeb Classical Library; Cambridge: Harvard University, 1961).

striven for virtue, knowing well that they would be praised
(εὐλογήσονται) more highly than those whom they had
excelled in merit (Evag. 5).

. . . (1) must make the effort and see if it is possible in prose
to eulogize (εὐλογεῖν) good men in no worse fashion than their
encomiasts (ἐγκωμιαζόντων) do who employ song and verse
(Evag. 11).[18]

In a work believed to have been influenced by Isocrates,[19] the fourth
century *Rhetorica ad Alexandrum*, Anaximenes understands εὐλογεῖν to
mean the same as ἐγκωμιάζειν. While considering the qualities in a
person to which the encomiast ought to call attention, he lists "the just,
the lawful, the expedient, the noble," etc., and then comments, "when
eulogizing (εὐλογοῦντα) one must show in one's speech that one of these
things belongs to the person in question . . ." (*Rhet. ad Alex.* 3.1426a.3-5).
Of significance for our discussion of terminology is the fact that although
εὐλογεῖν is clearly used to refer to the composition of encomia, the
genre, or more properly the εἶδος, is not called eulogy (εὐλογία). Rather
at the head of Anaximenes' treatment of this type of oratory, it is specifically called encomium. That heading begins, "In short, therefore, the
encomiastic species (τὸ ἐγκωμιαστικὸν εἶδος) is the amplification of
purposes and actions and noble speeches . . ." (*Rhet. ad Alex.* 3.1425b.36-
38).[20] Thus, by the time of the fourth century rhetors, the appropriate
term by which this type of speech was known was that of encomium. And
although "eulogy" (εὐλογία) or "to eulogize" (εὐλογεῖν) appear in such
compositions, and in theoretical treatments of them, εὐλογία is not used
as the title of the εἶδος.

---

[18] The emphasis is mine. The texts and translations of Isocrates, both
here and below, are those of George Norlin, *Isocrates: I, II* (Loeb Classical
Library; New York: G. P. Putnam's Sons, 1928, 1929), and LaRue Van
Hook, *Isocrates: III* (Loeb Classical Library; Cambridge: Harvard University, 1954). For other passages where Isocrates places εὐλογεῖν/εὐλογία
in apposition to ἐπαινεῖν/ἔπαινος and ἐγκωμιάζειν/ἐγκώμιον, cf. e.g.,
his *Letter 9: to Archidamus* 1-2, and *Panathenaicus* 206.

[19] Cf. Rackham, *Pliny*, 258.

[20] The translation is mine. Rackham chose to render encomiastic
(ἐγκωμιαστικόν) by "eulogistic."

## 3. ἔπαινος

In the foregoing we observed that not only is εὐλογεῖν sometimes regarded as equivalent to ἐγκωμιάζειν, but that it is also identified with ἐπαινεῖν. Like εὐλογεῖν, ἐπαινεῖν can be used in the general sense of "to praise" as well as to describe the action of composing an encomium. Isocrates, for example, uses ἐπαινεῖν in the latter sense when he outlines the possible forms in which he could structure his self-defense in the *Antidosis:*

> I saw, however, that if I were to attempt a eulogy of myself (ἐπαινεῖν ἐμαυτὸν ἐπιχειροίην), I should not be able to cover all the points which I proposed to discuss, . . . ( *Antidosis* 8).

Here ἐπαινεῖν appears to be synonymous with ἐγκωμιάζειν.

When it comes to the noun ἔπαινος, we sense that—unlike εὐλογία, which is not used to describe an εἶδος—it seems to represent a particular type of speech. Thus to return to the *Antidosis,* Isocrates—after including an encomium of Timotheus, his former pupil (107-128)—refers back to the composition by calling it τὸν ἔπαινον ἐκείνου ( *Antidosis* 129). Moreover, Thucydides, in describing the Athenian funeral rites for those who fell in the Pelopennesian War, comments:

> But when the remains have been laid away in the earth, a man chosen by the state, who is regarded as best endowed with wisdom and is foremost in public esteem, delivers over them an appropriate eulogy (ἔπαινον τὸν πρέποντα) (Thucydides, *War* 2.34.6-7).[21]

In the *Symposium,* Phaedrus begins his encomium of love in response to Eryximachus' call that each ought "to offer a commendation-speech of Love" (λόγον εἰπεῖν ἔπαινον Ἔρωτος) (177d).[22] And in the *Phaedrus* itself, λόγον ἔπαινον is again employed to designate a type of speech, viz., the encomium. (Pl., *Phdr.* 260b).[23]

---

[21] The translation is from the edition of C. F. Smith, *Thucydides: I* (Loeb Classical Library; Cambridge: Harvard University, 1962).

[22] The translation is mine. Lamb's translation is ". . . we ought each of us to make a speech in turn, from left to right, praising Love. . . ."

[23] συντιθεὶς λόγον ἔπαινον κατὰ τοῦ οὔου. . . . The context here

Thus there is evidence that ἔπαινος was apparently equivalent to ἐγκώμιον; both were used to identify a given εἶδος of oratory. Yet, on the part of some rhetors, ἔπαινος, while still regarded as the name of a particular speech-form, is nevertheless distinguished from ἐγκώμιον. Aristotle makes such a distinction in his *Rhetoric:*

> Now praise (ἔπαινος) is language that sets forth greatness of virtue (ἀρετῆς); hence it is necessary to show that a man's actions (πράξεις) are virtuous. But encomium (ἐγκώμιον) deals with achievements (ἔργων) . . . (*Rh.* 1.9.33)

And in his *Eudemian Ethics:*

> And again, there are the praises (οἱ ἔπαινοι) given to goodness (ἀρετῆς) on account of its deeds (ἔργα), and panegyrics (ἐγκώμια) describing deeds (ἔργων) . . .
> . . . . . . . . . . . . . . . . . . . . . . . . . . . . .
> Hence felicitation (εὐδαιμονισμός), and praise (ἔπαινος) and panegyric (ἐγκώμιον) are different things: panegyric (ἐγκώμιον) is a recital of a particular exploit (τοῦ καθ' ἕκαστον ἔργου), praise a statement of a man's general distinction (ὁ δ' ἔπαινος τοῦ τοιοῦτον εἶναι καθόλου) felicitation (εὐδαιμονισμός) is bestowed on an end achieved (*E. E.* 1.1.11-12).

Aristotle's distinction between ἔπαινος and ἐγκώμιον, as the general from the particular, appears to have continued in rhetorical theory for some time. For in the second century C.E. *Progymnasmata* of Hermogenes,[24] ἔπαινος refers to brief, general statements of praise, while ἐγκώμιον is used to describe a lengthy treament of the specific qualities and deeds of the subject.

> Encomium differs from praise (in general) in that the latter may be brief, as "Socrates was wise," whereas encomium is developed at some length.

---

is Socrates' proposal to Phaedrus that he could compose an encomium of an ass, calling it a horse, and portray it as a most valuable beast at home and in battle. Cf. H. N. Fowler, *Plato: I* (Loeb Classical Library; Cambridge: Harvard University, 1960).

[24] For a general discussion of Hermogenes, cf. George Kennedy, *The Art of Rhetoric in the Roman World: 300 BC-AD 300* (Princeton: Princeton University, 1972) 619-33.

('Επαίνου δὲ διαφέρει τὸ ἐγκώμιον, ὅτι ὁ μὲν ἔπαινος
καὶ ἐν βραχεῖ, γένοιτ' ἄν, οἷον 'Σωκράτης σοφός,' τὸ
δὲ ἐγκώμιον ἐν μακροτέρᾳ διεξόδῳ).25

Such a differentiation between ἔπαινος and ἐγκώμιον, however,
despite the evidence of Hermogenes, was not generally made.26 And even
in Aristotle, as much as he sought to contrast the two, there are contexts
in which they appear to mean the same. For example, there is a passage in
the *Rhetoric* where he describes the similarity between two different
genres of oratory—the ἔπαινος and the deliberative (συμβουλαί)—and
notes that by a simple change of phrase, one type can become the other.
Yet, having said this, when he resumes his discussion of the speech of
praise, he does not call it ἔπαινος, but rather ἐγκώμιον:

> Praise (ἔπαινος) and counsels (συμβουλαί) have a common
> aspect; for what you might suggest in counselling becomes
> encomium (ἐγκώμιον) by a change in phrase (*Rh*. 1.9.35-36).27

Given the fact (1) that despite Aristotle's attempt to differentiate,
ἔπαινος is used with the same meaning as ἐγκώμιον; (2) that in other
authors, e.g., Isocrates and Plato, the two terms are equivalent; and
(3) that even in later rhetoricians—e.g., Hermogenes—who viewed
ἔπαινος as distinct, treatments of it came under the general heading of

---

25The translation is that of C. S. Baldwin, *Medieval Rhetoric and
Poetic* (reprint of the 1928 ed.; Gloucester, MA: Peter Smith, 1959) 30.
For the Greek text, cf. H. Rabe, *Hermogenes Opera* (Rhetores Graeci: VI;
Leipzig: B. G. Teubner, 1913) 15, 11.6-8.

26"The distinction was not generally held to, although some rhetoricians, e.g., Hermogenes, tried to maintain it." From a private conversation with George Kustas, Classics Department, SUNY, Buffalo, in
November 1975 when he was a Visiting Professor of Rhetoric at the University of California, Berkeley.

27Note also the parallel between ἔπαινος and ἐγκώμιον in *Rh*. 1.9.41:

ἐκ τίνων . . . οἱ ἔπαινοι καὶ οἱ ψόγοι

. . . . . . . . . . . . . . . . . . . . .

καὶ ἐκ τίνων τὰ ἐγκώμια γίγνεται καὶ τὰ ὀνείδη

The antecedents of τίνων here are the topics out of which the speeches
are created, e.g., examples and enthymemes.

περὶ ἐγκωμίου,[28] it appears that the preferred term for this category
was ἐγκώμιον and not ἔπαινος.

### 4. ἐπιτάφιος

Although commentators do not employ it in their discussions of Sirach
44-50, another term that shows up in rhetorical treatises as related, or
even equivalent, to encomium is ἐπιτάφιος, the funeral speech. In illustrating the use of ἔπαινος above, attention was called to Thucydides'
report on the Athenian funeral rites for her soldiers fallen in battle. His
description in 2.34 is followed by his quotation of the text of Pericles'
oration (2.35). Aristotle, however, in referring to the ἔπαινος offered by
Pericles, called it an ἐπιτάφιον (Rh. 1.7.34). Evidently, at one time no
differentiation was made between the ἐπιτάφιος and the ἐγκώμιον (or
ἔπαινος). In fact, Burgess comments that the ἐπιτάφιος is "the oldest
form of prose encomium extant, . . ."[29] Later on the ἐπιτάφιος became a
more specialized form. Being understood as an "encomium of the dead,"[30]
it was characterized by the addition of the lament (θρῆνος) and the consolation (παραμυθία) to the ἔπαινος proper.[31] While the ἔπαινος in the
funeral oration developed the same topics as one would find in any encomium, the lament would add such themes as the appropriateness of sorrow
and the greatness of the loss, and the consolation would add such commonplaces as "it is fortunate to have died honorably," "death is common
to all," and "their bodies are mortal, but their fame is immortal."[32]

### 5. πανηγυρικός

The term commentators have most frequently used in order to emphasize that Sirach 44-50 is in praise of men is that of panegyric. Among
those who have described it as such are Bigot, Lévi, and Siebeneck.[33] Yet
they seem to employ the term in its most general sense. For example, The
Oxford English Dictionary defines panegyric to be "a public speech or

---

[28]The comments of Hermogenes on ἔπαινος are in section 7 of his Progymnasmata, Περὶ ἐγκωμίου.
[29]Burgess, "Epideictic Literature," 117, 170.
[30]Ibid., 114.
[31]Ibid., 148.
[32]Ibid., 155-56.
[33]Cf. above, n. 3.

writing in praise of some person, thing, or achievement; a laudatory discourse, a formal or elaborate encomium or eulogy."[34]

Such an understanding, however, is in contrast to the original sense that a πανηγυρικός was a particular speech composed for the πανήγυρις or national assembly. The movement from the restricted, or proper, sense of the term to the more general meaning is evident by the time of the third century C.E. rhetor Menander.[35] Of the two treatises on epideictic oratory attributed to him,[36] the one entitled περὶ ἐπιδεικτικῶν lists twenty-three different species of epideictic with rules for the composition of each. Among the twenty-three are treatments of the encomium, discussed under the headings περὶ βασιλικοῦ, the funeral oration (περὶ ἐπιταφίου), et al., but nowhere is there an entry bearing the title περὶ πανηγυρικοῦ.[37]

> Menander's failure to include the πανηγυρικός may perhaps be accounted for by the changed status of the πανήγυρις and the degeneration of the speech attending it to a mere personal encomium.[38]

The origins of this broader understanding of panegyric may be traced back from Menander to the Epicurean Philodemus (ca. 110-40/35 B.C.E.). Philodemus employed the term to refer to the εἶδος instead of ἐγκώμιον.[39] Thus for Philodemus, panegyric became the category within which the encomium was placed.

---

[34] *The Compact Edition of the Oxford English Dictionary: Vol. II* (London: Oxford University, 1971) 2064.

[35] On Menander, cf. Kennedy, *The Art of Rhetoric*, 636-37.

[36] There are questions as to whether or not Menander composed both the treatise, *The Division of Epideictic* (διαίρεσις τῶν ἐπιδεικτικῶν), and the work, *On Epideictic* (περὶ ἐπιδεικτικῶν). Bursian, for example, believes Menander wrote the former, but not the latter. Cf. Bursian, *Der Rhetor Menandros*, 17-28. This, however, does not alter the fact that the omission here of πανηγυρικός as a distinct species of epideictic suggests that πανηγυρικός was synonymous with ἐγκώμιον by the 3rd-4th century C.E. date of the treatise.

[37] For the Greek text of the περὶ ἐπιδεικτικῶν, cf. Bursian, *Der Rhetor Menandros*, 69ff. The heading περὶ βασιλικοῦ reflects a later name for the encomium, the λόγος βασιλικός, cf. below, 99.

[38] Burgess, "Epideictic Literature," 108.

[39] K. Ziegler, "Panegyrikos," *PW: XVIII*, 3, 561. Cf. τὸ πανηγυρικὸς αὐτῆς (= ῥητορικῆς) εἶδος, in *Philodemus Volumina Rhetorica: II* (S. Sudhaus, ed.; 2 vols.; Leipzig: B. G. Teubner, 1892, 1896) 251, ll. 19-20.

Alongside the identification of πανηγυρικός with ἐγκώμιον, there developed an even more general use of the term as an adjective to describe any type of oratory that was festive, showy, or ostentatious.[40] Plutarch employed it in this way:

> . . . when students of philosophy pass from the ostentatious (πανηγυρικῶν) and artificial to the kind of discourse which deals with character and feeling . . . (Plut. *Mor.* 79b).[41]

A curious combination of the two general meanings the term came to have—viz., an adjective describing an elevated style and a designation for an encomiastic species of rhetoric—is present in Hermogenes. On the one hand πανηγυρικός was used by him as the title of the third division of oratory alongside of the deliberative and the forensic. Yet, in the same treatise, περὶ ἰδεῶν, he also employs it to refer to any literature other than political or forensic. Thus for Hermogenes, Homer, Thucydides, Xenophon, Plato, and Demosthenes are all panegyricists.[42]

Such later understandings of the term are in contrast, as was mentioned, to its original use. That the original sense continued in the works of some rhetors beyond the time it had become generalized in others (e.g., Philodemus) is evident in the *Rhetoric* attributed to Dionysius of Halicarnassus. Among the various species of epideictic speeches described by Dionysius is one known as the πανηγυρικὸς λόγος. It is understood to be the speech delivered at the festival or πανήγυρις.[43] Dionysius outlines its structure in this way:

> The panegyric . . . is to begin with praise of the god who presides over the festival, listing his attributes. Then comes

---

[40]According to Ziegler, "Panegyrikos," 559, this even more general sense is first attested in Polybius 5.34.3 (200-118 B.C.E.) where the comparative πανηγυρικώτερον is used to refer to the pomp of Ptolemy Philopator.

[41]The translation is from the edition of F. C. Babbitt, *Plutarch. Moralia: I* (Loeb Classical Library; Cambridge: Harvard University, 1949). Cf. also πανηγυρικῶς "elevated style" in *Moralia: IX,* 756c, and the discussion in Ziegler, "Panegyrikos," 563.

[42]Cf. Ziegler, "Panegyrikos," 563-65; and D. A. Russell and M. Winterbottom (eds.), *Ancient Literary Criticism: The Principal Texts in New Translations* (London: Oxford University, 1972) 575, n. 4.

[43]Kennedy, *The Art of Rhetoric,* 635; and Burgess, "Epideictic Literature," 112.

> praise of the city where the festival is located: its location, origin, founder, history, size, beauty, power, public buildings, rivers, legends. The next theme is the festival itself, its origins, legends, and history. Other festivals may be compared unfavorably. Then comes the program of the festival: ... The prize is then described and praised. ... Finally there is to be praise of the emperor or king or others in charge.[44]

But this form critical use of the term, however, seems to be new with Dionysius. Prior to him πανηγυρικός appears to be employed with respect to the occasion of a speech—viz., at a public assembly—rather than describing a particular oratorical form. Such was the case with Isocrates. On the one hand he uses the term to designate the occasion:

> ... there are men who ... have chosen rather to write discourses, not for private disputes, but which deal with the world of Hellas, with affairs of state, and are appropriate to be delivered at the Pan-Hellenic assemblies (πανηγυρικούς) (*Antidosis* 46).[45]

And on the other hand he also employs the term as the title for one of his own compositions, *The Panegyricus* (= Oration 4) of 380 B.C.E. In it Isocrates extols Athens as the only Greek city capable to lead a united Hellas against the Persians.

> The title was chosen by Isocrates himself, no doubt to signify its appropriateness to be delivered before a pan-Hellenic gathering at Olympia.[46]

In subsequent orations, Isocrates referred back to this specific composition by using the term:

> ... this was, in fact, the course which I had already advocated in the *Panegyric* discourse (ἐν τῷ πανηγυρικῷ λόγῳ) (*To Philip* 9).[47]

---

[44]Kennedy, *The Art of Rhetoric*, 636.

[45]Cf. also ἐν τοῖς ὄχλοις τοῖς πανηγυρικοῖς, translated by Norlin as "before the crowds at the national festivals," Isoc., *Panathen*. 263.

[46]Ibid., 119.

[47]In Norlin, *Isocrates: I*. Cf. also *To Philip* 84, ". . . my *Panegyricus*, which has enriched the other men who make philosophy their business. . . ."

And others use it to refer to the same work of Isocrates:

> He may do the same when he has gripped his audience and
> filled it with enthusiasm, . . . as Isocrates does at the end of
> his *Panegyricus* (ἐν τῷ πανηγυρικῷ ἐπὶ τέλει) . . . (Aristotle,
> *Rh.* 3.7.11).

On the basis of this brief survey, then, it seems that at least down
through the time of Aristotle's *Rhetoric* (ca. 330 B.C.E.), πανηγυρικός is
employed generally to identify the occasion for certain types of oratory
(viz., the national assembly), as well as to refer to a specific work of
Isocrates. Between the *Rhetoric* and the first century B.C.E. two contrasting developments appear to have taken place: (1) πανηγυρικός came
to be a term describing any oratory that is festive or pompous in style (cf.
its use in Polybius and Plutarch); and (2) πανηγυρικός became at the same
time a technical term in rhetoric. As a technical term, however, it was
employed in two different ways. On the one hand, it designates a particular species of oratory composed for the national assembly, in continuity
with the original use of the term (cf. Dionysius of Halicarnassus), while on
the other hand, it came to be synonymous with ἐγκώμιον in the works of
other rhetoricians (e.g., Philodemus). Since these changes in usage show
up first in authors and rhetors of the second-first centuries B.C.E. (Polybius, Philodemus, and Dionysius), it would seem that prior to this—in Ben
Sira's time—πανηγυρικός still was a word which identified an occasion for
a speech and did not yet refer to an εἶδος identical to that of the encomium. Thus for commentators to speak of Sirach 44-50 as a panegyric is
anachronistic. If in fact Sirach 44-50 proves to be a composition incorporating the various topics (τόποι) and having the arrangement (τάξις) of
that rhetorical εἶδος whereby a man or men are praised, the preferred
term would be the one which was consistently used throughout antiquity—
ἐγκώμιον and not πανηγυρικός.

## 6. ἐγκώμιον

In our survey of epideictic terminology thus far, the term to which we
have repeatedly returned is that of ἐγκώμιον. The frequency with which
it has entered our discussion should not surprise us, for as Burgess notes:

No single term represents the aim and scope of epideictic
literature so completely as the word ἐγκώμιον. That the
encomiastic feature is the most distinctive characteristic of
this branch of literature is clear from the fact that the title
ἐγκωμιαστικόν is frequently used to designate the εἶδος,
from the discussion of its theory by the rhetors, as well as
from the examination of its literature.[48]

Thus, in contrast to terms such as ἔπαινος, πανηγυρικός, et al.,
whose meanings and usages varied, we would expect ἐγκώμιον to have
been used throughout antiquity with far more consistency—viz., that at
the mention of the term a specific form of oratory would have been
understood. That this was the case will be evident, I believe, from the
following historical sketch of the use of ἐγκώμιον (ἐγκωμιάζειν, ἐγκωμιαστικόν) from Pindar down to the rhetors of the Common Era.

Pindar, who employed εὐλογία as a general term to describe the praise
given to the victors in his Epinician Odes, titled those odes ἐγκώμια. For
example, he opens his ode from Chromius of Aetna, winner of the chariot
race (476 B.C.E.), with "Tis the chariot of Chromius and Nemea that
impel me to harness a song of praise (ἐγκώμιον) for deeds of victory"
(Nem. 1.7).[49]

As might be expected, both ἐγκώμιον and ἐγκωμιάζειν are not lacking
in Isocrates, who, as was noted earlier and will be discussed again later, is
considered the father of the prose encomium. In his Helen (ca. 370
B.C.E.), Isocrates criticizes Gorgias' attempt to compose a piece in praise
of the same subject with the comment

. . . for although he asserts that he (Gorgias) has written an
encomium (ἐγκώμιον) of Helen, it turns out that he has actually spoken a defence (ἀπολογίαν) of her conduct (Isoc., Helen
14).[50]

Also, in addition to the instance of ἐγκωμιάζειν in the Evagoras cited in
our discussion of εὐλογεῖν above, we may include Isocrates' use of it at
Evagoras 8:

---

[48]Burgess, "Epideictic Literature," 113.
[49]Cf. also ἐγκώμιον in Ol. 2.47, and Pyth. 10.53.
[50]In Isocrates: III, cf. Van Hook.

I am fully aware that what I propose to do is difficult—to eulogize (ἐγκωμιάζειν) in prose the virtues of a man.

And from his *Letter 9: To Archidamus:* "Since I know, Archidamus, that many persons are eager to sing the praises (ἐγκωμιάζειν) of you . . ." (1).[51]

Xenophon, who wrote his *Agesilaus* in praise of the Spartan king not long after Isocrates' *Evagoras,* called it an encomium:[52]

However, let it not be thought, because one whose life is ended is the theme of my praise (ἐπαινεῖται), that these words are meant for a funeral dirge (θρῆνον). They are far more truly the language of eulogy (ἐγκώμιον) (*Ages.* 10.3).

Encomium was also employed in Plato. Despite the fact that our earlier reference to the *Symposium* was in terms of the call to the banquet guests to offer an ἔπαινος of love, the speech in praise of love is also called an ἐγκωμίου τῷ Ἔρωτι (*Symp.* 194d), and the verb ἐγκωμιάζειν is used to describe the process of composing such a speech (cf. *Symp.* 177d and 198cd).

From the rhetorical literature of the fourth century we have already cited several passages in Anaximenes' *Rhetorica ad Alexandrum* in which ἐγκώμιον, ἐγκωμιάζειν, or ἐγκωμιαστικόν appear.[53] And in Aristotle, although he prefers ἔπαινος in his discussion of epideictic oratory, ἐγκώμιον and ἐγκωμιάζειν are not only employed as well, but they seem to be synonymous with ἔπαινος/ἐπαινεῖν despite Aristotle's attempt to distinguish them.[54]

Polybius (200-118 B.C.E.), in discussing Philopoemen in Book X of the *Histories,* made reference to an earlier work of his which dealt with the Achaean general and sought to contrast that work with his present treatment of him:

For just as the former work, being in the form of an encomium (ἐγκωμιαστικός), demanded a summary and somewhat exaggerated account of his achievements, so the present

---

[51]Ibid.

[52]E. C. Marchant, *Xenophon: VII, Scripta Minora* (Loeb Classical Library; Cambridge: Harvard University, 1971) xviii.

[53]Cf. above, 84, 87.

[54]Cf. above, 89-90.

history, which distributes praise (ἔπαινου) and blame impartially, demands a strictly true account . . . (Polyb. 10.21.8).

This second century use of ἐγκώμιον in Polybius is worth noting in that from the time of Aristotle's *Rhetoric* down to the time of Augustus we have no surviving handbooks of Greek rhetorical practice.[55] A possible exception here may be Demetrius' *On Style* (περὶ ἑρμηνείας), which tradition ascribes to Demetrius of Phaleron (ca. 350-280 B.C.E.). Although it is no longer believed that the work was composed by the famous Alexandrian librarian, there are grounds for dating it still in the third century,[56] while others argue for a first century C.E. date.[57] Regardless of the date to which we might assign it, *On Style* does make mention of the type of language employed in encomia:

For my own part, I can forgive the rhetorician Polycrates who eulogized (ἐγκωμιάζοντι) . . . with antitheses, metaphors, and every trick and turn of eulogy (πᾶσι τοῖς ἐγκωμιαστικοῖς τρόποις) (*On Style* 2.120).[58]

That the use of ἐγκώμιον continued down into the rhetors of the Common Era may be illustrated from the writings of Theon (late first or early second century),[59] Hermogenes (second century), and Menander (third century). Theon, for example, treated ἐγκώμιον in his *Progymnasmata* as one of the required oratorical exercises and defined it that ἐγκώμιόν ἐστι λόγον ἐμφανίζων μέγεθος τῶν κατ᾽ ἀρετὴν πράξεων ("An encomium is a speech which elucidates the magnitude of deeds according to virtue . . .").[60]

In like manner ἐγκώμιον is one of the forms outlined in Hermogenes' *Progymnasmata*. As was noted in our treatment of ἔπαινος, even though

---

[55]Kennedy, *The Art of Persuasion*, 264.

[56]Ibid., 285-86.

[57]Cf. the introductory comments of W. R. Roberts in W. H. Fyfe and W. R. Roberts, *Aristotle: The Poetics; "Longinus": On the Sublime; Demetrius: On Style* (Loeb Classical Library; Cambridge: Harvard University, 1965) 268-81.

[58]The translation is that of W. R. Roberts, *Aristotle*.

[59]On Theon, cf. Kennedy, *The Art of Rhetoric*, 615-16; and Bryant, *Ancient Greek*, 97-98.

[60]The translation is mine. The Greek text is that of L. Spengel, *Rhetores Graeci: II* (Leipzig, 1854), sec. 20, as cited by Burgess, "Epideictic Literature," 113, n. 3.

ἐγκώμιον and παραδείγματα                                                        99

Hermogenes attempted to differentiate between ἐγκώμιον and ἔπαινος,
this was done within the framework of a section which bore the title περὶ
ἐγκωμίου.[61] That section opens with the definition: ἐγκώμιόν ἐστιν
ἔκθεσις τῶν προσόντων ἀγαθῶν τινι κοινῶς ἤ ἰδίως . . . ("An
encomium is a setting forth of the good qualities which belong to someone
publicly or privately . . .").[62] And finally, while Menander in his list of the
twenty-three types of epideictic orations does not use the heading περὶ
ἐγκωμίου, he clearly knows and makes use of encomia. The category,
however, under which encomia are discussed is rather that of περὶ βασιλικοῦ. And the βασιλοκὸς λόγος, as he defines it, is identical to the
encomium known from the works of earlier rhetoricians:

    ὁ βασιλοκὸς λόγος ἐγκώμιόν ἐστι βασιλέως, οὐκοῦν αὔξη-
    σιν ὁμολογουμένην περιέχει τῶν προσόντων ἀγαθῶν
    βασιλεῖ . . . (The royal speech is an encomium of a king.
    Accordingly it embraces an agreed upon amplification of the
    good qualities belonging to a king . . .).[63]

From this brief survey, then, it appears that the technical term which
is used with the most consistency in Greek rhetoric to designate the type
of speech which was offered in praise of an individual is that of ἐγκώμιον.
And if our proposal can be sustained, that it is this type of speech that
provided the inspiration for the form of Sirach 44-50, then it is our task to
examine those chapters of Sirach in light of the ἐγκώμιον-form itself.


                    C. ἐγκώμιον AND παραδείγματα

In our discussion of the Beispielreihe, the point was made that in classical texts παραδείγματα may appear as a subordinate genre within other
compositions.[64] At the same time we acknowledged that Sir 44:16-49:16
is in the form of a series of examples. Thus the question that must be
considered, if we are going to describe the larger context of Sir 44:1-

---

[61]Cf. above, 89-90.
[62]The translation is mine. The Greek text is that of Rabe, Hermogenis
Opera, 14, ll. 17-18.
[63]The translation is mine. The Greek text is that of Bursian, Der
Rhetor Menandros, 95, chap. 5:1.
[64]Above, 44, 48.

50:24 as an encomium, is whether or not encomia were among those compositions which employed παραδείγματα.

In the rhetorical treatises which are extant from the fourth century B.C.E. down to and beyond Ben Sira's time, παραδείγματα were generally described as one of the proofs (πίστεις) which, though particularly appropriate to forensic rhetoric, were used in epideictic and deliberative oratory as well. Anaximenes, for example, commenting on the use of proofs, writes: ". . . though it is necessary to use them for all departments of oratory, (proofs) are most useful in accusations and defences" (Rhet. ad Alex. 6.1428a.5-7). He then proceeds to detail the various kinds of proof available to the orator and among these he lists παραδείγματα (7.1428a.20).

Aristotle, too, mentions the "proofs common to all branches of rhetoric" (περὶ τῶν κοινῶν πίστεων ἅπασιν) and notes that "the common proofs are of two kinds, example and enthymeme" (αἱ κοιναὶ πίστεις δύο τῷ γένει, παραδείγματα καὶ ἐνθύμημα) (Rh. 2.20.3).

That this fourth century custom of employing examples in all types of oratory continued to be the practice down to the first century C.E. is evident in Quintilian. Discussing proofs in the Institutio Oratoria, he writes:

> The most important of proofs of this class is that which is most properly styled example (exemplum), that is to say the adducing of some past action real or assumed which may serve to persuade the audience of the truth of the point we are trying to make.
>
> . . . . . . . . . . . . . . . . . . . . . . . . . . . . . . . . .
> The same divisions apply also to such forms of proof in panegyric (probandorum) or denunciation (culpandorum) (5.11.6-7).[65]

Thus we may tentatively conclude that since the use of παραδείγματα in epideictic oratory was accepted by the ancient rhetoricians, and since the encomium was but a species of epideictic, it should be possible to find encomia incorporating examples, either individually or in a series. There is nothing, then, to prevent us from proposing Sirach 44-50 to be an encomium of Simon II which, in turn, has employed the Beispielreihe of 44:16-49:16 as one of its topics (τόποι).

---

[65]Exemplum here has the same meaning for Quintilian that παραδειγμα had for Aristotle. Cf. McCall, Ancient Rhetorical Theories, 189.

Earlier, when we treated the integrity of Sirach 44-50, we noted that
Sirach often describes the forefathers in chaps. 44-49 in such a way that
it forces us to compare them with Simon II in chap. 50.[66] Instances of this
comparison, to which we directed our attention, are the vestments of
Aaron and those of Simon (45:7-11; 50:5, 9, 11); and the engineering feats
of Solomon (47:13), Hezekiah (48:17), Zerubbabel-Joshua (49:12), and
Nehemiah (49:13) compared with those of Simon (50:1-4). Such a comparison between the subject, Simon, and the appearance and accomplishments of other famous men, was one of the ways in which encomia would
make use of παραδείγματα. Isocrates, for example, in his *Evagoras*,
included a comparison of the Cypriot king with Cyrus of Persia. This
σύγκρισις was introduced as follows:

> . . . from what I have said the valour of Evagoras and the
> greatness of his deeds would be readily manifest: nevertheless,
> I consider that both will be yet more clearly revealed from
> what remains to be said. For of all the many sovereigns since
> time began, none will be found to have won this honour more
> gloriously than Evagoras. If we were to compare (παρα-
> βάλλοιμεν) the deeds of Evagoras with those of each one, such
> an account would perhaps be inappropriate to the occasion,
> and the time would not suffice for the telling. But if we select
> the most illustrious of these rulers and examine their exploits
> in the light of his, our investigation will lose nothing thereby
> and our discussion will be much more brief (*Evagoras* 33-34).[67]

This technique of incorporating παραδείγματα in encomiastic syncrisis,[68] seen here in Isocrates, was an accepted principle in ancient
rhetoric. Aristotle's discussion of epideictic bears this out:

> If he (viz., the subject of the encomium) does not furnish you
> with enough material in himself, you must compare (ἀντι-
> παραβάλλειν) him with others, as Isocrates used to do, . . . And
> you must compare him with illustrious personages (δεῖ δὲ
> πρὸς ἐνδόξους συγκρίνειν), . . . (*Rh.* 1.9.38).

---

[66]Above, 13-21.
[67]The emphasis is mine.
[68]On παραδείγματα in encomiastic syncrisis, cf. Lumpe, "Exemplum,"
1233.

Likewise Anaximenes,

> You must also compare (παριστάναι) the distinguished
> achievements (ἐνδόξους πράξεις) of other young men and
> show that they are surpassed by his, . . . (Rhet. ad Alex.
> 35.1441a.25).

The syncrisis with famous examples may extend as well to the implicit
comparison which comes with the presence in the encomium of the subject's genealogy. The genealogy, like syncrisis, is—as will be discussed
later—one of the fixed topics in encomia. And it is employed in such a
way so that what is said concerning each of the subject's ancestors
reflects favorably on the subject himself. Thus in the Evagoras, Isocrates
introduces the king's genealogy:

> In the first place, with respect to the birth and ancestry of
> Evagoras, even if many are already familiar with the facts, I
> believe it is fitting that I should recount them for the sake of
> the others, that all may know that he proved himself not
> inferior to the noblest and greatest examples (καλλίστων καὶ
> μεγίστων παραδειγμάτων) of excellence which were of his
> inheritance (Evag. 12).

And in his Busiris Isocrates faults Polycrates for his misuse of genealogical syncrisis in his attempt to praise the mythical Egyptian king:

> But the greatest absurdity is this—though you (viz., Poly-
> crates) have made a specialty of genealogies, you have dared
> to say that Busiris emulated those whose fathers even at that
> time had not yet been born! (Bus. 8)

The theory of such a use of genealogy is seen in Anaximenes:

> . . . we shall place first after the introduction (προοίμα) the
> genealogy (γενεαλογίαν) of the person we are speaking of . . .
> . . . . . . . . . . . . . . . . . . . . . . . . . . . . . .
> so in eulogizing (εὐλογοῦντες) a human being or a domestic
> animal we shall state their pedigree (γενεαλογήσομεν), . . .
> (Rhet. ad Alex. 35.1440b.20-25).

> The proper way to employ genealogy is this. If the ancestors
> are men of merit, you must enumerate (ἀναλαβόντα) them all

from the beginning down to the person you are eulogizing (ἐγκωμιαζόμενον), and at each of the ancestors summarily mention something to his credit (ἐνδόξον τι παρατιθέναι) (35.1440b.30).

The examples which make up the genealogy, then, and the comparison which the author intends to be drawn between them and the subject of the encomium, would seem to offer an additional parallel to what Sirach has done in his juxtaposition of the fathers of old and Simon II. The *Beispiel-reihe* of 44:16-49:16 may either be serving the purpose of an encomiastic genealogy—as in the above examples—and/or it may be understood as the section which furnishes the formal syncritistic element in the encomium —in much the same way as the section dealing with Cyrus in Isocrates' *Evagoras*.

## D. THE ENCOMIUM: A HISTORICAL SKETCH

I do not intend that what follows be thought of as an exhaustive treatment of the history and form of the Greek encomium. Such discussions are available elsewhere.[69] Rather my purpose is to survey the writings of those individuals who shaped the encomium into what it was by the time Ben Sira could have conceivably employed it as an inspiration for the form of Sirach 44-50. And in addition to commenting on the works produced by these individuals, I propose to identify the features of the encomium which tended to recur throughout the several periods of its development, and which came to be the principal characteristics of the form.

For purposes of our analysis I have chosen to divide the history of the encomium into three periods: an early period, which begins with the mid-sixth century B.C.E. and extends to the time of Isocrates (436-338 B.C.E.); an intermediate period which commences with Isocrates and includes those encomia extant down to the second century B.C.E., i.e., encomia in circulation by Ben Sira's time; and a later period extending from the second century to the rhetoricians of the first few centuries of the Common Era.

---

[69]Cf. V. Buchheit, *Untersuchungen zur Theorie des Genos Epideiktikon von Gorgias bis Aristoteles* (Munich: Max Hueber, 1960); Burgess, "Epideictic Literature," 113-42; Crusius, "Enkomion," *PW V,2*, 2581-83; and G. Fraustadt, *Encomiorum in Litteris Graecis usque ad Romanam Aetatem Historia* (Leipzig: Typis Roberti Noske Bornensis, 1909).

The reason for proposing that the transition from the early to the intermediate period occurred at the time of Isocrates is due to the pivotal role he appears to have played in the development of the encomium. Mention of his importance here has been made already.[70] Isocrates, for example, regarded himself as the creator of the prose encomium (*Evag.* 8,11), although Aristotle gives that honor to an encomium composed in Thessaly for one Hippolochus, otherwise unknown, early in the fourth century (*Rh.* 1.9.38).[71] At any rate, Isocrates is credited as one who was critical of the then encomiastic fascination with mythical subjects, and who, by his practical and theoretical elaboration of the form, made the encomium into a rhetorical εἶδος.[72]

The question may be raised as to the value for our study of including a discussion of the third period of development outlined above, viz., the encomium from Sirach's time down to its treatment in the rhetorical handbooks of the Common Era. Consideration of the form of the encomium in this later period, however, may be valuable owing to the conservatism of ancient rhetoric. For the handbooks of rhetors such as Theon (first-second century C.E.), Hermogenes (second century), Menander (third century) and Aphthonius (ca. 400 C.E.) evidence little originality over the encomiastic theory discussed centuries earlier by Aristotle and Anaximenes.[73]

> The ideal for the encomium of a person, both in theory and practice, was remarkably uniform. It agrees in general conception, and even largely in details, from almost the earliest to the latest period of Greek literature.[74]

---

[70] Above, 96.

[71] Cf. Momigliano, *The Development,* 49; and U. von Wilamowitz-Mölendorff, "Lesefrüchte LVII," *Hermes* 35 (1900), 533-34.

[72] Burgess, "Epideictic Literature," 115; Leo, *Die griechisch-römische Biographie,* 91; G. Misch, *A History of Autobiography in Antiquity: I* (International Library of Sociology and Social Reconstruction, K. Mannheim, ed.; trans. from the 3rd German ed. of 1949-50; Westport, CT: Greenwood, 1973) 161.

[73] On the conservatism of rhetoric and rhetorical forms, cf. Volkmann, *Die Rhetorik,* 326; H. J. Rose, *A Handbook of Greek Literature: From Homer to the Age of Lucian* (4th ed.; New York: E. P. Dutton and Co., 1951) 417; D. A. Russell and M. Winterbottom, *Ancient Literary Criticism,* 172, 579.

[74] Burgess, "Epideictic Literature," 119-20. Prof. George Kustas of the Classics Department, SUNY, Buffalo, made the same point in a private

Thus information on the form of the encomium which can be gained from examination of the theoretical discussions which post-date Ben Sira —those of Theon, et al., mentioned above, as well as those of the earlier *Rhetorica ad Herennium* (first century B.C.E.) and Quintilian (first century C.E.)—may aid us in identifying the form-critical features of the εἶδος which continued in use down to and beyond Sirach's time.

### 1. The Early Period: From the Lyric Poets to Isocrates

Although it is with the prose encomia both of, and subsequent to, Isocrates that we are concerned, such encomia were heirs to a long history of poetic precedent.[75] For in the mid-sixth century, poets began to deal in new hymnic forms whose subjects were men instead of the gods. Among these new forms were dirges (θρῆνοι), encomia, and victory-songs (ἐπινίκια) in honor of those who had met with success in one of the great games.[76] The latter, however, are but cognates of the encomium.[77] Thus, the epinician odes of the lyric poets—Simonides, Bacchylides, and Pindar —become the primary source for our knowledge of the early encomium.

Perhaps the earliest "encomium" which we may identify is a composition attributed to the lyric poet Ibycus of Rhegium which appears on a first century B.C.E. papyrus (POxy. 1790). The poem is an ode to Polycrates, the tyrant of Samos. Ibycus went to Samos during the rule of Polycrates' father, Aiakes (ca. 572-569 B.C.E.), and there he composed this ode in a style and triadic structure which were later to be perfected by Pindar.[78] From what is preserved of the poem, it appears that Ibycus sought to praise Polycrates through comparison of the tyrant's deed with those of the Greek expedition to Troy:

> But now 'tis my will to sing neither of Paris . . . nor yet of . . .
> Cassandra and other the children of Priam with the taking of
> Troy the high-gated, . . . nor shall I recount the proud valor of

---

conversation with me while he was a visiting professor of rhetoric at the University of California, Berkeley, in November 1975.

[75]Stuart, *Epochs*, 43.

[76]Rose, *Handbook*, 113-14.

[77]M. Hadas, *A History of Greek Literature* (New York: Columbia University, 1950) 46. Stuart, *Epochs*,15, refers to the epinician ode as a "cognate" of the encomium.

[78]Hadas, *History*, 56; Rose, *Handbook*, 109-10.

the Heroes, the Heroes so noble whom the hollow ships with
their nailed sides brought unto Troy . . .[79]

Ibycus, rather than praising the heroes of the Trojan War, presumably
turned to the task of praising Polycrates. But having introduced the
former, the audience's recollection of their exploits would no doubt reflect favorably on the poet's description of Polycrates' achievements.
Such a device whereby the presentation of the subject is somehow built
upon, or compared with, other praiseworthy figures is, as we will see, one
of the basic techniques of amplification (αὔξησις), and amplification is a
basic characteristic of epideictic or encomiastic literature (cf. Aristotle,
*Rh.* 1.9.40; and *Rhet. ad Alex.* 1428a. 2-4).

Moreover, as Ibycus continues, he comments that instead of attempting
to praise these heroic figures from the past, he will leave that task up to
the Muses, for ". . . never a mortal alive could tell of all the doings of the
ships, how came Menelaus from Aulis . . . .," etc. This protest of inadequacy on the part of the poet became, as we will see below, a commonplace in later encomia; the typical encomiast recites how he cannot do
justice to all the deeds/virtues of his subject.

With Simonides (556-468 B.C.E.) of Ceos we have at our disposal a
number of fragments upon which we may begin to fashion a clearer picture of early encomia. Simonides is said to have composed a variety of
encomiastic pieces, including dirges (θρῆνοι), epinician odes, and encomia
proper. Compositions which were regarded in antiquity as belonging to the
lattermost category are his ode to Scopas of Thessaly, to which Plato
refers in the *Protagoras,* and his commemorative hymn for the Spartans
who fell at Thermopylae. In discussing the hymn to Scopas, Plato has
Socrates comment:

And Simonides, as is probable, considered that he himself had
often to praise and magnify (ἐπαινέσαι καὶ ἐγκωμιάσαι) a
tyrant or the like, much against his will, . . . (*Prt.* 346b).[80]

---

[79]The translation is that of J. M. Edmonds, *Lyra Graeca: II* (Loeb
Classical Library; New York: G. P. Putnam's Sons, 1924) 115, 117.

[80]The translation is that of B. Jowett in I. Edman, ed., *The Works of
Plato* (The Modern Library; New York: Random House, 1956) 239. The
Greek text is that of J. Burnet, *Platonis Opera: III* (Oxford: Clarendon,
1903).

And Diodorus of Sicily referred to the praise of the Spartans at Thermopylae as an "encomium" of Simonides:

> . . . Simonides, the lyric poet, who composed the following encomium in their praise, worthy of their valor (ἄξιον τῆς ἀρετῆς αὐτῶν ποιήσας ἐγκώμιον): 'Of those who perished at Thermopylae . . .' (Diod. 11.11.6).[81]

Diodorus, however, may have been in error in calling this composition an encomium. C. M. Bowra argues that Diodorus has used the term in a more general sense and not in terms of a hymn which is in praise of a single individual.[82] To Bowra the poem would be best classified as a dirge, although it evidently was composed and sung not at Thermopylae over the graves of the fallen, but was employed as a cult-song in Sparta.

The principal sources, however, for our knowledge of Simonides' encomiastic poetry—given our only indirect knowledge of the hymn to Scopas and the fact that the ode for the Spartans at Thermopylae is in the nature of a dirge—are his epinician odes. Even though we possess only fragments, as quoted in later authors, we none-the-less can make some observations on Simonides' method. The first feature we can note is that he clearly makes use of the technique of amplification. For example, in his victory-song for Glaucus of Carystus, amplification is accomplished through syncrisis with mythical figures: "Neither the might of Polydeuces would have lift hand against him (viz., Glaucus), nay, nor the iron child of Alcmena (viz., Heracles)."[83] Another method of amplification utilized by Simonides—which was known and practiced in later periods (cf. Aristotle, *Rh.* 1.9.38)—is to describe the subject as the first or only person to have done something. Thus Simonides asks the rhetorical question concerning Astylus of Crotona:

> Who among those of our time ever bound upon him so many victories with leaves of myrtle or wreaths of roses in a contest of the men of those parts?[84]

---

[81]The text and translation are those of C. H. Oldfather, *Diodorus of Sicily: IV* (Loeb Classical Library; Cambridge: Harvard University, 1961).

[82]C. M. Bowra, "Simonides on the Fallen of Thermopylae," *Class. Phil.* 28 (1933) 277.

[83]The translation is that of Edmonds, *Lyra Graeca: II,* 303.

[84]Ibid., 301.

And Simonides practiced amplification by means of the particular expressions chosen to describe his subject. Aristotle, in his *Rhetoric*, refers to an occasion when Simonides, offered too small a fee for an epinician in honor of the victor in a mule-car-race, protested that he could not compose an ode in praise of mules. But when offered a more substantial honorarium, he took the assignment and glorified the mules with the words "Hail, ye daughters of storm-footed steeds!"[85] Such amplification by means of hyperbolic language, we will see, occupies a place in Quintilian's discussion of encomiastic theory half a millennium later.

The method of amplification whereby it is stated that the subject was the first or only person to have accomplished a certain feat is evident as well in Simonides' nephew and protege, Bacchylides. Born, as his uncle was, on the island of Ceos, he was about a dozen years older than Pindar, and was Pindar's closest rival for commissions in writing lyric poetry.[86] Examples of this type of amplification in his works include his description of Hiero of Syracuse, "Yet of all the dwellers that are in Greece, O illustrious Hiero, no man can say that any hath given to Loxias (Apollo) so much gold as thou,"[87] and in another poem celebrating a different victory of the same, "Yet we can crown him with wreaths as the only man on earth who hath achieved what he hath done in the glens of Cirrha by the sea, aye and we can sing of two victories Olympian."[88]

In addition, Bacchylides' epinicians include certain materials which would appear later as the fixed topics (τόποι) of rhetorical encomia. One of these is the section in which the genealogy of the subject is set forth. We have already mentioned the use of the genealogy in encomia,[89] and as will be discussed later on, it was one of the essential topics of the encomium as outlined even in the rhetorical handbooks of the Common Era. In Bacchylides' ode for Pytheas of Aegina, a victor in the Nemean games, he inserts the praise of the mythical offspring of Aegina—Aeacus, Peleus, Telamon, Achilles, and the Aeacidae of the Trojan War—for whom "there liveth nevertheless a glory by grace of the sweet-word Muses and by virtue of immortal songs (40.165-170)."[90] And from the praise of these Aeacidean ancestors, Bacchylides moves directly to the praise of the

---

[85]Ibid., 309.

[86]Hadas, *History*, 63.

[87]J. M. Edmonds, *Lyra Graeca: III* (Loeb Classical Library; New York: G. P. Putnam's Sons, 1927) 141.

[88]Ibid., 145.

[89]Above, 102-103.

[90]Edmonds, *Lyra Graeca: III*, 193, 195.

victor himself, singing that dame "Prowess" ('Αρετᾷ) has honored Aegina again by granting Pytheas victory:

> And lo, now she honoureth the enfaming isle of Aeacus, and guideth his city with aid of that lover of wreaths Good Name, . . . (40.182-185)

After the praise of Pytheas, the poem ends with an exhortation to others to extol his deeds:

> Chant ye the glorious victory of Pytheas, O youths, . . .
> . . . . . . . . . . . . . . . . . . . . . . . . . . . . . .
> Let all such as are not in bondage to blatant Envy give due praise to a man of skill (40.189-90, 199-202).

This type of a concluding exhortation appears as well in Bacchylides' victory-song for Automedes of Philius:

> Whoso winneth an honor of golden-sceptred Zeus, him let all men praise. With songs of revelry follow ye, I pray, the son of Timoxenus (viz., Automedes), for his victory in the five-events (36.100-104).[91]

Exhortations of this kind through which the audience was urged to join the poet in praise, or to emulate the subject's deeds became, as our discussion will show, a common element in the epilogue of the encomium.

The parallel here between the exhortation, with which Bacchylides closes his ode for Automedes, and the epilogue of later encomia, extends to additional points in the arrangement or τάξις of the encomium. Thus Bacchylides' opening lines anticipate one of the themes of later prooemia, the poet's or orator's reflection on the task of praising men: ". . . a divine spokesman of the violet-eyed Muses is ready to sing praise of Philius and the thriving plain of Nemean Zeus, . . . (36.3-6)." Following a mythical treatment of the origins of the Nemean games, he makes a transition to a unit in which he recites Automedes' victory in the current pentathlon:

> From those reknowned jousts at Nemea comes fame to any mortal that crowneth flaxen hair with wreath biennial; and now God hath given the same to the victorious Automedes. For

---

[91]Ibid., 171.

he was conspicuous among the five-event-men even as the
brilliant moon of the mid-month surpassesth the stars in
radiance; aye even thus shown the marvelous figure of him
amid the vast ring of Greeks, as he hurled the rounded quoit
. . . (36.21-32).

Such a portrayal of Automedes, employing techniques of amplification,
suggests the narration of the πράξεις, which rhetoricians considered to be
the chief topic of the encomium. Thus in Bacchylides we already sense
what would become the basic arrangement of τόποι: the prooemium, the
genealogy, the narration of the subject's accomplishments, and the epilogue with its concluding exhortation.

A similar outline or arrangement is evident when we turn to the epinician odes of Pindar (518-438 B.C.E.), a far greater poet than Bacchylides.[92] His epinicia are collected in four books, each of which consists of
the odes composed for one of the four great festivals: those of Olympia,
Pythia, Isthmia, and Nemea. These four books are the only works out of
the seventeen books attributed to Pindar that have come down to us in
manuscript tradition.[93] Lost are one book of encomia and one of dirges.
The epinicia, however, represent Pindar's favorite form, the form upon
which his reputation was based even in antiquity, and within the four
books which we have, forty-four separate odes have survived.

Now the importance of Pindar's epinicia for our survey of the history of
the encomium is due to the fact that, as Burgess has observed, the Pindaric form basically corresponds to that of the encomium or βασιλικὸς
λόγος of the Common Era rhetors:

> With allowance for the poetic form and the unfettered strain
> of the lyric master's genius, many of the odes of Pindar are
> βασιλικοὶ λόγοι. The very composition, as well as the pur-
> pose of a Pindaric ode, involves some of the most essential
> features of a βασιλικὸς λόγος. As a rule, the introduction
> names and praises her hero, frequently including his native
> city. The myth is apt to owe its presence to its direct or
> implied praise of the hero's ancestry. The conclusion comes
> back to the hero, often with an enumeration of his qualities
> and deeds, ending with a prayer.[94]

---

[92]Hadas, History, 63.
[93]Ibid., 59.
[94]Burgess, "Epideictic Literature," 129-30. Also, cf. Fraustadt, Encomiorum, 32, 38, where he outlines Pindaric odes in terms of the arrangement of later encomia.

Within this general arrangement which he shares with Bacchylides on
the one hand, and later encomiasts on the other, Pindar employs a number
of topics characteristic of encomia. Some of these we have identified
already in Simonides and Bacchylides, while others appear for the first
time in Pindar. Among these are:

### a. Elements Proper to the Prooemium

One feature that recurs in the introductions to encomia is where the
poet or rhetor comments in some way on the task at hand. In the above
example from Bacchylides (no. 36 in the Loeb edition), that comment was
in the form of a statement to the effect that the poet was ready, with the
Muses' help, to begin the praise of Automedes. Similarly Pindar reflects
on the task of praising a man. This may be in terms of acknowledging the
occasion for the hymn and how appropriate it is that praise be offered.
Olympian 2, for example, opens with the question, "Ye hymns that rule
the lyre! What God, what hero, aye, and what man shall we loudly praise
(Ol. 2.1-2)?" To which Pindar's answer is: ". . . Theron (of Acragas, 476
B.C.E.) must be proclaimed by reason of his victorious chariot with its
four horses, . . .(Ol. 2.5-6)."[95] Other examples of the same sort of thing
may be seen in:

> Lo, I come from splendid Thebes, and I bring a song that
> telleth of the race of the four-horse chariot that shaketh the
> earth, that race in which Hieron (of Syracuse, 475 B.C.E.) was
> victorious . . . (Pyth. 2.3-5)

> . . . when anyone is victorious by aid of toil, then it is that
> honey-voiced odes are a foundation for future fame, even a
> witness to noble exploits. Far beyond envy is the praise that is
> thus stored up for victors at Olympia; and such praises my
> tongue would fain feed and foster; . . . For the present rest
> assured, Hagesidamus (of Locri Epizephyrii, 476 B.C.E.), son of
> Archestratus, that for the sake of thy victory in boxing, I shall
> loudly sing a sweet strain . . . (Ol. 11.4-9, 11-14)

In addition to specifying that the victory calls for the praise of the
hero, Pindar believes that praise of the hero's city is also appropriate. In

---

[95]The translation is that of Sandys, *Odes.*

his ode for Epharmostus of Opus, winner in the wrestling match of 468 B.C.E., he urges that the city be praised as well for the victory of her son:

> Praise herself and her son; praise her whom Themis and her glorious daughter, the Saviour Eunomia, have received as their portion . . .
> . . . . . . . . . . . . . . . . . . . . . . . . . . . . . . . .
> Lo! I am lighting up that city dear with dazzling songs of praise, . . . (Ol. 9.14-16, 21-22).

In like manner, the praise of Xenophon of Corinth is joined with the praise of his city: "While I laud a house, thrice victor at Olympia, . . . I shall take knowledge of prosperous Corinth, portal of Isthmian Poseidon, glorious with her noble youths (Ol. 13.1-5)." And Pindar's hymn for Megacles of Athens, winner in the Pythian chariot race of 486 B.C.E., begins with the note that "The mighty city of Athens is the fairest prelude of song, . . . (Pyth. 7.1-2).

In each case, however, the city is not praised merely for the victory of its particular son. Rather the city is remembered for the deeds of all her sons—viz., all of the subject's ancestors—perhaps going as far back as the mythical exploits of the city's eponymous ancestor. It is through such a comparison of subject and city, or better, subject and ancestors, that later encomiasts practiced one form of syncrisis. Syncrisis, about which comment has already been made and to which we will return later, is one of the basic techniques of amplification in the encomium.

The prooemium in some instances might include comment on the methods, especially if they were new or novel, which the encomiast had chosen to employ in his composition. Something of this sort in Pindar may be his remark that the ode will be crafted in such a way that it can be sung to the accompaniment of both flute and lyre: ". . . not only often with the sweetly-sounding lyre, but also amid the varied notes of the flute. And now to the music of both, have I come with Diagoras to laud, . . . that so I may honour for his fairness in fight . . ." (Ol. 7.12,15,16; cf. also Ol. 3.8).

Pindar's epinician odes also make use of a feature, seen as early as Ibycus, which became a commonplace of encomiastic prooemia: the protest of the poet's inadequacy. This element may be considered but another form of amplification in that, as the poet protests his inability to do the subject justice, the subject is made to appear all the greater. Although Pindar's expressions of protest do not appear in the opening lines of his odes, they are none-the-less present and are remarkably similar to those we find later in the prooemia of Isocrates *et al.*:

. . . whereas sand can never be numbered, and who could even count up all the joys that he (viz., Theron, the subject) hath given to others (Ol. 2.98-100)?

In commenting on this passage, Burgess notes that "This ode, like many others, contains the distinctly epideictic plea of inadequacy."[96] Other examples of this type of protest are in his ode for Xenophon of Corinth,

. . . too long would be the songs which shall attain to all the victories . . . For, in truth I could not have the skill to tell the number of the pebbles of the sea (Ol. 13.41-42,46; cf.also Isth. 6.55-56).

And in his praise of Theaeus of Argos,

My mouth is of small measure to tell all the story, to wit all the fair things, of which the holy precinct of Argos hath a share (Nem. 10.19).

### b. Elements Proper to the Genealogy (γένος)

In our discussion of Bacchylides' epinician ode for Pytheas of Aegina, it was noted that the poem includes a section in praise of the mythical sons of Aegina. Such sections were features of Pindar's epinicia as well. As we have already seen, the opening lines of a number of Pindar's odes contain statements that the victor's city is to be praised, not simply in that it is the subject's home, but that its sons—from the immediate forbearers of the victor back to the city's mythical first sons—have excelled in the games and in battle. This praise of the ancestors, anticipated or implied in some of Pindar's introductions, is then taken up again in a section in-and-of-itself. This section, referred to by commentators on Pindar as the myth, seems to correspond to what later rhetors identified as the genealogy or γένος of the encomium. Commenting on the myth, Rose writes:

The legend may be a saga relating to the country or family of the man in whose honour the ode is composed; thus, the many epinikians written for Aiginetans regularly contain some episode of the long history of Aiakos and its descendants; while in many of the shorter odes there is no myth, or at most

---

[96]Burgess, "Epideictic Literature," 130.

but the hint of one. Again, the connexion between the story
and the general subject of the ode may be so slight as to be
almost undetectable; . . .[97]

That is to say, evidently in the longer epinicians Pindar felt obligated to
include a mythical section whose purpose was to describe favorably the
ancestry of the subject. Moreover, the sense that this element was necessary or desirable led him to include some kind of myth even on those
occasions when no myths were available that would lend themselves
directly to the story of the victor's ancestry or city.

To illustrate Pindar's use of myth here, first of all, there are those odes
where Pindar creates a section that brings together his knowledge of the
actual genealogy of his subject and elements of myth. An illustration of
this is Olympian 13, in honor of Xenophon of Corinth, which begins with
the recollection of the exploits of Xenophon's father, Thessalus (ll. 35-36),
and those of other Corinthian relatives, Terpsias, Eritimus, and Ptoe-
ödorus (ll.40-42).[98] Then, however, Pindar moves on to sing of the mythical heroes of Corinth:

> . . . but I, in the fleet of common joy, setting forth on a course
> of my own, and telling of the craft and the warrior-worth of
> the men of yore, shall, in the tale of heroic prowess (ἐν ἡρωΐ-
> αις ἀρεταῖσιν), truly speak of Corinth. I shall tell of Sisyphus,
> who, like a very god, was most wise (πυκνότατον) in his coun-
> sels; and of Medea, who . . . thus saved the ship Argo and her
> seamen (ll. 49-54).

Pindar continues with lines on Glaucus, Sisyphus' son (ll. 60-82), and
Bellerophon, his grandson (ll. 83-92). Finally, after this extensive treatment of Sisyphus' descendants, Pindar returns to the praise of his subject's
family: "For gladly I have come, as a champion . . . of the race of Oligae-
thus. As to their victories . . . with a few words shall I make all of them
manifest; . . ." (ll. 96-98)

Similarly, in the epinician (Pythian 5) for the Battiad king of Cyrene,
Arcesilas IV, Pindar extols the founder of the dynasty and leader of the

---

[97]Rose, *Handbook,* 120.
[98]It is unclear as to what the relationship is of these three to
Thessalus, Xenophon's father. From the ode itself we might assume Pto-
eödorus to be Thessalus's father, but the scholia make him another son of
Thessalus. Cf. Sandys, *Odes,* 137, n. 1.

Theran colonization of Cyrene, Battus I, as "that tower of the city of Cyrene, and that light most radiant to strangers from afar" (l. 56). The section in praise of Battus continues to l. 107, but within it Pindar digresses into a treatment of the legendary pre-Battiad inhabitants of Cyrene, who are said to have come from Troy:

> . . . bronze-armed Trojans from a foreign shore, even by the descendants of Antenor. For they came with Helen, after they had seen their native city burnt in war, . . . (ll. 82-85)

The apparent necessity of including such a section may be seen, in the second place, in those odes where Pindar did not have a myth or genealogical material directly relevant to his subject. An example of this is Olympian 6, written for Hagesias of Syracuse. Here Pindar makes a recognizable transition (ll. 22-27) from his introduction to a unit in which he states he will describe "the descent (γένος) of our heroes" (ll. 24-25). But rather than presenting Hagesias' ancestry, he extols the clan of Olympia by telling the myth of Evadne and her son Iamus (ll. 27-70). The purpose of the myth, then, is in the comparison that is to be drawn between the Iamidae, whose prowess has been demonstrated in the Olympian games, and Hagesias who, though not of their clan, has shared in their victories (cf. ll. 71-76).

Another example is that of Olympian 2 composed for Theron where the myth does not deal at all with the victor's city, Acragas in Sicily. In contrast, the myth employed by Pindar tells of various personalities associated in some way with Thebes: Cadmus of Tyre, the legendary founder of Thebes, and his daughter Semele, who had a cult at Thebes (ll. 22-34). At this point Pindar narrates a line of descent that begins with Laius, king of Thebes, his son Oedipus, Oedipus' son Polyneices, Polyneices' father-in-law Adrastus, and Polyneices' son Thersander (ll. 35-45). Thereupon Pindar asserts that his Sicilian subject Theron is descended from this line by way of his father Aenesidamus, and how he, then, should be met with "songs of praise and with notes of the lyre" (ἐγκωμίων τε μελέων λυρᾶν τε τυγχανέμεν) (ll. 46-47).

A final example will illustrate those occasions, referred to above by Rose, when the myth has no apparent relationship to the praise of the hero. In Pythian 2, the subject is Hieron I, but the myth is that of Ixion, the Greek "Cain." The story of the latter has nothing to do with the tyrant of Syracuse whose victory is being extolled by Pindar. Rather it is offered to teach the lesson that "men should requite (their) benefactors with fresh tokens of warm gratitude" (l. 24), a lesson that the city of Locri

Epizephyrii will now heed as it gives praise to its benefactor Hieron (ll. 18-19).

With the exception of odes such as the latter, where the myth has no connection with the subject, and those brief odes which, as Rose pointed out, omit the myth altogether, the epinicia of Pindar exhibit, then, a treatment of the subject's genealogy either in the form of a myth or in some combination of myth and genealogical fact. Thus in Pindar we already have the presence of one of the elements that was to become a fixed topic in later encomia. We have had occasion to comment on this topic, the γένος, above, and we will return to it again when we consider the form of the Isocratean encomium.[99]

## c. Elements Proper to the πράξεις

The recitation of the subject's deeds—in war and peace—became the chief topic in the encomia of the rhetors.[100] And the same may be said for the narration of the victories being celebrated in the epinician odes. Already we had occasion to cite Bacchylides' narration of the victory of Automedes in the pentathlon at Nemea,[101] in which attention is given to his prizes in the discus, the javelin, and the wrestling match (ll. 32-37). No mention is made of the remaining running and jumping events, which Automedes evidently did not win. Success in the three former contests, however, was sufficient to gain the victory.[102] As he narrates Automedes' accomplishments, Bacchylides has the opportunity to practice the technique of amplification by comparing his subject to the other competitors in terms of "the brilliant Moon of the mid-month" which surpasses the stars in radiance (ll. 27-31).

In Pindar, we have seen that a recitation of the πράξεις is anticipated already at the beginning of some of his odes (e.g., Ol. 2.5-6, 7.15-17; Pyth. 2.3-5). But in each of these the "foretaste" of the subject's accomplishments is expanded upon in a later section which would appear to correspond to the πράξεις of later encomia. Thus in Olympian 2, he returns to the theme of Theron's victory in the chariot-race, an event that Theron's brother has won as well in the Pythian and Isthmian games (ll. 46-52). And at the same point in Olympian 7, Pindar adds up the total number of

---

[99]Above, 102.
[100]Burgess, "Epideictic Literature," 123-24.
[101]Above, 109.
[102]Edmonds, *Lyra Graeca: III*, 167, n. 1.

prizes won by his subject, Diagoras, in all of the games together (ll. 81-87).

Such a narration of games and prizes won is characteristic, moreover, of those epinicia which do not have the anticipatory statement or summary of the victor's accomplishments at the outset of the poem. In this type of ode, the recital of the πράξεις is confined to a particular section within the body of the composition. For example, similar to Olympian 2 and 7 above, are Olympian 13, which totals the number of victories won by Xenophon and his family at the several games (ll. 32-46), and Olympian 4 and Isthmian 6. In the case of the latter two, however, the specific remembrance of the athletic events won is broadened to include other deeds and virtues which the subjects have accomplished or which they possess. Similarly, Pythian 2, which like Olympian 2 and 7, employs a preliminary description of the event won by its subject, goes on in the narration of the πράξεις proper to include mention of Hieron's wealth, his wise counsels, and his military prowess (ll. 57-67). In the case of Olympian 4 and Isthmian 6, this broadening of the grounds upon which the victor is praised includes the fact that he is ". . . one who is right ready in the rearing of coursers, one who rejoiceth in welcoming his guests, and one who in pure heart devoteth himself to Peace that loveth the state" (Ol. 4.13-16). And in Isthmian 6, Phylacidas is remembered for

> . . . bringing a general fame to his own city, . . . his good deeds
> to strangers also, in heart pursuing the true mean, and holding
> to that mean in act beside; and his tongue departeth not from
> his thoughts (ll. 69-72).

Within his narration of the πράξεις, Pindar, like Bacchylides, Simonides, and Ibycus before him, employs techniques of amplification in order to enhance the stature of his subjects. One common method of amplification, seen already in Bacchylides, is for the poet to portray his subject's deeds as unique. Extolling his subjects, then, Pindar writes:

> He (Xenophon of Corinth) hath thus attained what no mortal
> man ever yet attained before (Ol. 13.30-31).

> . . . for these hundred years, no city hath given birth to a man
> more munificent in heart, more ungrudging in hand, than
> Theron (Ol. 2.93-95).

> But if, when wealth and honour are in question, any one saith
> that among the men of old any other king hath surpassed thee

(viz., Hieron) in Hellas, in his idle fancy he striveth in vain
(Pyth. 2.58-61).

A second method of amplification, also evident in the earlier lyric
poets, is that of σύγκρισις or comparison. In addition to the comparisons
implicit in the above examples (viz., that no one else has done what
Pindar's subject has) and in the mention of the hero's γένος, Pindar employs a formal σύγκρισις within his narration of the πράξεις. Thus, as he
extols the victory of Chromius of Aetna in the chariot race at Sicyon
(Nem. 9), he expands the theme of his praise to include the military
exploits of Chromius. And to amplify his subject as a military hero he
compares Chromius' bravery in battle (with the Syracusans on the banks of
the Helorus River) to that of Hector (on the banks of the Scamander) (ll.
39-43). And in Nemean 5, the victory of Pytheas is compared with that of
his maternal uncle, Euthymenes, at Isthmia (ll. 41-43).[103] Amplification
through comparison, moreover, is practiced not only by likening the
subject to some other heroic personality, but by employing the language
of metaphor and/or simile. Thus Pindar compares Phylacidas of Aegina to
the famous emerystones of the island of Naxos:

> You might say, amid the athletes, he was a very stone of
> Naxos among all others, the metal-mastering whetstone (Isth.
> 6.72-73).

And within the praise of the wrestler Alcimidas, he honors as well the
boy's trainer, Melesias, by comparing him to the swiftness of the dolphin:

> Of Melesias, as a a trainer deft in strength of hands, I would
> say that in speed he is a match for the dolphin that darteth
> through the brine (Nem. 6.66-69).

### d. Elements Proper to the ἐπίλογος

In his outline of Pindaric epinicia, Burgess calls attention to the presence in each ode of a definite concluding section.[104] The feature that

---

[103]Cf. also Isth. 8.61-65, where the victory of Cleandros is amplified
by comparison with that of his cousin, Nicocles.

[104]Burgess, "Epideictic Literature," 130; and cf. above, 110.

recurs within such sections is that of a prayer,[105] and/or as was seen in our discussion of Bacchylides, the epilogue may include some type of exhortation to others to join in praise of the victor.

In those cases where the poet ends with a prayer—generally to Zeus—the petition is offered either for the continued well-being of the subject, or that he will experience victory in games yet to come. Petitions of the former type appear in Olympian 6, where the prayer is for the safe journey of Hagesias back to this home in Syracuse (ll. 105-106); Olympian 5, with its request that Psaumis may know health, wealth and fame (ll. 17-24; cf.also Ol. 8.84-88 and Pyth. 5.118-24); and Olympian 7, where Zeus is asked to insure that Diagoras will receive the honor and respect of his countrymen:

> But do thou, O father Zeus, . . . grant honour to the hymn ordained in praise of an Olympian victor, and to the hero who hath found fame for his prowess as a boxer; and do thou give him grace and reverence in the eyes of citizens and of strangers too (ll. 87-90).

On the other hand, petitions for future victories are found at the close of Isthmian 1, where Pindar prays that Herodotus of Thebes may also enjoy success at the Olympian and Pythian contests (ll. 64-67). Likewise the prayer in Isthmian 7 is that Strepsiades, winner in the Isthmian pancratium, might experience the same at the next Pythian games (ll. 49-50). That the two types of prayer, however, are not mutually exclusive is shown by Olympian 1, in which Pindar prays both for Hieron's future prosperity (l. 115) and that he may know future victories (ll. 109-110).

In those instances where Pindar ends with an exhortation to others to offer their praise of the hero, the audiences vary. The appeal can be to deities or mythical figures. Thus in Olympian 11.16-17 the Muses are asked to join in the victory-song, while in Olympian 14.20-24, the nymph Echo is bid to "bear the glorious tidings" of Asopichus' victory to his father, Cleodamus, in Hades.

Pindar, like Bacchylides, chooses to exhort the victor's fellow-citizens as well, calling upon them to continue the praise he has begun. For example, to the citizenry of the Attic deme of Archanae, upon the victory of Timodemus, Pindar writes:

---

[105]Ibid. Also cf. Burgess, "Epideictic Literature," 126, where he notes that throughout the history of the encomium the epilogue has ended "most appropriately with a prayer."

Praise him O ye citizens, with the song of triumph, at the
bidding of Timodemus, when he cometh home again with glory,
and begin the song with sweetly-sounding strains (Nem. 2.24-
25).

And concerning Cleandros of Aegina, the wish is expressed that:

Therefore let a bright crown of myrtle, in honour of the pancratium, be entwined for Cleandros by one of his comrades,
. . . 'Tis fitting for the good to praise him, for he hid not the
spirit of his youth in a hole unknown to fame (Isth. 8.65-70).

Another feature of some Pindaric epilogues is for the poet to return to
the first-person note with which he began the ode; viz., as he began with a
declaration that "I am/we are" going to praise the victor, so he ends with
a wish or a prayer that the praise he has now offered will be considered
appropriate. In the case of Isthmian 4 he opened by acknowledging in the
first person (cf. Ἔστι μοι, l. 1) that he has before him the opportunity to
laud Melissus of Thebes. At the close of the ode, again in the first person
cf. κωμάξομαι, l. 72), he writes that the song he has now composed will
befit this occasion. Similarly, he opens Nemean 9 with the statement, in
the first-person plural, that he with the Muses will sing of Chromius of
Aetna (cf. κωμάσομεν, l. 1). This first-person declaration of intention,
then, is balanced at the conclusion by Pindar's prayer:

O father Zeus, I pray (εὔχομαι) that I may sound the praises of
this deed of prowess by the favour of the Graces, and that I
may excel many a bard in honouring victory by my verses,
shooting my dart of song nearest of all to the mark of the
Muses (ll. 53-55).

### e. Additional Encomiastic Features in Pindar

A topic which would later show up in the epilogues of prose encomia,
and which in a sense is related to the prayers for the continued well-being
of the subject, is that of the catalogue of blessings. Stuart calls attention
to how this motif was a traditional device in Greek commemorative
literature:

The items of felicity are: lineage, noble beyond compare;
unequaled physical and mental gifts; sovereignty gloriously
achieved and coextensive with life; immortal fame; a life

prolonged to old age but immune from the ills that aflict old
age; and lastly, that rare combination, offspring both numerous and goodly, blessings phrased by the Greek as *polypedia*
and *eupedia*.[106]

Such blessings may be inventoried within the body of an encomium or
they may appear as the object of the prayer in the epilogue. The presence
of the blessings catalogue, however, did not begin with later prose encomia, but in Pindar. It is from Pindar that the catalogue passed into prose
*epitaphioi* and encomia as a traditional element.[107]

One epinician that contains such an inventory of blessings is Pindar's
Pythian V in which he begins his praise of Arcesilas by calling him "O
blest of heaven" (ὦ θεόμορ', l. 5), after which he lists the blessings
enjoyed by him: his prosperity and his sovereignty over great cities (ll. 14-
19). The catalogue ends with the most recent blessing, that of his Pythian
victory: ". . . even today art thou happy (μάκαρ) in that thou hast already,
. . . won glory from the famous Pythian festival, . . . " (ll. 20-21).[108] That
a victory in the games should be considered a blessing is sounded as well
in the ode for Hippocleas of Thessaly (Pyth. 10):

> . . . but by poets wise that man is held happy (εὐδαίμων), and is
> a theme for their song, whosoever, by being victorious with his
> hands or with the prowess of his feet, gaineth the greatest
> prizes by courage or by strength, and who, while still living,
> seeth his youthful son by fate's decree happily win two Pythian
> crowns (ll. 22-26).

Another theme which appears in later prose encomia, especially in
Isocrates, and which seems to have a precedent in Pindar, is at those
points where he contrasts his poetic effort with the attempts of others.
Toward the end of Olympian 2, for example, Pindar speaks of his ability in
composing epinicia at the expense of, evidently, his two rivals Simonides
and Bacchylides:

---

[106]Stuart, *Epochs*, 85.
[107]Ibid., 86.
[108]Similarly, Nem. 11.11-14 catalogues the blessings of Aristagoras:
his imposing stature, his calmness of soul, his riches, his handsome form,
and his courage in the games.

> The true poet is he who knoweth much by gift of nature, but
> they that have only learnt the lore of song, and are turbulent
> and intemperate of tongue, like a pair of crows, chatter in
> vain against the god-like bird of Zeus (ll. 86-88).[109]

Thus far we have attempted to sketch how a number of elements, which were characteristic of later encomia, had their origins in the epinicia of the lyric poets. Yet to describe the early history of the encomium exclusively in terms of a poetic form would be to tell only part of the story. For although the encomium may have begun with the poets, the further development and popularization of the form came to be in the hands of the rhetors, beginning with Isocrates. Thus, in treating the history of the encomium in this early period, attention must be given to the question of what role a prose encomium may have had in rhetoric prior to the time of Isocrates.

Tradition holds that Greek rhetoric had its beginnings in Sicily with the expulsion of the tyrants from Syracuse in 467 B.C.E.[110] With the consequent establishment of democracy, families who had suffered expropriation of property under the tyrants began litigation to reestablish their claims. Thus there arose a demand for those who could either teach citizens the art of arguing a case in court, or who could compose a speech for them to use on such an occasion. It is in this context that we hear of the two earliest teachers of oratory, and composers of rhetorical handbooks (τέχναι), Corax and Tisias.

Because of the practical need for deliberative and judicial speeches in the new democracies of Sicily, Corax is remembered for his work with the former, while Tisias, his student, seems to have been concerned with the latter.[111] From the references which Plato, Aristotle, and others make to

---

[109]Sandys, Odes, 27, n. 1, regards the identification of the "pair of crows" as Simonides and Bacchylides to be preferable.

[110]Hadas, History, 160; Kennedy, The Art of Persuasion, 26; Rose, Handbook, 279.

[111]There is a story that Tisias, as a student of Corax, refused to pay his teacher for his instruction. Whereupon Corax took Tisias to court. Tisias, however, argued that if he won the case in court, he would not have to pay Corax due to the decision in his favor. If, however, he lost the case, he noted that payment would be unfair since the skills in oratory taught him by Corax would have been proved worthless. Corax responded by reversing the same set of arguments. The court turned both of them out with the epigram "a bad egg from a bad crow (korax)." Cf. Kennedy, The Art of Persuasion, 59.

the two of them, Corax appears to have devised a tripartite scheme of oratory—prooemium, ἀγών, and epilogue, appropriate for deliberative speeches—to which Tisias added a fourth element, the narration, for those speeches employed in the law-court.[112] This four-part outline generally corresponds to the τάξις or arrangement enjoined by later rhetorical theory, and it came to be the framework not only for deliberative and forensic speeches, but for epideictic pieces as well.[113] Thus even though Corax and Tisias did not work with or develop display speeches—such as the encomium—their work with judicial and political oratory provided the structure which subsequent rhetors would employ for the encomium. To such an arrangement the topics of the encomium would easily lend themselves in that, as we've seen above, the basic elements were already present in a similar order in the epinicia. For example, the narration of the speech presented the natural place for the recitation of the hero's victories, and thus became the πράξεις of the encomium. Another indirect contribution of Tisias to the eventual development of the prose encomium may be seen in his adoption of amplification as a rhetorical device. Amplification, already employed in poetry, is, as we've had occasion to point out, a favorite tool of the encomiast. That Tisias used it in his practice of rhetoric is suggested by a comment of Plato in the *Phaedrus* where he links Tisias with Gorgias and describes them as proficient in the art of making "the small seem great, the great small, the new old, and the old new" (cf. *Phdr.* 267a6).[114]

It is in the works of Gorgias, however, that we have the first examples of encomia composed by an orator. Commenting on this other Sicilian, with whom Plato linked Tisias in the passage from the *Phaedrus*, Stuart writes:

> . . . it would appear that the prose encomium and its counterpart,the vilification, came as conscious literary modes to Athens in the ship that brought Gorgias of Leontini in the year 427 B.C. He it is whom ancient literary critical opinion regarded as the exponent *par excellence* of these methods. Not

---

[112]Kennedy, *The Art of Persuasion*, 59. Cf. also G. Kennedy, "The Earliest Rhetorical Handbooks," *American Journal of Philology* 80 (1957) 177-78.

[113]Cf. Kennedy, *The Art of Persuasion*, 113, 119-22, for an overview of *taxis* in Aristotle's *Rhetoric* and in Anaximenes' *Rhet. ad Alex.*

[114]Ibid., 63; cf. also Stuart, *Epochs*, 57-58.

that he can be credited with having invented the weapons;
they had been forged, at least rudely, . . . in the fires of
litigation kindled in Sicily . . . Disparagement of an adversary,
praise of a friend were bound to be the spontaneous issue of
actual conflicts in the ancient court of law.[115]

The success of Gorgias' embassy in 427 B.C.E., which led to an alliance
between Athens and Leontini, was no doubt due to his rhetorical skill. The
Athenians, both the crowds and the officials, were astonished by his
unfamiliar style of speaking, and from that time on Gorgias was in
demand as a public speaker and as a teacher of rhetoric.[116] Among his
many students, whom he taught by assigning them various discourses to be
memorized,[117] were Isocrates, Agathon, and perhaps Xenophon.[118]
Isocrates was the greatest of his pupils, and not only did he owe Gorgias
credit for his stylistic devices,[119] but individual works of Isocrates were
based on or inspired by comparable works of Gorgias. Hence Isocrates'
*Helen* sought to improve upon the *Helen* of his teacher, and with his
*Panegyricus* he desired to have it rival Gorgias' *Olympicus.*[120]

What is new in Gorgias is that he was not concerned, as were Corax and
Tisias, with the practical type of oratory which could be of use in the
assembly and the lawcourt. Rather he produced display speeches and is
credited, then, with being the "father" of epideictic.[121] All of his
speeches of which we have knowledge, or which have survived, represent
this type. Moreover, even in antiquity he was known for his epideictic
oratory. Dionysius of Halicarnassus is quoted as saying that he knew of no

---

[115]Stuart, *Epochs,* 57-58.

[116]K. Freeman, *The Pre-Socratic Philosophers: A Companion to Diels,
Fragmente der Vorsokratiker* (3rd ed.; Oxford: Basil Blackwell, 1953) 354-
55.

[117]Kennedy, *The Art of Persuasion,* 52.

[118]The suggestion that Xenophon might possibly have been a student of
Gorgias is made by Stuart, *Epochs,* 73, where he notes that ". . . he had
imbibed a working knowledge of the stylistic devices of which Gorgias was
the leading exponent and which are traditionally connected with the great
sophist's name."

[119]Freeman, *Pre-Socratic Philosophers,* 356.

[120]E. Norden, *Die Antike Kunstprosa: I* (5th ed.; Stuttgart: B. G.
Teubner, 1958) 116.

[121]Freeman, *Pre-Socratic Philosophers,* 364; Burgess, "Epideictic
Literature," 102, n. 1; Hadas, *History,* 160.

forensic speeches composed by Gorgias and that he was aware of only a few of his political speeches.[122]

The epideictic quality of his oratory is represented both in those speeches which have survived and in the distinctive style Gorgias employed. Of his epideictic compositions whose titles and/or contents have come down to us, we may list: an *epitaphios*, his *Olympicus*, a Pythian oration of which nothing remains, a defense of Palamedes,[123] and then of interest to us, two encomia—an encomium on the Eleans, of which only the opening line survives, and his *Helen*. To the *Helen* and what it may contribute to our understanding of the early encomium we will return below.

Gorgias' epideictic style, however, deserves some comment at this point. One thing that needs to be said, especially in view of our earlier discussion that the encomium first appeared in lyric poetry, is that "epideictic is the form of oratory closest in style and function to poetry,"[124] and "in essence Gorgias simply borrowed a number of the techniques of poetry and developed to an extreme the natural Greek habit of antithesis."[125] In his *Helen*, Gorgias recognized the power of poetry, that it could produce various emotions—terror, pity, "sad longing," pleasure (*Helen* 9, 10)—and that oratory could now do the same (*Helen* 14).[126] Thus rhetoric found a model in poetry and poetic style,[127] and in Gorgias, that influence came to expression in the so-called Gorgian figures: antithesis, isocolon, parison (parallelism), homoeoteleuton, paronomasia, etc.[128] It

---

[122]Freeman, *Pre-Socratic Philosophers*, 359.

[123]Hadas, *History*, 160, curiously refers to the speech concerning Palamedes as an encomium. Others, however, describe it as a defense of this rival of Odysseus. The speech, although epideictic, for "display," has a forensic quality and takes the form of a courtroom defense on a charge of treason. Cf. Kennedy, *The Art of Persuasion*, 64, 169; and for a translation of the text, cf. K. Freeman, *Ancilla to the Pre-Socratic Philosophers: A Complete Translation of the Fragments in Diels, Fragmente der Vorsokratiker* (Cambridge: Harvard University, 1957) 134-38.

[124]Kennedy, *The Art of Persuasion*, 153.

[125]Ibid., 64.

[126]The paragraph numbering, both here and below, is that of Freeman, *Ancilla*, 131-33.

[127]Cf. the discussion of the influence of poetry on Gorgias' rhetorical style in J. de Romilly, *Magic and Rhetoric in Ancient Greece* (Cambridge: Harvard University, 1975) 1-11.

[128]For a brief survey of the Gorgian figures, cf. Kennedy, *The Art of Persuasion*, 64-66; and for a more comprehensive treatment, cf. Norden, *Die Antike Kunstprosa*, 16-29.

should not be surprising, then, that what was once a poetic form—the encomium in our case—became a speech form in the hands of Gorgias and the rhetoricians who followed him.

It was mentioned above that the *Helen* is the only composition we have upon which we can make a judgment as to what a Gorgian encomium was like. That Gorgias considered it an encomium is indicated by the fact that he identifies it as such at the close of his text (*Helen* 21): "I . . . have chosen to write this speech as an encomium (ἐγκώμιον) on Helen and an amusement (παίγνιον) for myself." Yet Isocrates, in his *Helen*, criticizes his teacher for not writing an encomium on Helen, but a "defence (ἀπο-λογίαν) of her conduct" (Isocrates, *Helen* 14).[129] What we seem to have here, then, is not a formal prose encomium by Gorgias, but a composition that makes use of encomiastic techniques.

> Die Helena in ihrer merkwürdigen Mischung von Lobpreisung und Apologie ist nicht als von Gorgias bewusst eingeführte Frühform der Lobrede zu verstehen; sie ist viel mehr aus dem Programm und der Zielsetzung seiner Rhetorik, die Macht des Logos zu erweisen, erwachsen.[130]

This mixture of encomiastic and forensic[131] elements in the *Helen* may be seen in the following description of its outline and contents.

First of all, Gorgias begins with two paragraphs which appear to correspond to the encomiastic prooemium. Within the first of the two he includes a statement of the task at hand: "Now a man, woman, discourse, work, city, deed, if deserving of praise, must be honoured with praise, but if undeserving must be censured" (*Helen* 1).[132] Such an introductory statement not only is reminiscent of the opening lines of some epinicia,

---

[129]The text and translation of Isocrates' *Helen*, both here and below, are those of van Hook, *Isocrates: III*.

[130]Buchheit, *Untersuchungen zur Theorie*, 236.

[131]Although Gorgias wrote no forensic speeches as such, Freeman, *Pre-Socratic Philosophers*, 363, notes that his *Helen* has a forensic tone to it.

[132]The translation of Gorgias's *Helen* is out of van Hook in his third volume of Isocrates, *Isocrates: III*, 55-57. He does not, however, provide paragraph notations. I have used here the paragraph numberings employed by Freeman in her summary/translation. Cf. Freeman, *Ancilla*, 131-33.

but it reflects as well the kind of language used by Isocrates and other encomiasts in their prooemia.

In the second of his two introductory sections, however, Gorgias moves from discussing the purpose of his oration in encomiastic terms to forensic terms. Helen, "a woman concerning whom there has been uniform and universal praise of poets" has had her detractors. Gorgias, then, desires by means of this speech to "free the lady's reputation" and "by revealing the truth, to put an end to error" (*Helen* 2). Yet, following this forensic turn in his introduction, he begins the speech proper by utilizing the γένος characteristic of the encomium. As he describes her parentage —Leda, Tyndareüs, Zeus—amplification abounds: she "was the fairest flower of men and women," Tyndareüs is called "the greatest of humanity," and Zeus "the lordliest of divinity" (*Helen* 3-4). Because of this ancestry she possessed a beauty which attracted numerous suitors. And having said this, he makes a transition—as would be expected in an encomium—from the γένος to the πράξεις:

> Passing over in my present discourse the time now past, I will proceed to the beginning of my intended discussion and will predicate the causes by reason of which it was natural that Helen went to Troy (*Helen* 5).

Having introducted the next section in this way, however, Gorgias does not provide us with the narrative we would expect. Rather he supplies a defense which seeks to prove, by means of the apagogic method,[133] that Helen is not at all culpable in the matter of her journey to Troy with Paris. Gorgias sets out four possible reasons which might explain why she went—viz., because of fate, by means of force, by the persuasion of speech, and on account of love—and dealing with each in turn he concludes that she is not to be blamed for what happened to her (*Helen* 6-20).[134] In each case she was powerless to resist and do otherwise. Within this section, which represents the principal division of the oration, Gorgias devotes more lines to the argument on the power of speech than to the other three possible reasons for Helen's conduct. But this sub-section on the power of oratory—although its purpose is forensic, to prove that Helen was powerless to resist the persuasion of the spoken word—

---

[133]Kennedy, *The Art of Persuasion*, 168.

[134]N. B. van Hook's translation omits sections 11-14, the details of the argument regarding the force of speech, and 16-18, on the force of love. For summaries of these sections, cf. Freeman, *Ancilla*, 132-33.

evidences a number of encomiastic features. There is a recitation of the spoken word's πράξεις (*Helen* 8-14), illustrated by the use of παραδείγματα, (13) and utilizing σύγκρισις, where the power of speech is compared to the effects of drugs upon the body (14).

Following the main unit of sections 6-20, where he has now made his defense of Helen, Gorgias concludes the speech by a brief comment which forms an inclusion with his statement of purpose in the prooemium:

> I have kept the promise which I made in the beginning; I have essayed to dispose of the injustice of defamation and the folly of allegation; . . . (21)

His final remark is the one referred to earlier: that he has written this piece as an encomium of Helen and an amusement (παίγνιον) for himself (21).

It is this encomiastic treatment of Helen upon which Isocrates sought to improve, and in so doing, Isocrates with his *Helen, Busiris,* and above all, his *Evagoras,* gave the encomium the shape it was to have for centuries to come. We now want to turn to examine what the encomium became under him.

### 2. The Intermediate Period: From Isocrates to the Second Century B.C.E.

#### a. Isocrates

That Isocrates played a pivotal role in the history of the encomium is indicated by the number of times we have had occasion to refer to him already.[135] Born in 436 B.C.E., he lived to the age of ninety-eight, a lifespan that embraced the Peloponnesian War on the one hand and the battle of Chaeronea on the other.[136] Among his teachers was Gorgias, whose

---

[135]Cf. above, 96-97, 101-103.

[136]For treatments of Isocrates' life, cf. the introduction in Norlin, *Isocrates: I,* ix-xlvi; Kennedy, *The Art of Persuasion,* 174-203; R. C. Jebb, *The Attic Orators from Antiphon to Isaeus: II* (London: Macmillan and Co., 1893) 1-33; A. Lesky, *A History of Greek Literature* (Trans. by J. Willis and C. de Heer from the 2nd German ed. of 1963; New York: Thomas Y. Crowell, 1966) 583-91.

influence appears to have been far stronger than that of any other.[137] His influence appears, for example, in Isocrates' use of the Gorgian figures —e.g., parison, homoioteleuton, and antithesis—although he did not employ them to the extreme that Gorgias did.[138] Another early rhetorician, whom we have mentioned, Tisias, may have served as another of Isocrates' teachers.[139] Alongside of the influence of Gorgias, Isocrates was acquainted with Socrates and considered himself to be one of his followers.[140]

Isocrates' professional career can be divided into two distinct periods. From his return to Athens from Chios in 403 B.C.E., following the restoration of democracy, to the year 393 B.C.E., he was a logographer, viz., a writer of forensic speeches for those who were in need of them. It is this first stage of his career about which he subsequently felt embarrassed. In later life he spoke with contempt of those who wrote judicial speeches; such speeches are merely written for hire and their themes are mundane rather then noble.[141] The second period of his career began in 393/2 B.C.E. with his opening of a school in Athens near the Lyceum. In his school he taught "philosophy" and rhetoric to many of those who would come to be the most important men of that day,[142] e.g., the general Timotheus, historians Theopompus and Ephorus, and Nicocles, the king of Cyprus.[143] It was during these fifty years as an educator that Isocrates composed his more ambitious political and epideictic works.

Among Isocrates' speeches—speeches which were never given orally by him in public, but which were written as specimens for his students to imitate, or published for distribution beyond the confines of his school— are several which represent either complete encomia or employ the encomium as a subordinate genre. In chronological order they are: the encomiastic treatment of Alcibiades which appears in the forensic speech

---

[137]Jebb, *Attic Orators*, 5.

[138]W. Eisenhut, *Einführung in die antike Rhetorik und ihre Geschichte* (Darmstadt: Wissenschaftliche, 1974) 28; Lesky, *History*, 590.

[139]Kennedy, *The Art of Persuasion*, 61, 174; but Jebb, *Attic Orators*, 4, n.1, believes Plutarch wrongly identified Tisias as a teacher of Isocrates.

[140]Kennedy, *The Art of Persuasion*, 179-84; Jebb, *Attic Orators*, 4, 47.

[141]Kennedy, *The Art of Persuasion*, 177; Jebb, *Attic Orators*, 7.

[142]Rose, *Handbook*, 285. Note that Rose lists 388 B.C.E. as the year Isocrates opened his school.

[143]Kennedy, *The Art of Persuasion*, 174.

*Concerning the Team of Horses* (ca. 397 B.C.E.);[144] the encomia on
*Busiris*, the mythical king of Egypt (ca. 391/390 B.C.E.), *Helen* (370
B.C.E.), and *Evagoras* (365 B.C.E.);[145] *The Letter to Archidamus*, with its
encomiastic description of Archidamus III and his father, Agesilaus of
Sparta (356 B.C.E.); the encomium of Timotheus in the *Antidosis* 353
B.C.E.); and the encomia of two mythical figures, Heracles and
Agamemnon in *Oration 5: To Philip* (346 B.C.E.) and the *Panathenaicus*
(339 B.C.E.) respectively.[146]

As a transitional figure in the history of the encomium, Isocrates stood
in continuity with the efforts of earlier poets and rhetors, and at the same
time, he gave encomiastic theory and practice a new direction. The
element of continuity is, first of all, suggested in his relationship to
Gorgias. Not only did he continue to use the Gorgian figures, as we have
noted, but he chose to compose the same types of encomia that had
become popular with Gorgias and his circle. The sophists were known for
their encomia on mythical or legendary personages, e.g., Gorgias' treatment of Helen, and what is more, they took delight in composing encomia
on trivial subjects. Polycrates, another of the students of Gorgias, is said
to have written encomia on mice, pots, and stones, in addition to more
traditional treatments, such as his on the figure of Clytemnestra.[147] Thus
Isocrates continued in this tradition—though not to the extent that he
dealt with trivia—with his encomia on Busiris, Helen, Heracles, and Agamemnon.

Isocrates' link with earlier encomiasts, however, extended as well to
the encomium's roots in poetry. He was of the opinion that he was doing
the same thing in his compositions that the lyric poets had done in their
encomia and epinicia. In his *Antidosis* he compares his work with that of
Pindar:

> It would be even more absurd if, whereas Pindar, the poet, was
> so highly honoured by our forefathers because of a single line
> of his in which he praises Athens as 'the bulwark of Hellas'
> that he was made 'proxenos' and given a present of ten

---

[144]The date is that of van Hook, *Isocrates: III*, 174.

[145]The dates are those of Jebb, *Attic Orators*, 9-10. Volkmann, *Die
Rhetorik*, 327, would date the *Evagoras* a few years later, ca. 360 B.C.E.,
while Momigliano, *The Development*, 49, dates it earlier, ca. 370 B.C.E.

[146]The dates are all those of Jebb, *Attic Orators*, 18, 10-11, 11 and 12
respectively.

[147]Volkmann, *Die Rhetorik*, 317.

thousand drachmas, I, on the other hand, who have glorified
Athens and our ancestors with much ampler and nobler en-
comiums (ἐμοὶ δὲ πολὺ πλείω καὶ κάλλιον ἐγκωμιακότι),
should not even be privileged to end my days in
peace (166).[148]

Isocrates, too, is in the business of composing encomia. The only difference is that, while the poets worked with "meter and rhythm" (Evag.
10), Isocrates has chosen the medium of prose; everything else remains
basically the same:

> . . . although poetry has advantages so great, we must not
> shrink from the task, but must make the effort and see if it
> will be possible in prose to eulogize good men in no worse
> fashion than their encomiasts (ἐγκωμιαζόντων) do who employ
> song and verse (Evag. 11).[149]

It is reasonable to expect, then, that we fill find the same topics and
arrangement in the Isocratean encomium which were observed in the odes
of Pindar, et al. Later, when we summarize the shape of the encomium
(see below, 178-206), I believe we will find this to be the case.

Short of that, however, particular mention can be made of one feature
which was identified in Pindar—the catalogue of blessings—and which
passed into the encomia of Isocrates and Xenophon where it became a
traditional element. It was ". . . introduced especially at the close of the
tribute, where the consolatory mood, indigenous to literature of this kind,
naturally held sway and the thought would turn to summing up the blessings that had attended a human life."[150] In Isocrates' Evagoras the catalogue appears within the epilogue:

> . . . the life he lived on earth has been more blessed (εὐτυ-
> χέστερον) and more favoured by the gods (θεοφιλέστερον)
> than theirs [viz., other immortals ]
> · · · · · · · · · · · · · · · · · · · · · · · · · ·
> Evagoras continued from the beginning to be not only the most
> admired, but the most envied for his blessings.
> · · · · · · · · · · · · · · · · · · · · · · · · · ·

---

[148]The translation is that of Norlin, Isocrates: II, 281.
[149]In van Hook, Isocrates: III, 11.
[150]Stuart, Epochs, 86.

Such ancestors Fortune gave to him as to no other man, . . .
and so greatly in body and mind did he excel others that he
was worthy to hold sway over not only Salamis but the whole
of Asia also; . . . and though a mortal by birth, he left behind a
memory of himself that is immortal, and he lived just so long
that he was neither unacquainted with old age, nor afflicted
with the infirmities attendant upon that time of life. In addition to these blessings, that which seems to be the rarest and
most difficult thing to win—to be blessed with many children,
(πολυπαιδίας) who are at the same time good (εὐπαι-
δίας)—not even this was denied him, . . . And the greatest
blessing was this: of his offspring he left not one who was
addressed merely by a private title; on the contrary, one was
called king, others princes, and others princesses (70-72).

The blessings which Isocrates lists here—physical and intellectual excellence, sovereignty, fame, health, and children—are all in harmony with
those catalogued by Stuart as characteristic of this element,[151] and with
those which were seen earlier in Pindar.[152]

Although both the evidence offered by his compositions, and his own
comments about himself, point to Isocrates' link with earlier encomiastic
traditions, the evidence suggests at the same time that he was an innovator. It is due to the new direction he gave to the writing of encomia--
especially in the case of his *Evagoras*—that Leo[153] and Misch[154] refer to
him as the creator of a new εἶδος, the prose encomium of a historical
personage.

While it is true that Isocrates in his own words viewed the *Evagoras* as
a successor to the poetic encomium (cf., *Evag.* 11, cited above), he clearly
indicated at the same time that it is something new. In his estimation, no
one had yet attempted to compose a prose encomium on a contemporary
subject:

I am fully aware that what I propose to do is difficult—to
eulogize (ἐγκωμιάζειν) in prose the virtues of a man. The best
proof is this: Those who devote themselves to philosophy
venture to speak on many subjects of every kind, but no one

---

[151]Ibid., 85; and cf. above 120-21.
[152]Above, 121.
[153]Leo, *Die griechisch-römische*, 91.
[154]Misch, *History*, 161.

of them has ever attempted to compose a discourse on such a theme (*Evag.* 8).

To Isocrates the difference between poetic encomia and what he is attempting to do in prose is substantial:

> For to the poets is granted the use of many embellishments of language, since they can represent the gods as associating with men, conversing with and aiding in battle whomsoever they please, and they can treat of these subjects not only in conventional expressions, but in words now exotic, now newly coined, now in figures of speech, . . . Orators, on the contrary, are not permitted the use of such devices; they must use with precision only words in current use and only such ideas as bear on the actual facts (*Evag.* 8-10).

Despite Isocrates' claims about the originality he has shown in the *Evagoras,* we have already noted the dissenting opinion of Aristotle, who regarded an encomium on Hippolochus to be the first attempt in prose to praise a contemporary.[155] To be sure, there no doubt were such prose attempts prior to Isocrates. Yet, as Stuart suggests, they were not in harmony with the conception Isocrates held of "how the prose encomium should continue the poetic tradition," and therefore he did not acknowledge them at all.[156] And what is important for our purposes, is to remember that it was not these earlier prose encomia that shaped the form for generations to come, but it was Isocrates, who, through his own compositions and the rhetorical training he offered, determined what would be the accepted scope, topics and structure of the encomium.

Over and above the change in medium from poetry to prose, Isocrates' innovations included the selection of a contemporary subject. Thus the *Evagoras* was written within a decade or so of the death of the king of Cyprus whom it extols. Other historical personages celebrated by Isocrates are: his student, Timotheus, whom he praises in the encomiastic portion of his *Antidosis* (107-128); and the Athenian general, Alcibiades (ca. 450-404 B.C.E.), is the subject of an encomiastic presentation in the early forensic speech, *Concerning the Team of Horses* (15-36).[157]

---

[155]Above, 104.

[156]Stuart, *Epochs,* 105-6.

[157]Although his treatment of Alcibiades antedates the *Evagoras,* and

Besides proposing that contemporaries were fit subjects for encomia, Isocrates sought to move the treatment of traditional encomiastic themes in a different direction. Noted already was Isocrates' lack of patience for those orators who engage in trivial themes (e.g., "to praise bumble-bees and salt and kindred topics," *Helen* 12).[158] Encomia on such topics present no real challenge to the orator. The real test, if one is going to deal with traditional themes, is to praise "those subjects recognized as good or noble, or of superior moral worth . . . ;" it is here that orators "have all fallen far short of the possibilities which these subjects offer" (*Helen* 12).[159] He encouraged, then, his students not to engage in the novelty of composing encomia on non-sensical topics, but to strive to surpass those who have treated the noble themes of the past.

> . . . since oratory is of such a nature that it is possible to discourse on the same subject matter in many different ways . . . to recount the things of old in a new manner . . . it follows that one must not shun the subjects upon which others have spoken before, but must try to speak better than they.
> . . . . . . . . . . . . . . . . . . . . . . . . . . . .
> And it is my opinion that the study of oratory as well as the other arts would make the greatest advance if we should admire and honour, not those who make the first beginnings in their crafts, but those who are the most finished craftsmen in each, and not those who seek to speak on subjects on which no one has spoken before, but those who know how to speak as no one else could (*Paneg.* 7-10).

---

thus would be his first attempt at a prose encomium of a historical person, Isocrates saw the *Evagoras* as an innovation in that it was his first prose encomium as an independent work. The encomium of Alcibiades, in contrast, was employed as a part of a forensic speech. Cf. Stuart, *Epochs*, 93-94, and Leo, *Die griechische-römische*, 92.

[158]Cf. the *Panathenaicus*, sec. 1, where Isocrates says that "When I was younger, I elected not to write the kind of discourse which deals in myths nor that which abounds in marvels and fictions. . . ." Even though he, in fact, dealt with such themes, his attempt to divorce himself here from these types of encomia may reflect his conviction that his own encomia on mythical personages were different from the types then in vogue.

[159]Cf. also the *Panathenaicus* 36: ". . . while it is easy to magnify little things by means of discourse, it is difficult to find terms of praise to match deeds of surpassing magnitude and excellence."

In three of his works Isocrates offers examples of how oratory ought to deal with the great themes of the legendary past. First of all, his encomium of Busiris, the mythical Egyptian king, is intended to be an improvement on Polycrates' treatment of the same subject. Isocrates opens his version with the observation that although Polycrates prides himself on his portrayal of Busiris, his effort does not do the topic justice:

> Having observed, therefore, that you take especial pride in your *Defence of Busiris* (τῇ βουσίριδος ἀπολογία) and in your *Accusation of Socrates,* I shall try to make it clear to you that in both these discourses you have fallen far short of what the subject demands ( *Bus.* 4).

He goes on to point out Polycrates' errors in employing syncrisis ( *Bus.* 7) and genealogy ( *Bus.* 8), after which he introduces his example of a proper encomium of Busiris with these words:

> I will try briefly to expound the same subject—even though it is not serious and does not call for a dignified style—and show out of what elements you ought to have composed the eulogy (ἔπαινον) and the speech in defense ( *Bus.* 9).[160]

Similarly, Isocrates' *Helen* is offered as a corrective to Gorgias' encomium on the same.[161] Although he commends his teacher's effort—"I praise especially him who chose to write of Helen, because he has recalled to memory so remarkable a woman, . . ."—he has his criticisms: Gorgias has not written an encomium as such, but a defense (ἀπολογία) of Helen's conduct ( *Helen* 14). And, he goes on to say that

> . . . the composition in defence does not draw upon the same topics as the encomium, nor indeed does it deal with actions of the same kind, but quite the contrary; for a plea in defence is appropriate only when the defendant is charged with a crime, whereas we praise those who excel in some good quality (15).

---

[160]Although Isocrates refers to Polycrates' speech as a *Defense of Busiris* (cf. *Bus.* 4), the reference here suggests that Polycrates had composed an encomium which was part of a forensic speech. The analogy here would be Isocrates' encomium of Alcibiades within his speech *Concerning the Team of Horses.*

[161]Cf. Buchheit, *Untersuchungen zur Theorie,* 237; and our discussion of Gorgias' *Helen,* above 125-128.

Whereupon Isocrates begins his own encomium on Helen as an illustration of how the theme ought to be treated:

> But that I may not seem to be taking the easiest course, criticizing others without exhibiting any specimen of my own, I will try to speak of this same woman, disregarding all that any others have said about her (15).

Within his *Oration V: To Philip* there is an encomium on Heracles which, as was the case with the *Busiris* and the *Helen*, Isocrates regarded as a departure from the traditional way this hero was extolled. Thus he contrasts his Heracles with the treatment others have given him:

> Coming now to Heracles, all others who praise him harp endlessly on his valour or recount his labours; and not one, either of the poets or of the historians, will be found to have commemorated his other excellences—I mean those which pertain to the spirit. I, on the other hand, see here a field set apart and entirely unworked . . . (*To Philip* 109).

The final example of an encomium on a traditional theme—that of Agamemnon in Isocrates' final work, the *Panathenaicus*, published when he was ninety-seven—is not set off by the kind of introductory comments seen above in the *Busiris*, the *Helen*, and the encomium of Heracles. Yet at the close of this presentation of Agamemnon, Isocrates apologizes for the inordinate amount of space he has devoted to the topic (*Panathenaicus* 84). But his reason for taking the space is his belief that the subject required it. Thus his apology would seem to be directed toward those critics who, in the interests of form, took liberty with the content necessary for an encomium on such a figure:

> I thought also that I should be applauded by the most cultivated of my hearers if I could show that I was more concerned when discoursing on the subject of virtue about doing justice to the theme than about the symmetry of the speech —and that too, knowing well that the lack of proportion in my speech would detract from my own reputation, while just appreciation of their deeds would enhance the fame of those whose praises I sing. Nevertheless I bade farewell to expediency and chose justice instead (*Panathenaicus* 86).

Isocrates, then, in this his final encomium, was no less concerned than he had been in his earlier works, to distinguish his encomia on traditional themes from those which had come to be the accepted fashion in sophistic rhetoric.

A third area in which Isocrates may be seen as an innovator is suggested in his defense, referred to above, of the space he gave to the description of Agamemnon's virtue. Here, and in other encomia, he gave an emphasis to the virtues possessed by his subjects.

> He is the first to make portrayal of character the real theme. . . . Moral qualities had found a place in Pindar, but only in single sentences as a general characterization. There is no analysis of character. To introduce the deeds as an evidence of virtues, to bring out the character of the one praised, was a new point of view.[162]

This new dimension, which began with Isocrates, became incorporated in subsequent encomia. Thus Stuart, commenting in general on the prose encomium of the fourth century B.C.E., writes:

> The encomiast approached his work with the hypothesis that there were foreordained excellencies without which lofty character could not be imagined as existing. The four cardinal virtues, valor, wisdom, temperance, and justness, which, evolving naturally in the moral consciousness of Greece, were systematized into criteria of ethical valuation, furnished measuring rods. Taking these in hand, the encomiast would seek to show that his hero lived up to this standard of all that did become a man.[163]

In Isocrates the recitation of deeds as illustrative of the cardinal virtues is best seen in the *Evagoras,* but it is present in other encomia as well.[164] All four virtues are evident in Evagoras by the time he attained manhood; as a boy he already possessed temperance or modesty (σωφρο-σύνη) (22), and when he became a man, "were also added manly courage (ἀνδρία), wisdom (σοφία), and justice (δικαιοσύνη)"(23). And as Isocrates

---

[162]Burgess, "Epideictic Literature," 115-16.

[163]Stuart, *Epochs,* 65.

[164]Burgess, "Epideictic Literature," 115-16, writes that "Isocrates does this for the first time in the *Evagoras.*" Yet the link between virtue and deed is already established in his earlier *Helen.*

moves on to recount Evagoras' deeds, his recitation is punctuated with
reminders that his virtue is revealed in those deeds:

> I think that even if I should mention nothing more, but I should
> discontinue my discourse at this point, from what I have said
> the valour of Evagoras . . . would be readily manifest . . .
> (ῥᾴδιον ἐκ τούτων εἶναι γνῶμαι τὴν τ' ἀρετὴν τὴν 'Eυα-
> γόρου . . .) (33).

> That these attributes were inherent in Evagoras, and even
> more than these, it is easy to learn from his deeds themselves
> (46).

> In truth, how could one reveal the courage (ἀνδρίαν), the
> wisdom (φρόνησιν), or the virtues generally (σύμπασαν τὴν
> ἀρετὴν) of Evagoras more clearly than by pointing to such
> deeds (τοιούτων ἔργων) and perilous enterprises? (65)

Such a link between virtue and deed is present in his encomium of
Timotheus where, in sections 117-18 of the *Antidosis*, the wisdom of his
subject is manifested in his military strategy:

> Well, in this kind of sagacity there has never been anyone like
> him or even comparable with him, as may easily be seen from
> his deeds themselves (ῥᾴδιον δ' ἐξ αὐτῶν τῶν ἔργων γνῶ-
> μαι). For, although he undertook most of his wars without
> support from the city, he brought them all to a successful
> issue, and convinced all the Hellenes that he won them justly.
> And what greater or clearer proof of his wise judgment could
> one adduce than this fact? (118)

Among his other works, the encomium of Agamemnon, as was mentioned, devotes space to a description of the Greek commander's virtues.
Isocrates begins by stating that Agamemnon possessed not "one or two of
the virtues (ἀρετάς) merely, but . . . all which anyone can name—and
these, not in moderate, but in surpassing degree" (*Panathenaicus* 72).
Having said this, however, he recognizes that this claim of virtue must be
supported by reference to Agamemnon's actions: ". . . I am ashamed, after
having said so much about the virtue (ἀρετῆς) of Agamemnon, to make no
mention of the things which he accomplished . . ." (74). And in the *Helen*,
as Isocrates seeks to amplify his picture of her by means of extolling
Theseus, her abductor, he links the virtues and deeds of Theseus:

. . . while in the case of other men who have won reknown we shall find that one is deficient in courage (ἀνδρίας), another in wisdom (σοφίας), and another in some kindred virtue, yet this hero [Theseus] alone was lacking in naught, but had obtained consummate virtue (παντελῆ τὴν ἀρετήν) (21).

Continuing in secs. 25-29 with specific illustrations of Theseus' courage, Isocrates then concludes: "His courage Theseus displayed in these perilous exploits which he hazarded alone . . ." (31).

Finally, mention should be made of Isocrates' earliest encomium, that of Alcibiades in the speech *Concerning the Team of Horses*, which contains a catalogue of the virtues possessed by Pericles, Alcibiades' guardian. That Pericles should have the qualities of being "most temperate" (σωφρονέστατον) and "most just" (δικαιότατον) and "most wise" (σοφώτατον) was interpreted to be a blessing inherited by Alcibiades, his ward (*Concerning the Team* 28).

### b. Xenophon's Agesilaus

Ranked equally with Isocrates' *Evagoras* as an important witness to the form of the fourth century encomium is the *Agesilaus* of Xenophon (430-356 B.C.E.).[165] The work, written shortly after the death of the Spartan king whom it celebrates (361/60 B.C.E.),[166] is called an encomium by its author:

However, let it not be thought, because one whose life is ended is the theme of my praise, that these words are meant for a funeral dirge (θρῆνον). They are far more truly the language of eulogy (ἐγκώμιον) (*Ages.* 10.3).

Although the *Evagoras* and *Agesilaus* are equally valued, there are some differences to be noted between them. First of all, in terms of the pictures they present of the two respective kings, the portrayal of Evagoras is far more idealistic, ". . . als den idealen Fürsten und

---

[165]A Dihle, *Studien zur griechischen Biographie* (Abhandlungen der Akad. der Wiss. in Göttingen, Philologisch-historische Klasse, III: 37; Göttingen: Vandenhoeck und Ruprecht, 1956) 27; cf. also Stuart, *Epochs*, 31-33, and Leo, *Die griechische-römische*, 91.
[166]Rose, *Handbook*, 307.

Monarchen."[167] In contrast Xenophon's description of Agesilaus as the consummate general is illustrated with concrete, life-like examples of what a good general is and does. The difference here is no doubt due to the relationship the two encomiasts had with their subjects. In the case of Isocrates, he writes of Evagoras from some distance, linked only to the late Cypriot king through his son, Nicocles, a former student. Xenophon, on the other hand, stands nearer to his subject, having served under the Spartan soldier-king.[168]

A second difference between the two encomia is one of arrangement. In Isocrates we observed that the virtues of the subject are illustrated through the recitation of his deeds. But in the *Agesilaus*, Xenophon creates two separate sections in order to treat virtues and deeds separately. First, there is a rehearsal of Agesilaus' deeds, the πράξεις, in chronological order (1.6-2.31), followed by a catalogue of his virtues (3.1b-8.8), listed according to categories. The transition from one section to the other is at 3.1a:

> Such, then, is the record of my hero's deeds (ἔργων), so far as they were done before a crowd of witnesses. . . . But now I will attempt to show the virtue (ἀρετήν) that was in his soul, the virtue through which he wrought those deeds . . .

In addition to the four cardinal virtues, Xenophon adds the qualities of piety (εὐσέβεια), patriotism (φιλοπόλις), and urbanity (εὔχαρις). Under each of the seven headings are gathered proofs (τεκμήρια) of the particular virtue. Such proofs may be in the form of examples (παραδείγματα), as in the case of illustrating Agesilaus' piety (3.3-5), or enthymemes (ἐνθυμήματα), like those listed under the rubric of justice (4.2-4). It is the separate consideration of virtue apart from deeds that is the principal characteristic of the Xenophontic encomium.[169]

At other points, however, the *Agesilaus* parallels the Isocratean and pre-Isocratean structure. The prooemium contains the commonplace regarding the difficulty of the encomiast's task (1.1); there is a treatment of Agesilaus' genealogy (1.2-5); and following Xenophon's double-division of πράξεις and ἀρεταί, the encomium concludes with a formal σύγκρισις —comparing Agesilaus with the Persian king (9.1-7)—and an epilogue

---

[167]Dihle, *Studien*, 28. Cf. also Stuart, *Epochs*, 77-78.

[168]Dihle, *Studien*, 28. On the relationship between Xenophon and Agesilaus, cf. Lesky, *History*, 616; Rose, *Handbook*, 305-6.

[169]Leo, *Die griechische-römische*, 91.

(10.1-11.16). In the epilogue we encounter the Xenophontic inventory of virtues for the second time: in 11.1-16 he recapitulates each of the seven virtues introduced earlier in the work.

Because of the similarities which exist, coupled with the fact that the *Evagoras* probably antedated the *Agesilaus* by perhaps five years, Leo is of the opinion that Xenophon was dependent on the *Evagoras* for his encomium of the Spartan king.[170] Since Leo's time, however, the question of dependence has become more complex. Stuart, for example, is critical of Leo, and is of the opinion that

> The relation between Isocrates and Xenophon is not that of mentor and imitator respectively. Both should be ranged side by side as co-heirs of an older tradition, starting from which each traveled his own road.[171]

Momigliano takes an intermediate position:

> Xenophon, however, was not the man to follow Isocrates blindly. To begin with, he was much more interested in Agesilaus' actual achievements than Isocrates had been in Evagoras' deeds. He also had greater historical sense than Isocrates.
> . . . . . . . . . . . . . . . . . . . . . . . . . . . . . .
> The untidy mixture of static eulogy and chronological account was not easily acceptable to the historian of the *Anabasis* . . .
> He therefore divided the encomium of Agesilaus into two parts.[172]

The division of the encomium, or more precisely the πράξεις, into the chronological account of deeds and the systematic review of virtues, though, was not entirely new with Xenophon. Momigliano acknowledges this,[173] and Stuart points out that ultimately such a division may have had its origins in Gorgias.[174] For the same type of separation is employed by Plato in Agathon's encomium of love (*Symp.* 194e-197e), a speech to which we will return later. But given that in real life Agathon had been under the influence of Gorgias, and that Plato clearly gives Agathon's speech a Gorgianic coloring (cf. Socrates' comment that in Agathon's

---

[170]Ibid.; cf. also Fraustadt, *Encomiorum,* 69.
[171]Stuart, *Epochs,* 81.
[172]Momigliano, *The Development,* 50.
[173]Ibid., 51.
[174]Stuart, *Epochs,* 89.

oration he heard Gorgias speaking, 198c), the deeds/virtues division may have been introduced by Plato as a typical feature of Gorgias' technique.

Other considerations point to the probability that Xenophon is heir to earlier encomiastic models and not just those of Isocrates. Stuart speaks of Xenophon's use of Gorgian figures.[175] and speculates that he may have even been a student of the latter.[176] Another pre-Isocratean feature present in the *Agesilaus* is the blessings catalogue. This element, examples of which we saw both in Pindar and Isocrates, appears in the epilogue at 10.4: "Justly may the man be counted blessed (μακαρίζοιτο) who . . ." Thus, in Xenophon, we seem to have an encomiast who, while under the stimulus of the *Evagoras*, was not solely dependent on it for the design of his tribute to Agesilaus.

The *Agesilaus* is not the only work of Xenophon that has been characterized as an encomium. Diogenes Laertius, for example, refers to the *Cyropaedia* as an ἐγκώμιον Κύρου (Diog. Laert. 4.84), and Dihle admits that in a certain sense, it is.[177] The same could be said of the Memorial Address of Cyrus in the *Anabasis*.[178] The encomiastic quality of the latter is evident in Xenophon's amplification of Cyrus through the use of superlatives: "Most kingly and most worthy of all the Persians since Cyrus the elder" (*An.* 1.9.1), and ". . . while he was still a boy and was with his brothers . . . [he was] regarded as the best of them . . ." (1.9.2).[179] Yet, though they are encomiastic, they do not exhibit all the formal characteristics of the encomium in the way that the *Agesilaus* does.[180] For this reason only the *Agesilaus* will be used when we attempt later to summarize the form of the encomium for the purpose of comparing it with Sirach 44-50.

---

[175]Ibid., 69.

[176]Ibid., 73. Cf. above, 124, no. 118.

[177]Dihle, *Studien*, 27.

[178]Ibid. Also, Leo, *Die griechisch-römische*, 88, notes that "Der Nachruf des Kyros ist ganz enkomiastisch."

[179]Cf. the edition of C. L. Brownson, *Xenophon, III: Anabasis, Books I-VII* (Loeb Classical Library; Cambridge: Harvard University, 1922).

[180]Momigliano, *The Development*, 51-52, refers to the portraits of Cyrus et al. in the *Anabasis* as "character sketches of contemporaries" and says that they "are not *encomia*." He would classify the *Cyropaedia* as a "philosophical novel," ibid., 8.

## c. The Stimulus of Isocrates

Above, in our discussion of Isocrates, mention was made of both his school and the number of famous individuals who studied with him. Although one had to pay tuition (1000 drachmas), his school was open to all and had none of the closed-sect-characteristics of the Academy.[181] Students, who would study with Isocrates in groups of no more than nine at a time,[182] pursued a three or four year course of study (cf. *Antidosis* 87). The total number of pupils trained by him over the years is said to have been no less than one hundred.[183] And because of the "practical" dimensions of the education Isocrates offered, with its emphasis on training men to "speak well" (τὸ εὖ λέγειν) and preparing them for political life, it can be said, as Marrou has, that "on the whole it was Isocrates, not Plato, who educated fourth-century Greece and subsequently the Hellenistic and Roman worlds; . . ."[184]

The key to Isocrates' teaching was in his requirement that his students learn through the actual practice of oratory, rather than spending an inordinate amount of time on rhetorical theory. Such practice came by the study and imitation of model speeches. The best models were, of course, Isocrates' own compositions.[185] Thus his students were educated by means of their study of the *Evagoras*, et al., and in turn, they were moved to fashion comparable encomia after the manner of their teacher. Moreover, the fact that Isocrates' speeches were written and published, meant that his influence extended beyond just those individuals who were his students or those who might have occasion to "hear" him.[186] The fourth century, then, was a period when those who composed encomia were, in one-way-or-another, indebted to the standards set by Isocrates.

The tradition holds that at least three of his students composed encomia of which we have some knowledge. Perhaps the best known of the three is the historian Theopompus of Chios, b. ca. 378 B.C.E. Aelius Theon, in his *Progymnasmata*, secs. 2 and 8, mentions that Theopompus wrote encomia on Philip and Alexander, and his encomia are linked by Theon with those of Isocrates and the *Agesilaus* of Xenophon.[187] Also,

---

[181]H. I. Marrou, *History of Education*, 82.
[182]Ibid., 86.
[183]Ibid., 82.
[184]Ibid., 79.
[185]Ibid., 84.
[186]Cf. Jebb, *Attic Orators*, 428-29.
[187]Cf. fragments F255 and F256 in F. Jacoby, *Die Fragmente der*

there is a report in the second century C.E. *Attic Nights* of Aulus Gellius on the competition sponsored by Artemisia, widow of Mausolos (377-353 B.C.E.) satrap of Caria, for encomia to be composed on the occasion of the dedication of her husband's tomb (the Mausoleum) at Halicarnassus (*NA* 10.18.5-7).[188] Gellius writes that Theopompus, Theodectes, and Naucrates, "three men distinguished for their eminent talent and eloquence are said to have come to contend in this eulogy" (6). He continues by mentioning that some even believe that Isocrates himself entered the competition, but the winner of the prize was Theopompus, who "was a disciple of Isocrates" (6).

Although Theopompus' prize-winning encomium was evidently known to Gellius by name only, he mentions that Theodectes' entry was still extant in his day: *Extat nunc quoque Theodecti tragoedia, quae inscribitur Mausolus* (7). Curiously, he refers to the work as a tragedy rather than as a laudation. Theodectes (375-334 B.C.E.), likewise, was a student of Isocrates (cf. the comment of Hermippus quoted by Ath. 10.451e), and is remembered as well for an encomium he composed on Alexander of Epirus (viz., Alexander I, king of Molossia, 342-330 B.C.E.)[189] The third student of Isocrates known to have written encomia is Philiscus of Miletus (400-325 B.C.E.), who wrote an encomium on the orator Lycurgus.[190]

The philosopher Speusippus (407-339 B.C.E.), Plato's nephew and successor as head of the Academy, is known to have produced an encomium of his uncle and teacher. Diogenes Laertius includes it in his list of Speusippus' works: Πλάτωνος ἐγκώμιον (Diog. Laert. 4.5). Jebb is of the opinion that Speusippus may have been a pupil of Isocrates as well, and if so, his encomium on Plato may have had an Isocratean form.[191]

At any rate, the influence of Isocrates is not restricted solely to either his alleged students, such as Speusippus, or those who were in fact his pupils, Theopompus et al. Rather, an indication of the stimulus he provided to others beyond his circle of students is perhaps to be seen in Diogenes Laertius' reference to the fact that ". . . there were innumerable authors of epitaphs and eulogies upon Gryllus," the son of Xenophon who

---

griechischen Historiker: Zweiter Teil B: Nr. 106-261 (Leiden: E. J. Brill, 1962) 591; and the comment of Momigliano, *The Development*, 82.

[188]Cf. the Loeb edition of J. C. Rolfe, *The Attic Nights of Aulus Gellius: II* (Loeb Classical Library; New York: G. P. Putnam's Sons, 1927).

[189]Momigliano, *The Development*, 64, n. 21.

[190]Leo, *Die griechische-römische*, 93, n. 2.

[191]Jebb, *Attic Orators*, 13.

died in the battle of Mantinea in 362 B.C.E. Diogenes adds that Hermippus, in his *Life of Theophrastus,* mentioned that Isocrates was one of
these encomiasts of Gryllus,[192] and Leo believes that the example and
stimulus of Isocrates was behind the attempts of others to write on the
same theme.[193]

Specific encomiasts who continued to write according to the form laid
down by Isocrates may have included Clearchus, Callisthenes, and
Xenocrates. Clearchus (340-250 B.C.E.), of Soli on Cyprus, is known to
have written an encomium on Plato, and his choice of a title suggests that
he intended it to be of the same form as Speusippus' composition.[194]
Callisthenes (370-327 B.C.E.) wrote an encomium of Hermias, the tyrant
of Atarneus, shortly after the latter's death in 342/1 B.C.E.,[195] which
belonged to the same genre as well. Leo believes the same to be true of a
speech by a certain Xenocrates, who is named by Diogenes Laertius as a
relative of the more famous Xenocrates, head of the Academy after
Speusippus.[196] This speech of the lesser known Xenocrates, titled λόγος
Ἀρσινοητικός, is described by Diogenes as "treating of a certain deceased Arsinoë" (Diog. Laert. 4.15).

To the above we might add the name of Demetrius of Phaleron (ca.
350-283 B.C.E.), among whose writings were both a *Lobrede* on Socrates
and a collection of biographical materials on various authors, including
Isocrates.[197] Because of Demetrius' interest in, and practice of, rhetoric,
it is reasonable to assume that his *Socrates* was influenced by the shape of
the Isocratean encomium. That this was perhaps the case is supported by
the reference Plutarch makes to this work in his life of Aristides. There
Plutarch cites three points Demetrius regarded as "proofs" (τεκμήρια) of
Aristides' "opulent circumstances" in contrast to the general opinion that
Aristides died a poor man (Plut., *Aristides* 1.2-3).[198] This bit of

---

[192]Ibid., 76, n. 2. Jebb believes that Hermippus, in his reference to an
encomium of Gryllus by Isocrates, may mean Isocrates of Apollonia. Yet
the latter was a student of Isocrates and succeeded his teacher as the
head of his school (cf. 13). Thus either way this particular encomium of
Gryllus is Isocratean.

[193]Leo, *Die griechische-römische,* 93 n. 2.

[194]Momigliano, *The Development,* 77.

[195]Jacoby, *FrGH: IIB, 2,* 416; Momigliano, *The Development,* 82.

[196]Leo, *Die griechische-römische,* 93 n. 2.

[197]Susemihl, *Geschichte,* 140.

[198]Cf. the Loeb volume of B. Perrin, *Plutarch: The Parallel Lives: II*
(Loeb Classical Library; Cambridge: Harvard University, 1914).

information appears to have been introduced into the *Socrates* for the purpose of amplification through syncrisis: Demetrius wanted to compare Socrates to a wealthy Aristides. Thus Plutarch concluded: "In fact, Demetrius is clearly ambitious to rescue not only Aristides, but also Socrates from what he deems the great evil of poverty" (*Aristides* 1.9). It would seem, then, that Demetrius' *Socrates* may well have been of the type of encomium that Isocrates and his school had made popular.

Demetrius' encomium of Socrates, moreover, had its own influence. With his move to Alexandria, he provided that city with "its chief link to Athens," and "His encomium on Socrates, as well as his popular and ambassadorial speeches, prompted Josephus to call him the most learned man of his day."[199] Cicero, too, who was indebted to Isocrates,[200] held Demetrius in high regard.[201] Thus in the person of Demetrius the Isocratean type of encomium found its way to Ptolemaic Alexandria.

The influence of Isocrates on oratory in general, and hence on the composition of epideictic works such as encomia, may be seen not only in the speeches written by others, but in the surviving handbook of sophistic rhetoric from the fourth century, the *Rhetorica ad Alexandrum*. While Isocrates is remembered as having produced a handbook or τέχνη of rhetoric, it has not survived.[202] Yet it appears to have left its mark on this work addressed to Alexander,[203] which is traditionally attributed to Anaximenes of Lampsacus (ca. 380-320 B.C.E.),[204] and evidently was

---

[199]R. W. Smith, *The Art of Rhetoric in Alexandria: Its Theory and Practice in the Ancient World* (The Hague: Martinus Nijhoff, 1974), 38. On the reference in Josephus, cf. *Contra Apion* II: 46.

[200]Jebb, *Attic Orators*, 69.

[201]R. W. Smith, *The Art of Rhetoric*, 38.

[202]Cf. Jebb, *Attic Orators*, 78, 258-60; and the introduction to the Loeb edition of the *Rhet. ad Alex.*, Hett and Rackham, *Aristotle*, 258-59.

[203]McCall, *Ancient Rhetorical Theories*, 21, n. 63; and cf. Kennedy, *The Art of Persuasion*, 115-16, where he lists similarities between the rhetorical style practiced by Isocrates and that taught by Anaximenes.

[204]The identification of Anaximenes as the probable author is based upon a reference in Quintilian (3.4.9), "Anaximenes regarded forensic and public oratory as *genera* but held that there were seven *species*: . . ." The mention of seven *species* corresponds to the list given in *Rhet. ad Alex.* 1.1421b.7-11. On the difference between Quintilian's reference to two *genera* and Anaximenes' τρία γένη (1.1421b.7), it is suggested that someone later adjusted the text of Anaximenes so that it would correspond to Aristotle's tripartite division of oratory. Cf. Kennedy, *The Art of Persuasion*, 114.

written sometime between 341 and the publication of Aristotle's *Rhetoric*.[205]

Two of the handbook's 38 chapters are devoted exclusively to rules on the composition of encomia—chapter 3, which deals with amplification:

> The eulogistic species (ἐγκωμιαστικὸν εἶδος) of oratory consists, to put it briefly, in the amplification (αὔξησις) of creditable purposes and actions and speeches and the attribution of qualities that do not exist, . . . (3.1425b. 36-38).

And chapter 35, which discusses the arrangement or τάξις of such speeches:

> Next let us set before us for examination the oratory of eulogy (ἐγκωμιαστικόν) . . . (35.1440b. 5-6)
>
> · · · · · · · · · · · · · · · · · · · · · · · · · · · ·
>
> We shall first arrange (τάξομεν) the introduction (προοίμια) in the same way as in speeches of exhortation and dissuasion (1440b. 14-15)
>
> · · · · · · · · · · · · · · · · · · · · · · · · · · · ·
>
> The proper way to employ genealogy is this (γενεαλογεῖν δὲ δεῖ ὧδε) (1440b.29).

In like manner the rest of the chapter continues with Anaximenes' presentation of those features which should be included in each of the traditional sections or topics of an encomium.

In addition to the two chapters which deal exclusively with encomiastic oratory, chapters 6-28 are relevant in that they treat those elements common to all types of speeches: forensic, deliberative and epideictic. Anaximenes introduces this major section of the handbook at 1427b.38-40: "Having thus defined the various species of oratory, let us next enumerate their common requirements, and discuss their proper mode of employment." Whereupon he begins his discussion, for example, of style, types of

---

[205]The *terminus post quem* of 341 B.C.E. is given by Kennedy, *The Art of Persuasion*, 114, in that Anaximenes makes reference to the Corinthian expedition to Sicily which took place in 341. That the *Rhet. ad Alex.* antedates Aristotle's *Rhetoric* is the conclusion of McCall, *Ancient Rhetorical Theories*, 21 n. 63. He notes that Anaximenes seems to be unaware of Aristotle's work: "It seems doubtful that Aristotle could have been ignored to such an extent if the *Rhetoric* had already been written."

proof, etc. Among the proofs which may be admitted in all classes of oratory is the παράδειγμα to which we referred earlier in this study.[206] In the summary of the form of the encomium that will follow this historical survey, we will have an opportunity to place Anaximenes' rules alongside examples of their use in the encomia of various authors.

### d. The Response of Plato and Aristotle

In Plato (427-347 B.C.E.) and Aristotle (384-322 B.C.E.) we have two individuals who, while not rejecting the place of rhetoric outright, made a critique of rhetoric as it was practiced in their day, proposing that it ought to be grounded on sound philosophical priniciples. Plato's criticism was, on the one hand, directed toward the type of sophistic rhetoric represented by Gorgias and his students. This is the concern of his earliest work on the subject, *Gorgias* (387 B.C.E.), which he directed against the notion that rhetoric is a part of a political education.[207] In his later work, the *Phaedrus*, there is evidence that we are at a new stage in Plato's attitude towards rhetoric—an attitude now shaped by the rhetoric being taught, not by Gorgias, but by Isocrates.[208] And in the case of Aristotle, his initial work on rhetoric, the dialogue *Gryllus*, no longer extant, and his three volume *Rhetoric*, are to be seen as responses to Isocratean rhetorical practice.[209]

Restricting ourselves to strictly encomiastic oratory, there is ample evidence that—like rhetoric in general—Plato saw a place for it, even though he questioned the manner in which it was being taught. In fact, Plato held the encomium in high esteem. For in his ideal state, encomia would be one of the two types of poetic literature permitted: ". . . you must be clear in your mind that the only poetry admissible in our city is hymns to the gods (ὕμνους θεοῖς) and encomia to good men (ἐγκώμια τοῖς ἀγαθοῖς) (*Republic* 10.607a).[210] Another indication that the encomium had a legitimate role in Plato's scheme of things appears in the *Ion*

---

[206]Cf. above, 33-35.

[207]Kennedy, *The Art of Persuasion*, 15.

[208]Cf. W. Jaeger, *Paideia: The Ideals of Greek Culture. III: The Conflict of Cultural Ideals in the Age of Plato* (New York: Oxford University, 1944), 185.

[209]Kennedy, *The Art of Persuasion*, 83.

[210]For the Greek text see J. Burnet, *Platonis Opera: IV* (Oxford: Clarendon, 1902). The translation here is that of D. A. Russell in Russell and Winterbottom, *Ancient Literary Criticism*, 74.

where, while describing that poetry is something produced by divine
inspiration, and is not an art or craft that can be learned, he writes how
an individual poet can be moved by the Muses to compose only certain
categories of song: ". . . this man dithyrambs, another laudatory odes
(ἐγκώμια), another dance-songs, another epic or else iambic verse; . . ."
(*Ion* 534c).[211]

The specific points which Plato seeks to make about the composition of
encomia appear in three of his works: the *Phaedrus*, the *Symposium*, and
the *Menexenus*. The *Phaedrus*, it is suggested, was written as Plato's
response to Isocrates' encomium of Helen:

> That dialogue (viz., the *Phaedrus*), which is structurally a
> reverse image of the *Helen* in that it consists of specimen
> speeches followed by a theoretical discussion, contains not
> only reminiscences of Isocrates but a "direct and comprehen-
> sive attack on the education system of Isocrates in which
> Isocrates' own words and methods . . . are turned against
> him."[212]

Although written as an answer to the *Helen*, the *Phaedrus* is neither in
the form of an encomium nor does it deal with encomia in the strict
sense. It is concerned rather with rhetoric in general, and only insofar as
the composition of encomia is a rhetorical task, does the *Phaedrus* concern itself with encomiastic literature.[213] The three specimen speeches
offered therein on the theme of love are not encomia on love, but are
speeches of a forensic nature which argue the relative advantages to a
youth of favoring the friendship of either a lover or a non-lover. The first
speech is represented by Plato as one spoken originally by Lysias. It is
repeated by Phaedrus for Socrates' benefit and it argues for the case of
the non-lover. Plato intends it to be an example of bad oratory.[214] Socrates responds to it by offering a speech on the same theme, arguing as

---

[211]The text and translation are those of W. R. M. Lamb in H. N.
Fowler and W. R. M. Lamb, *Plato: III* (Loeb Classical Library; Cambridge:
Harvard University, 1952).

[212]Kennedy, *The Art of Persuasion*, 188. It should be noted that Plato's
wish to respond to the *Helen* was due in part to the fact that Isocrates had
there made a critical allusion to Plato. Cf. *Helen* 1, and Jebb, *Attic
Orators*, 49.

[213]Buchheit, *Untersuchungen zur Theorie*, 92.

[214]G. J. de Vries, *A Commentary on the Phaedrus of Plato* (Amsterdam: Adolf M. Hakkert, 1969) 25.

well for the advantage of the youth to accept the non-lover. But in contrast to Lysias' speech, Socrates' effort is commendable. It evidences the full four-part structure of a forensic speech: prooemium (237a.7-237b.1), narration (237b.2-237b.6), proof (237b.7-241c.6), and epilogue (241c.6-241d.3).[215] Though from a rhetorical standpoint it is a fine speech, Socrates regards it to be as poor as the one of Lysias (242d.4). He then goes on in the third speech to treat the theme as he believes it ought to be handled, arguing now for the reverse—that the lover should be preferred by the youth. This third speech is characterized by Socrates as a recantation (παλινῳδία, cf. 243b.5 and 257a.4), which he has offered for any offense he has committed against Eros through the arguments advanced in his previous speech. These three specimen speeches, then, become the basis for the discussion of rhetoric, or of "persuasive speech,"[216] that is Plato's concern for the balance of the dialogue. The dialogue concludes interestingly enough, with a complimentary reference to Isocrates (279a).[217]

The link between the specimen speeches and the criteria which Plato advances for oratory is introduced in the first speech of Socrates when he remarks that an orator ought to have knowledge of his subject: "All good counsel begins in the same way; a man should know what he is advising about" (237b.7-237c.2).[218] Following the second of his speeches, that theme is picked up and developed as Plato's principal criticism of contemporary rhetoric: "Before there can be any question of excellence in speech, must not the mind of the speaker be furnished with knowledge of the truth of the matter of which he is going to speak?" (259e.4-6). Without such knowledge of the truth, which comes from philosophy (216a.4), rhetoric can only persuade falsely and bring about not the good, but its reverse (260c.6-260d.2).

---

[215]Kennedy, The Art of Persuasion, 77.

[216]De Vries, Commentary, 27.

[217]Jaeger, Paideia, 184, regards the positive evaluation here of Isocrates as indicative of a new stage in Plato's assessment of the type of rhetoric taught by Isocrates. While the Phaedrus began with the speech of Lysias, which Plato dismissed as an example of bad sophistic rhetoric, the dialogue ends with this favorable comment regarding Isocrates. For a contrary opinion, in which the compliment paid to Isocrates is seen as a taunt, cf. de Vries, Commentary, 17.

[218]The translations of the Phaedrus are those of Jowett, Works. Cf. Buchheit, Untersuchungen zur Theorie, 92-93, for a discussion of the Phaedrus and Plato's critique of rhetorical practice.

While the speeches and the rhetorical principles of the *Phaedrus* seem
to apply more to questions of forensic and deliberative oratory, where the
merits of a particular case are being argued, the *Symposium* represents a
work which speaks to the shortcomings of epideictic as it was practiced
by the sophists.[219] The setting of the *Symposium* is a banquet which took
place in the home of Agathon (who had been one of Gorgias' students) for
the purpose of honoring him for the recent competition he won with his
first tragedy. At the banquet Eryximachus, one of the guests, proposes
that each one present, in turn, offer an encomium on Eros. His suggestion
was the result of an observation by Phaedrus, also a guest, that the other
gods have all been honored by the poets (177a), and even salt and other
trivial subjects have been celebrated in encomia (177b), but no one as yet
has composed a fitting hymn in praise of love (177c). All the guests agree
to the proposal, and Phaedrus is bid by Socrates to lead off: "So now let
Phaedrus, with our best wishes, make a beginning and give us a eulogy
(ἐγκωμιαζέτω) of love" (177e). After Phaedrus come the speeches of
Pausanius, Eryximachus, and Aristophanes. At this point Plato introduces
the speech of Agathon in such a way that it is clear that this encomium is
intended to be a showpiece of sophistic rhetoric. Thus Socrates remarks to
Eryximachus that if the latter were in Socrates' position of having to
follow Agathon in this encomiastic competition, ". . . you would be fitly
and sorely afraid, and would be as hard put to it as I am" (194a). This
element is framed at the close of Agathon's speech by a remark Socrates
again makes to Eryximachus:

> But surely, my good sir . . . I am bound to be hard put, I or
> anyone else in the world who should have to speak after such a
> fine assortment of eloquence. . . . when we drew towards the
> close, the beauty of words and phrases could not but take one's
> breath away. . . . I was so conscious that I should fail to say
> anything half as fine, that for very shame I was on the point of
> slinking away, had I had any chance. For his speech so
> reminded me of Gorgias . . . (198bc).[220]

---

[219]Cf. Buchheit, *Untersuchungen zur Theorie*, 96. On the close relationship between the *Phaedrus* and the *Symposium*, cf. Jowett, *Works*,
107; and Rose, *Handbook*, 266.

[220]For the translation of the *Symposium* used here, as well as for the
text and translation employed below, cf. W. R. M. Lamb, *Plato: V* (Loeb
Classical Library; Cambridge: Harvard University, 1946).

The speech of Agathon, then, bracketed in this way by Socrates' comments, is to be interpreted as an illustration of the type of current encomiastic rhetoric of which Plato was critical. It may be that his criticism here, however, is not so much directed towards Isocrates, but to Gorgian or sophistic rhetoric in general. There is on the one hand, Socrates' assessment that the speech "so reminded me of Gorgias," and on the other hand, we already have had occasion to note that Agathon's division of the narration into two parts—viz., ". . . we praise him (Eros) first for what he is and then for what he gives" (195a)—parallels the division in the *Agesilaus* of Xenophon (and hence Gorgias?), rather than the practice of Isocrates.[221] At other points Agathon's τάξις and use of amplification are reminiscent of features common to encomia in general—including those of Isocrates, Xenophon, and the Pindaric epinicia. In the prooemium, for example, Agathon contrasts his work with the attempts of others to eulogize the same subject (cf. 194e), while the epilogue contains a wish (cf. the prayer in other epilogues) that everyone should "follow (Eros), joining tunefully in the burthen of his song, . . ." (197e). And included as well is the catalogue of the four cardinal virtues: justice and temperance (196c), valor and wisdom (196d).

Plato's criticism of the speech, and hence his criticism of fourth century epideictic, begins at 198c where, after Socrates has made his comment that Agathon reminded him of Gorgias, he protests against continuing the contest. For with Agathon's speech it has become apparent to Socrates that the rules by which the others compose encomia are not those which he believes should be used:

> And so in that moment I realized what a ridiculous fool I was
> to fall in with your proposal . . . when really I was ignorant of
> the method in which eulogies ought to be made (ἐγκωμιάζειν)
> at all. For I was such a silly wretch as to think that one ought
> in each case to speak the truth about the person eulogized; on
> this assumption I hoped we might pick out the fairest (κάλ-
> λιστα) of the facts and set these forth in their comeliest guise
> (εὐπρεπέστατα). . . . But now, it appears that this is not what
> is meant by a good speech of praise; which is rather an ascrip-
> tion of all the highest (μέγιστα) and fairest (κάλλιστα) quali-
> ties, whether the case be so or not; it is really no matter if
> they are untrue (198c-198e).[222]

---

[221]Above, 140-41.
[222]The emphasis is mine.

While Plato recognizes that amplification is the basic characteristic of the encomium, he believes that the practice of amplification has gotten out of hand. There must be, he says, truth to the qualities which the encomiast seeks to amplify. Plato's concern for truth in oratory is seen here with respect to epideictic, just as the same concern was expressed in the *Phaedrus* in terms of forensic rhetoric.

Having made this criticism, Plato has Socrates offer his encomium of Eros as an example of how the truth about love should be treated. The speech (201d-212c) is Socrates' narration of a conversation he once had with the legendary priestess Diotima, and although, with its question-and-answer form it is unlike conventional encomia, it employs none-the-less some encomiastic elements. The Diotima speech is called an ἐγκώμιον by Socrates (212c); it follows the pattern whereby the subject's virtues and acts are considered separately (201e), and it includes a γένος or genealogy of Eros (203a-204a).

A third work of Plato in which he deals with the rhetorical fashions of the day is his *Menexenus*. The dialogue between Socrates and his young friend Menexenus, with which the work opens and closes, frames an extensive funeral oration which Socrates claims to have learned from Aspasia, the mistress of Pericles. A funeral oration, however, as we've observed, is but an encomium to which a lamentation (θρῆνος) and a consolation (παραμυθία) have been added.[223] The *Menexenus*, then, may be of some value in supplementing the picture we have of the encomium in Plato.

The puzzling thing about this particular work, though, is that the funeral oration it contains is a good piece of oratory.[224] The quality of the speech is in sharp contrast to the commentary on contemporary funeral laments which Socrates offers in the opening part of the dialogue. There Socrates criticizes, in terms already familiar to us, that the praise given in honor of those who have fallen in battle does not correspond to the truth: thus a poor man (πένης) is awarded a magnificent funeral, a worthless fellow (φαῦλος) wins praise, and the orator ascribes to each—in stock speeches composed long beforehand—"both what he has and what he has not, . . ." (234C).[225] In order to explain the contrast between this criticism of funeral oratory and the specimen speech of Aspasia, one

---

[223]Cf. above, 91.

[224]Kennedy, *The Art of Persuasion*, 158.

[225]The text and translation are those of R. G. Bury, *Plato: VII* (Loeb Classical Library; New York: G. P. Putnam's Sons, 1929).

suggestion is that the speech is a satire on funeral orations.[226] Yet, as Kennedy points out, ancient authorities, such as Cicero, regarded the Aspasia speech as a serious work, and it is hard to imagine Plato engaging in satire on the subject of death and immortality.[227] On the contrary, it may be that Plato is quite comfortable here in presenting a philosopher as an accomplished orator. After all, since rhetoric to Plato is merely a craft (τέχνη), it is not in competition with philosophy, and need not be feared by the philosopher. Kennedy, therefore, interprets the speech to be a model of a proper funeral lament.[228]

The elements which are employed in the Aspasia speech, then, are in keeping with what we have come to recognize as characteristic of encomiastic oratory. There is the formal structure of prooemium (236d-237b), γένος (237b-239b), πράξεις (239d-246a), and epilogue (246b-248e). Plato makes use of the commonplace that it is impossible to praise adequately all the deeds of the fallen (246ab), he engages in amplification through syncrisis (240a,c), he treats the virtues of the subjects (e.g., σωφροσύνη, 243a), and he closes the speech with an exhortation that the children of the heroes ought to follow the example of their fathers (248e).

In contrast to Plato, whose views on rhetoric, and in particular the encomium, must be pieced together from the analysis of specimen speeches, like that of the *Menexenus,* or from his criticisms of sophistic rhetoric, Aristotle (384-322 B.C.E.) provides us with a systematic presentation of rhetoric and encomiastic theory. While Plato regarded rhetoric merely to be a knack, Aristotle took it far more seriously. He gave it a theoretical foundation and made it an integral part of the Academy's program.[229] Or as Baldwin summarizes it:

> The ultimate, the only final answer to Plato's challenge is the Rhetoric of Aristotle. . . . Aristotle amply vindicated rhetoric by defining its place among studies, its necessary correlation with inquiry and with policy, its permanent function. He settled the question of rhetoric philosophically. He established its theory. But this theory was oftener accepted than followed. The sophists had, indeed, been put in their place more surely

---

[226]Cf. Buchheit, *Untersuchungen zur Theorie,* 94; Rose, *Handbook,* 266.

[227]Kennedy, *The Art of Persuasion,* 159.

[228]Ibid., 160-61.

[229]Cf. Buchheit, *Untersuchungen zur Theorie,* 238; Eisenhut, *Einführung,* 29-30; Jaeger, *Paideia,* 186.

by Aristotle than by Plato; but they continued to thrive, until ancient rhetoric became more and more sophistic.[230]

Aristotle's theories on rhetoric evolved over the course of his career from his first work on the subject, the *Gryllus*, to the publication of his *Art of Rhetoric*. The *Gryllus* was a dialogue that was no doubt prompted by the flood of encomia produced in honor of Gryllus, Xenophon's son, upon his death in 362 B.C.E.[231] What we know of Aristotle's *Gryllus* comes from Quintilian (2.17.14) who mentions it in the context of a discussion regarding those who say rhetoric is not an art:

> Aristotle, it is true, in his *Gryllus* produces some tentative arguments to the contrary, which are marked by characteristic ingenuity. On the other hand he also wrote three books on the art of rhetoric, in the first of which he not merely admits that rhetoric is an art, but treats it as a department of politics and also of logic.

Quintilian evidently saw a discrepancy between Aristotle's views on rhetoric in the *Gryllus* and those which came to be systematized in the three-volume *Rhetoric*. Thus Kennedy infers that at the time of the *Gryllus*, Aristotle's criticisms of oratory were not unlike those of Plato, but that by the time of the *Rhetoric* they had been modified through Aristotle's acceptance and application of rhetoric in his educational program.[232] The similarity between the views of the young Aristotle and those of his teacher is suggested further by the attack of Cephisodorus, a student of Isocrates, on both philosophers. He interpreted works like that of Aristotle's *Gryllus* to have been directed against Isocrates and himself.[233]

The second stage in Aristotle's developing concern with rhetoric is represented by another work, also lost, his Συναγωγὴ τεχνῶν.[234] It was a compendium of rhetorical instruction that he prepared out of the various rhetorical handbooks which were available to him. It may have come about as a consequence of the information gathering he did in preparation

---

[230]Baldwin, *Medieval Rhetoric*, 3.

[231]Cf. above, 144-45.

[232]Kennedy, *The Art of Persuasion*, 83.

[233]Ibid. Cf. also Eusebius, *Praeparatio Evangelica* 14.6.9, for the reference to Cephisodorus.

[234]Eisenhut, *Einführung*, 29.

for his own teaching on rhetoric.[235] If so, it suggests a movement on Aristotle's part away from the type of criticism that apparently was in the *Gryllus* to an appreciation of the possibilities rhetoric might have in education.

The third phase, then, is that period when Aristotle made the positive contributions to rhetorical theory which are set forth in his three-volume *The Art of Rhetoric*. Yet even here there are inconsistencies which suggest an ongoing development during the time it was being written. Proposals regarding how and when the *Rhetoric* took shape are available elsewhere,[236] but basically it is suggested that Books I and II, dealing with εὕρεσις or invention, were written first. Later, perhaps after Aristotle's return to Athens from Macedonia, the first two books were expanded and/or revised, and Book 3, covering style (λέξις) and arrangement (τάξις), was added.[237] McCall suggests that Book 3 may have been a posthumous addition drawn from lecture notes.[238] In its final form, whether edited by students after his death, or by Aristotle himself, it represented the culmination of his efforts to give rhetoric a solid theoretical foundation.

We had occasion earlier to refer to the *Rhetoric* in terms of Aristotle's division of oratory into three γένη: deliberative, forensic, and epideictic;[239] as well as his discussion of the παράδειγμα as a type of proof (πίστις) common to all three branches.[240] When Aristotle moves from discussing the aspects of theory shared by all types of oratory to treat the characteristics of individual genres, most of his attention here is devoted to forensic and deliberative oratory. Specific concern with epideictic plays a relatively small role in the course of the three volumes. Be that as it may, however, Aristotle is to be credited with the more precise definition of epideictic as a genre, and with limiting epideictic to the topics of praise and blame.[241] He also makes the point that the epideictic orator is to be concerned with present time, "for it is the existing condition of things that all those who praise or blame have in view. It is not

---

[235]Kennedy, *The Art of Persuasion*, 58.

[236]Ibid., 84-85, and 84, n. 73.

[237]Ibid., 87-114, for a summary of Aristotle's theory of invention, style, and arrangement in the *Rhetoric*.

[238]McCall, *Ancient Rhetorical Theories*, 30.

[239]Above, 83.

[240]Above, 33, 100.

[241]Buchheit, *Untersuchungen zur Theorie*, 239; Burgess, "Epideictic Literature," 105.

uncommon, however, for epideictic speakers to avail themselves of other
times, of the past by way of recalling it, or of the future by way of antic-
ipating it" (1.3.4).[242] And within the epideictic genre he identifies four
speech types as the best or purest representatives of the category: the
ἐπιτάφιος, the πανηγυρικός, παράδοξα ἐγκώμια, and ἐγκώμια of persons
(cf. 1.7.34; 1.9.30; 3.10.7; 3.14.1-2; 3.14.11; 3.17.10-11).[243] Finally, in his
treatment of proofs (πίστεις) and arrangement (τάξις), he notes those
features which mark epideictic off from the other two genres. Thus, for
epideictic, amplification is the most appropriate type of proof:

> Speaking generally, of the topics common to all rhetorical
> arguments, amplification is most suitable for epideictic speak-
> ers (αὔξησις ἐπιτηδειοτάτη τοῖς ἐπιδεικτικοῖς), whose
> subject is actions which are not disputed, so that all that
> remains to be done is to attribute beauty and importance to
> them (1.9.40).

> Now, of the commonplaces (τῶν κοινῶν) amplification
> (αὔξειν) is most appropriate to epideictic rhetoric, as has been
> stated (2.18.5).

In Book 3 where he covers the arrangement (τάξις) of the speech,
Aristotle takes issue with the involved structures proposed in sophistic
handbooks.[244] In contrast, he insists that a speech need have only two
parts, the statement (πρόθεσις) and a proof, and at a maximum, four,
with the addition of a prooemium and an epilogue (3.13.2, 4).[245] When he
outlines the features of each of the four, however, he adds a discussion of
a fifth part, the narrative (διήγησις), in the case of epideictic (3.16.1).
The narration, though admitted in sophistic oratory, is a topic that Aristotle had excluded earlier from his four-part arrangement (3.13.3). Later
when we summarize the form of the encomium on the basis of our historical survey, we will have opportunity to note Aristotle's particular views
on the prooemium, the narration, proof by amplification, and the epilogue.

---

[242]Burgess, "Epideictic Literature," 105.
[243]Ibid.
[244]Eisenhut, Einführung, 34-35.
[245]Ibid., 35; and Kennedy, The Art of Persuasion, 113.

e. Late Poetic Encomia

In our survey thus far our concern has been with the history of the prose encomium during the fourth century B.C.E. As we move into the third century, we discover that it is a period from which little knowledge of epideictic oratory can be gained. While epideictic continued to be produced in abundance, "there is no extant [rhetorical] treatise of importance from the time of Aristotle to Dionysius of Halicarnassus, late in the first century B.C."[246] The void in what we know of the encomium in the third century, however, is offset by hellenistic poetry. For although we have not considered the poetic encomium since our discussion of Pindar, et al., the poetic form not only continued in use, but found itself stimulated by the popularity of its prose offspring. As poetry gave rise to the prose encomium, there came to be a reciprocal influence between poetry and rhetoric, such that the prose form of the encomium encouraged the poets' use of the genre.[247] In the third century poetry of Callimachus and Theocritus, then, we find encomia and encomiastic treatments which share the same or similar commonplaces, methods of amplification, and modes of arrangement with those employed in the prose texts of the fourth century.

Among the poems of Callimachus of Cyrene (ca. 305-240 B.C.E.),[248] who was employed in the Alexandrian library of Ptolemy II Philadelphus, are hymns which extol the Ptolemies as divine and which may be considered encomiastic.[249] Three hymns which exhibit such features are *Hymn I: To Zeus*; *Hymn II: To Apollo*; and *Hymn IV: To Delos*.[250] Callimachus' contemporary Theocritus (ca. 300-260 B.C.E.), a native of Syracuse, who migrated to Cos and thence to Alexandria,[251] composed two idylls which

---

[246]Burgess, "Epideictic Literature," 106.

[247]De Romilly, *Magic and Rhetoric*, 7. Cf. also Crusius, "Enkomion," 2582.

[248]For a general discussion of Callimachus, cf. Susemihl, *Geschichte*, 347-72.

[249]Thus Prof. George Kustas, Classics Department, SUNY, Buffalo, in a private communication while he was Visiting Professor of Rhetoric, University of California, Berkeley, November 1975.

[250]On the encomiastic quality to the Hymn to Apollo, cf. Crusius, "Enkomion," 2582. On the hymns to Zeus and Delos as paralleling Theocritus' Id. 16 and 17, cf. A. S. F. Gow, *Theocritus, II: Commentary* (Cambridge: Cambridge University, 1952), 325.

[251]On Theocritus, cf. Lesky, *History*, 719; and Rose, *Handbook*, 331. For a more extensive discussion, cf. Susemihl, *Geschichte*, 196-229.

have been called encomia. Burgess describes Idyll 17 as "an excellent example of a βασιλικὸς λόγος,"[252] while Gow notes that Idyll 16 is reminiscent of the epinicia of Pindar and Simonides, and that it stands far closer to the encomium of Idyll 17 than it does to any other of Theocritus' works.[253]

The most important of the above poems for our purposes is Idyll 17, Theocritus' encomium of Ptolemy Philadelphus which was written ca. 273/2 B.C.E.[254] It exhibits the arrangement familiar to us from prose encomia. There is a prooemium (1-12), where Theocritus outlines the task before him, ". . . but I who know how to praise must sing of Ptolemy" (7-8),[255] and where he at the same time employs the commonplace on the difficulty of praising his subject: "Of what am I to make mention first, for countless to tell are the blessings wherewith heaven has honoured the best of kings?" (11-12). The γένος follows in which Philadelphus' father and mother, Ptolemy I Soter and Berenice I are extolled (13-76). Ptolemy I's relationship to Alexander is mentioned and both are said to have been descendants to Heracles (18-27). Berenice is described as blest of Aphrodite (36-50), while the marriage of Berenice to Ptolemy I and the birth of Ptolemy II are compared to the unions of Deipyle to Tydeus and Thetis to Peleus, marriages that gave birth to the great warriors Diomedes and Achilles respectively (53-57). The narration of the πράξεις (77-134) comes immediately after the γένος. It includes a description of the Ptolemaic empire over which Philadelphus reigns (77-94), and a catalogue of his riches, skill, and acts of piety (95-134). The encomium closes with a brief epilogue (135-137) in which there is a call to prayer. The summons to prayer is addressed to Ptolemy himself; he is urged to pray to Zeus for ἀρετή such that he may have success in future exploits, success which, along with his riches, will assure him of immortality.[256]

---

[252]Burgess, "Epideictic Literature," 130. Cf. also Crusius, "Enkomion," 2582.

[253]Gow, Theocritus, II. Gow also notes, p. 326, that Id. 14 might be considered here as well in that it contains a "panegyric of Ptolemy."

[254]The dates are those of Gow, Theocritus, II, 326.

[255]For the translation, as well as the numbering of the lines of the Greek text, cf. Gow, Theocritus, I: Text (Cambridge: Cambridge University, 1952) 130-39.

[256]Note that Ptolemy is alive at the time Theocritus composed this tribute to him. Gow is of the opinion that at this point Ptolemy's exploits are still largely in the future. He suggests, then, a date of 273/2 B.C.E., prior to the close of the Syrian war. Gow, Theocritus, II, 347.

Gow points out that there are parallels in Callimachus to this encomium of Ptolemy that cannot be accidental:

> The *Hymn to Zeus* describes the birth of Zeus and his upbring-
> ing in Crete (10-63) as T. [Theocritus] (58-70) describes those
> of Ptolemy in Cos: Zeus' eagle, and his patronage of kings,
> appear in both poems and in the same order (Call. 68-86; T.
> 71-6): T's panegyric of Ptolemy (77ff.) is matched by a pre-
> diction of Ptolemy's greatness (Call. 85-90): and both poems
> end with a triplet concerning ἀρετή. The *Hymn to Delos*
> follows other lines, but it contains a description of Ptolemy's
> empire (166ff.), and Delos addresses the newborn Apollo (265)
> just as in T. (66) Cos addresses Ptolemy.[257]

By their praise of Ptolemy II in the guise of extolling Zeus, and Delos as
the home of Apollo, these two hymns are in effect covert encomia of
Philadelphus. The same may be said of *Hymn II: To Apollo*—but here the
king being praised is Ptolemy III Euergetes.[258] The occasion of the hymn
is the Carnean festival of Apollo at Cyrene, and Callimachus must have
composed it at the time when Ptolemy III became king of Cyrene through
his betrothal to Berenice, daughter of Magas of Cyrene, viz., 258 B.C.E.
or after.[259] One feature of the structure of this hymn that calls to mind
that of the prose encomium is the apparent division Callimachus has made
between Apollo's beauty and skill on the one hand (32-46), and the recitation of, in effect, Apollo's πράξεις (47-96) on the other. This suggests the
division of virtues and deeds employed by Plato, in his speech of Agathon,
and Xenophon in the *Agesilaus*.

Theocritus' Idyll 16, through which the poet sought to obtain the
patronage of Hiero II of Syracuse, is of interest in that it develops a
commonplace regularly employed in encomiastic prooemia, viz., that
unless a man be praised in song by a poet, he will not be remembered
after he has gone to the grave. Theocritus believes that it is the duty of
rulers, who have the financial means, to patronize the arts, thereby". . .
to honour the holy interpreters of the Muses, that even when thou art

---

[257] Ibid., 325.

[258] A. W. Mair in A. W. Mair and G. R. Mair, *Callimachus and Lycophron; Aratus* (Loeb Classical Library; New York: G. P. Putnam's Sons,
1921) 23-24. Note the identification of Apollo and Ptolemy III at line 27 in
Mair's text: ". . . he who fights with my king, would fight even with
Apollo."

[259] Ibid., 23.

hidden in Hades thou mayest be well spoken of and not mourn unhonoured on the chill shore of Acheron . . ." (16.29-31).[260] Theocritus proceeds to illustrate this point by citing the examples of those figures who would no longer be held in remembrance had there not been a poet to sing of them. He reviews the Thessalian patrons of Simonides: Antiochus, Aleuas, and the families of the Scopadae and Creondae (16.34-39).[261] And then, additional examples are offered of those legendary persons about whom no one would know, had not Homer sung of them: the Lycians, Priam, Cycnus,[262] Odysseus, Eumaeus, Philoetius, and Laertes (16.48-57). As these men are brought to memory through the poetry of Simonides and Homer, so too Hiero will need the poetry of Theocritus in order that his exploits in the forthcoming campaign against Carthage (16.76-79) may be remembered: "That man shall have need of me for his poet when he has done such deeds as great Achilles wrought, . . ." (16.73-74).

Another commonplace, identified already in the lyric poets, prose encomia, and in Theocritus' encomium of Ptolemy II, deals with the difficulty of the encomiastic task, given the abundance of material available on the subject. The same feature appears in the hymns of Callimachus. In the *Hymn to Zeus* it is sounded both at the opening and close of the poem:

> How shall we sing of him—as lord of Dicte or of Lycaeum? . . .
> (1.4)
> . . . . . . . . . . . . . . . . . . . . . . . . . . . . . . . . .
> Thy works (ἔργματα) who could sing? There hath not been, there shall not be, [one] who shall sing the works of Zeus
> (1.91-92).

---

[260]The translation of Theocritus, here and below, is that of Gow, *Theocritus, I*, 125.

[261]Gow is of the opinion that there is a redundancy in Theocritus' list in that the Scopadae and Creondae probably refer to the same family. Simonides wrote an ode for Scopas, but the father of Scopas was Creon. It also strikes Gow as curious that Theocritus looks to Thessaly for examples here. A more likely comparison for him to employ would have been in terms of Simonides' relationship to the court of Hiero I. But perhaps, he suggests, the political position of Hiero II at the time was such that a comparison with the tyrant of Simonides' day would have been unwelcome. Cf. Gow, *Theocritus, II*, 313.

[262]Ibid., 316, where Gow notes that the story of Cycnus appears in neither the *Iliad* nor the *Odyssey*, but in the *Cypria* whose Homeric authorship is doubted.

And in the *Hymn to Delos*, Callimachus takes note of the myriad of legends which could be used to praise Delos, and wonders, "Now if songs full many circle about thee, with what song shall I entwine thee?" (4.28-29).

Finally, in addition to the similarities in arrangement and commonplaces between these third century poems and the encomia/epinicia of the preceeding two centuries, there are the same techniques of amplification. Amplification by syncrisis appears in the γένος of Idyll 17, outlined above, and in Idyll 16 where Theocritus uses the *Beispielreihe* of those past heroes celebrated by Homer and Simonides, in order to amplify the coming deeds of Hiero which will need to be praised.

A second means of amplification, of which we've become aware, is the assertion that the subject is beyond comparison, viz., he is the first or only man to have done something. Several instances of this type of amplification are evident in Theocritus and Callimachus:

> In riches he [Ptolemy II] could outweigh (καταβρίθοι) all other kings, . . . (Idyll 17.95).

> Of men of old and of those the imprint of whose steps still warm the trodden dust holds beneath the foot, Ptolemy alone (μοῦνος) has founded fragrant shrines for his dear mother and father, . . . (Id. 17.121-123).

> But from Zeus come kings; for nothing is diviner (οὐδὲν θειό-τερον) than the kings of Zeus. . . .
>
> . . . . . . . . . . . . . . . . . . . . . . . . . . .
> One may well judge by our Ruler [Ptolemy II], for he hath clean outstripped (εὐρὺ βέβηκεν) all others (Callim. 1.78-79, 84-85).[263]

> None is so abundant in skill (τέχνη δ' ἀμφιλαφὴς οὔ τις τόσσον) as Apollo (Callim., 2.42).

> No (οὐ) other dance more divine (θεώτερον ) hath Apollo beheld [viz., the dance of the Carnean festival], nor (οὐδὲ) to any city hath he given so many blessings as he hath given to Cyrene, . . . Nor (οὐδὲ), again, is there any other god whom the sons of Battus have honoured above Phoebus (Callim. 2.93-96).

---

[263]The translations of Callimachus are those of Mair, *Callimachus*.

With the works of Theocritus and Callimachus, then, we find the presence of the poetic encomium in Ptolemaic Alexandria, even as its prose counterpart was known there in the *Socrates* of Demetrius of Phaleron. Could it not be that such encomia, together with their predecessors, were among the materials with which Sirach became acquainted in the course of his travels (cf. Sir 34:11; 39:4; 51:13)?[264] The value of travel in a person's education was itself a hellenistic idea,[265] and if Ben Sira journeyed to any educational centers at all, he would have gone to Alexandria.[266] And if he had not come into contact with Greek literature and rhetoric in Palestine, he certainly could not have escaped it in the Ptolemaic capital.

### 3. The Later Period: From the Second Century B.C.E. to the Rhetors of the Common Era

Thus far we have traced the development of the encomium from its poetic origins, through its establishment as a rhetorical εἶδος to its appearance in hellenistic poetry. With the beginning of the second century, a period critical to our study in that it is here that Ben Sira was engaged in his teaching and travels, we would welcome any evidence that

---

[264]At Sir 51:13a the reference to Sirach's travels is present in the Greek while the Geniza MS reads "and I took pleasure (וחפצתי) in her (viz., wisdom)." The cave 11 Psalms scroll has בטרם תעיתי. The verb תעה, however, can mean either "to err" or "to travel." Sanders, *Dead Sea Psalms Scroll*, 115 and P. W. Skehan, "The Acrostic Poem in Sirach 51:13-30," *HTR* 64 (1971) 388, opt for the former meaning here. But Marböck, *Weisheit*, 161, and Smend, *Commentary*, 504, whose conjecture concerning the original reading has been confirmed by 11QPsᵃ, are of the opinion that the latter sense of תעה, "to travel," is meant.

[265]Cf. Marböck, *Weisheit*, 162.

[266]Among those who believe Ben Sira travelled widely in the hellenistic world are Marböck, *Weisheit*, 162; Hengel, *Judaism*, 132; and Oesterley-Box, in Charles, *Apocrypha*, 292, who suggest that Ben Sira may have been in political service under Ptolemy IV Philopater. In contrast, Middendorp, *Die Stellung*, 170-73, believes Ben Sira would not have had to travel at all to become acquainted with Greek literature—for it was already available to him in Jerusalem. Middendorp suggests that had Sirach visited Alexandria, he would no doubt have incorporated into his lectures—and his book of wisdom—mention of the city's architectural wonders.

could be gained from encomia and rhetorical handbooks of the period.
Unfortunately, we are handicapped at this point. For although there was
an abundance of epideictic literature produced during the third, second
and first centuries, B.C.E., little is extant.[267] And when it comes to the
rhetorical treatises that could provide an understanding of encomiastic
theory at this time, none have survived. There is a lacuna between the
*Rhetoric* of Aristotle and the Roman handbooks of the first century; what
we can know of hellenistic rhetorical theory can only be inferred from
later Greek and Roman authors.[268]

One author, however, who offers indirect evidence concerning the
encomium in the second century and is roughly contemporary with Sirach,
though a generation or so younger, is the Greek historian Polybius (ca.
200-118 B.C.E.). In Book 10 of his *Histories,* in his discussion of Philopoemen, Polybius refers to a previous work he has written about this
distinguished Achaean soldier-statesman. The former work he describes as
". . . being in the form of an encomium (ἐγκωμιαστικός)," and as such, it
". . . demanded a summary and somewhat exaggerated (μετ' αὐξήσεως)
account of his achievements (πράξεων)" (10.21.8). In addition to identifying his use of amplification in the narration of Philopoemen's deeds,
Polybius comments that in his encomium he explained "who he and his
family were, and the nature of his training when young, . . ." (10.21.5).
Thus, although it comes only indirectly, we have the sense that this second century encomium possessed the topics of γένος and πράξεις, and
employed the technique of amplification.

It is known that the second century produced at least one rhetorical
handbook of importance, that of Hermagoras. It, however, is no longer
extant. From what information is known about Hermagoras—by way of
Cicero and Quintilian[269]—it appears that he represented a culmination in
the development of rhetorical theory that had begun with Aristotle.[270] To
Hermagoras rhetoric was an art for which all the rules can be learned, and

---

[267]Burgess, "Epideictic Literature," 106.

[268]Ibid. Cf. also Kennedy, *The Art of Persuasion,* 264; and McCall,
*Ancient Rhetorical Theories,* 53. One exception that could be mentioned
is the treatise *On Style* attributed to Demetrius of Phaleron. It does refer
to the encomium in discussing a work of the sophist Polycrates. But the
*On Style* is of uncertain date and is not now thought to be from the hand
of Demetrius. Cf. above, 98.

[269]Kennedy, *The Art of Persuasion,* 304.

[270]Ibid.

he ". . . had discovered virtually all the rules."[271] The rules he presents
—e.g., those on *stasis*, i.e., the crucial point at issue in a case, and those
by which he expanded the traditional four parts of an oration to include
partition and confirmation[272]—suggest that his concern was primarily for
the oratory that would be practiced in the lawcourt. Hermagoras, however, described rhetoric's task in somewhat broader terms. He preferred
to speak of rhetoric dealing with "political questions," viz., anything that
might involve the citizen, and as such, Kennedy is of the opinion that
epideictic would have been covered there as well.[273]

The emphasis on the "political" use of rhetoric in Hermagoras, coupled
with the assumption that his work was directed to a Roman audience,[274]
point to a characteristic that Roman oratory had during the last century
B.C.E. and the first century of the Common Era: the concern with practical oratory, such as that of the lawcourt, at the expense of epideictic.[275]
This lessened emphasis on epideictic is born out by the comments of the
Roman rhetors themselves. For example, out of the 287 sections that
make up Cicero's *de Inventione*, 263 deal with forensic, twenty two with
deliberative, and only two touch on epideictic.[276] And in the *de Oratore*,
Book 2, Cicero contrasts the practices of the Greeks and the Romans
when it comes to the writing of encomia:

> . . . we Romans do not much practise the custom of panegyrics
> (*laudationibus*), so consequently I put this department entirely
> on one side. For the Greeks themselves have constantly thrown
> off masses of panegyrics, designed more for reading and for
> entertainment, or for giving a laudatory account of some
> person, than for the practical purposes of public life with
> which we are now concerned: . . . (*de Oratore* 2.84.341).[277]

---

[271]Ibid., 318.
[272]Ibid., 314.
[273]Ibid., 304, 311.
[274]Ibid., 319.
[275]Kennedy, *The Art of Rhetoric*, 115.
[276]Forensic: all of Book 1 (secs. 1-109) and secs. 1-154 of Book 2;
political: secs. 155-76 of Book 2; epideictic: secs. 177-78 of Book 2. Cf.
the outline of the work in H. M. Hubbell, *Cicero: de Inventione; de Optimo
Genere Oratorum; Topica* (Loeb Classical Library; Cambridge: Harvard
University, 1959), x-xi. Cf. also Kennedy, *The Art of Rhetoric*, 111.
[277]The translation is that of E. W. Sutton and H. Rackham, *Cicero: de
Oratore, I-II* (Loeb Classical Library; Cambridge: Harvard University,
1959).

Be that as it may, however, the Romans did compose encomia and the two great teachers of first-century Roman rhetoric—Cicero (106-43 B.C.E.) and the author of the *Rhetorica ad Herennium* (written ca. 86-82 B.C.E.)[278]—devote some space at least to a discussion of epideictic. In the *de Inventione*, which was composed while Cicero was still a young man (ca. 91 B.C.E.) and may simply be an edition of class notes he made during his own rhetorical training,[279] Cicero includes the two sections we mentioned that treat epideictic (Book 2, 177-78). His brief discussion here addresses the topics for which a man can be praised (or censured). First of all, he refers back to the attributes of persons which he introduced earlier in a judicial context (Book 1.34-36)—viz., name, nature, manner of life, interests, achievements, etc.—and notes that praise may be offered on these grounds. Within the list of attributes, his category "nature" (*naturam*) includes the topic of genealogy which is essential to the Greek encomium, while "manner of life" (*victum*) and "achievements" (*facta*) correspond to the Greek πράξεις (1.34-35). Secondly, Cicero goes on to say that if the orator wants to treat the subject more systematically, he can divide the attributes among the three categories of "mind, body and external circumstances" (2.177). The category of attributes of the mind consists of the four cardinal virtues—wisdom (*prudentia*), justice (*iustitia*), courage (*fortitudo*), and temperance (*temperantia*) (2.159)—the treatment of which we recall from Isocrates, and in a separate, systematic way, from Xenophon. Thus Cicero's division between virtues and external circumstances parallels, in a way, the ἀρεταί/πράξεις division in Xenophon and the Agathon speech of the *Symposium*.

A later and more comprehensive treatment of rhetoric is Cicero's *de Oratore*, written in 55 B.C.E.[280] In Book 1 he has Crassus, his "mouthpiece" in the dialogue, speak of the place of epideictic as one of the three branches of rhetoric:

> . . . of such questions . . . , some have their place in courts of justice, others in deliberations; while there was yet a third kind (*genus*), which had to do with the extolling (*laudandis*) or reviling (*vituperandis*) of particular persons; and that there were prescribed commonplaces (*locos*) which we were to employ in the law-courts . . . others for use in deliberations,

---

[278]McCall, *Ancient Rhetorical Theories*, 58, suggests a date for the *ad Herennium* of between 86 and 82 B.C.E.

[279]Hubbell, *Cicero: de Inventione*, vii-viii.

[280]Sutton and Rackham, *Cicero: de Oratore*, x.

. . . and again others in panegyric (*laudationibus*), wherein the sole consideration was the greatness of the individuals concerned (*de Oratore* 1.141).

In Book 2 of the work Cicero devotes two chapters (84-85: sections 341-348) to the rules governing encomia. After noting the contrast between Greeks and Romans in regard to the practicality of epideictic, seen above, Cicero says that even though Romans do not write all that many encomia, there are occasions when they must be delivered, and therefore a treatment of the subject is in order (2.341). The basic ground for praise is that of virtue (2.343), and each of the several virtues has its own "appropriate form of commendation" (*laus propria*) (2.345). In addition to his presentation on the role of virtue, which brings to mind the treatment of the *de Inventione*, Cicero adds that in the narration of the person's achievements, ". . . one must select achievements that are of outstanding importance or unprecedented or unparalleled in their actual character; . . ." (2.347). In other words, Cicero commends the traditional practice of amplification by means of stating that the subject was the first or only person to have done something. Cicero, too, encourages other forms of amplification: "Moreover, a splendid line to take in panegyric is to compare (*comparatio*) the subject with all other men of high distinction (*cum ceteris praestantibus viris*)" (2.348). Here we're reminded of Aristotle's comment on amplification by syncrisis: "And you must compare him with illustrious personages, . . ." (*Rh.* 1.9.38).[281]

A second treatise of Roman rhetorical theory from the same period as Cicero is the anonymous *Rhetorica ad Herennium*. Written but a few years after Cicero's *de Inventione*,[282] it and the latter work both seem to be dependent on an earlier hellenistic source, or on a Roman rhetorician who had studied traditional Greek theory.[283] Because of the common ancestry of the two works, it is not surprising to find epideictic presented in the same way in the *ad Herennium* as in Cicero. Thus, the anonymous *auctor* recognizes the traditional three-fold division of oratory:

---

[281]Kennedy, *The Art of Persuasion*, 278, emphasizes the link between Cicero and Aristotle. For example, the *de Oratore* is based on "the broader and more philosophical concept of rhetoric found in Aristotle and his pupil (viz., Theophrastus)."

[282]Cf. the dates suggested by McCall, above, 166 n. 278.

[283]McCall, *Ancient Rhetorical Theories*, 57; Kennedy, *The Art of Persuasion*, 264-65.

> There are three kinds (*genera*) of causes which the speaker
> must treat: Epideictic (*demonstrativum*), Deliberative, and
> Judicial. The epideictic kind is devoted to the praise or cen-
> sure (*laudem vel vituperationem*) of some particular person
> (I.11.2).

And like Cicero, the *auctor* regards the practice of rhetoric to be geared
primarily to judicial and political needs, not to purely epideictic ends. But
since epideictic techniques can be of value in forensic and deliberative
arguments, there is a need for the student to master them:

> And if epideictic is only seldom employed by itself indepen-
> dently, still in judicial and deliberative causes extensive
> sections are often devoted to praise or censure. Therefore let
> us believe that this kind of cause also must claim some mea-
> sure of our industry (3.8.15).

As the *auctor* begins his treatment of epideictic, he outlines that there
are three bases upon which a man can be praised: external circumstances,
physical attributes, and qualities of character (*rerum externarum, corpo-
ris, animi*) (3.6.10). These are the same as the "external circumstances,
body, and mind" of Cicero's *de Inventione*. Likewise, the *auctor* subsumes
under each of the three headings the same virtues, gifts or achievements
which had been catalogued by Cicero, e.g., the four cardinal virtues under
"qualities of character," etc. The praise that is offered on the basis of the
attributes, qualities, or actions listed in these three categories becomes
the proof (*confirmatio*) and refutation (*confutatio*) of an epideictic speech
(3.6.11). Here we note the attempt to make the arrangement of an epideictic speech conform to the expanded six-part τάξις, advocated by
Hermagoras, which prescribes a refutation.

What the *ad Herennium* contains that was not present in the theory
outlined by Cicero is a discussion of invention in epideictic oratory in
terms of the several topics which make up a speech. Thus the *auctor*
writes that invention, with respect to a speech's introduction, will depend
on whether the orator wishes to start with his own self, with the person
being praised, or with the audience. If he begins with his own person, he
will want to say that he desires to praise the subject out of a sense of
duty or from "goodwill, because such is the virtue of the person under
discussion that everyone should wish to call it to mind; . . ." (3.6.11). If, on
the other hand, he starts with the person whom he is praising, the epideictic author will want to employ the commonplace of inadequacy: ". . .

if we speak in praise, we shall say that we fear our inability to match his deeds with words: . . ." (3.6.11).

Utilizing the six-part outline of Hermagoras, the next section of the speech for which the *auctor* discusses invention is the partition. While in judicial speeches the partition is a statement of those things in a case upon which both parties agree and those things still in dispute, in epideictic it appears to take the form of a simple statement of the grounds upon which the subject will be praised:

> The division (*divisione*) we shall make is the following: we shall set forth the things we intend to praise or censure; then recount the events, observing their precise sequence and chronology, . . .(3.7.13).

The partition, then, seems to be comparable to the chronological πράξεις of the Isocratean outline. But here we sense that the precise order of the six-part forensic outline doesn't quite suit the purposes of epideictic. For the *auctor* appears to be saying that prior to the chronological recitation in the partition, the subject's virtues, external circumstances, and physical advantages must be catalogued (3.7.13). The virtues again are the four cardinal ones (3.8.15); the external circumstances include, among other things, the genealogy:

> Descent (*genus*)—in praise: the ancestors of whom he is sprung; if he is of illustrious descent, he has been their peer or superior; if of humble descent, he has had his support, not in the virtues of his ancestors, but in his own (3.7.13).

And the physical advantages include strength, beauty, agility, good health, etc. The outline which the *auctor* seems to propose here for the main body of the speech, then, suggests once again the kind of division between virtues and deeds which we saw in the *de Inventione* and which can be traced back to the encomiastic practice of the fourth century B.C.E.

The discussion of epideictic ends in the *ad Herennium* with a brief comment concerning invention in the epilogue:

> Our conclusions will be brief, in the form of a summary (*enumeratione*) at the end of the discourse; in the discourse itself we shall by means of commonplaces (*per locos communes*) frequently insert brief amplifications (*breves amplificationes*) (3.7.15).

To judge from what we have seen in both Cicero and the *ad Herennium*, it appears that the principal features of the fourth century encomium were in like manner recognized and taught in first century Greco-Roman rhetoric.

Two first century Greek writers whose names have been linked with encomiastic theory are the Epicurean Philodemus (ca. 110-45/35 B.C.E) and Dionysius of Halicarnassus, who lived and taught in Rome from the year 30 B.C.E. on. Although the Epicureans were hostile to rhetoric, we do have a treatise, written in the mid-first century by Philodemus, which provides some discussion of epideictic.[284] By the examples which Philodemus uses, it is clear that he understands epideictic to be the kind practiced by Isocrates.[285] In terms of Dionysius, there is attributed to him an *Art of Rhetoric* of which Burgess makes use in outlining the τάξις of the encomium.[286] This, however, was done in error in that the *Art of Rhetoric*, with its extensive treatment of epideictic (7 out of 11 chapters), cannot have been written by Dionysius. The author or authors speak more highly of Plato than Dionysius ever did, and they deal with concerns which, as Kennedy notes, fit more appropriately the period of 150-250 C.E. than the time of Dionysius.[287]

With the advent of the Common Era, we are presented with two contrasting attitudes toward epideictic. First of all, in the person of Quintilian (ca. 30/35-100 C.E.), we have someone whose views on epideictic are in harmony with those of Cicero and the author of the *ad Herennium*. Quintilian, too, shares the Roman belief that oratory should be practical. In Book 3 of his *Institutio Oratoria* (ca. 96 C.E.), he notes that while epideictic was composed by the Greeks purely for entertainment, the "Roman usage on the other hand has given it a place in the practical tasks of life" (Quint. 3.7.2).[288] Such practical applications of epideictic included the funeral orations which a public official might be called upon to offer, as well as the role praise and blame could play within the context of forensic rhetoric. Thus in Book 2, where he presents his views on education and rhetoric, he sees the teaching of epideictic to be a necessary part of a young man's advanced training:

---

[284]The text of Philodemus' treatise, discovered on a papyrus at Herculaneum, was published by Sudhaus, *Philodemus*.

[285]Kennedy, *The Art of Persuasion*, 300-301.

[286]Burgess, "Epideictic Literature," 121.

[287]Kennedy, *The Art of Rhetoric*, 634-35.

[288]The translation of the *Institutio Oratoria* here, as well as below, is that of Butler, *Institutio Oratoria*.

> From this our pupil will begin to proceed to more important
> themes, such as the praise of famous men (*laudare claros
> viros*) and the denunciation of the wicked (2.4.20).

Contrasting somewhat with this practical Roman attitude is a resur-
gence of interest in pure epideictic that began with the second century of
the Common Era. With the rhetorical treatises of Theon, Hermogenes,
Aphthonius, et al., we witness rules for the composition of encomia and
other epideictic speeches spelled out in ever-increasing detail during the
300 year period known as the Second Sophistic.[289] In either case, however, whether in the practical emphasis of Quintilian, or in the more
traditional Greek view of epideictic seen in the Common Era sophists,
encomia continue to exhibit those principal characteristics which were
fixed by the fourth century B.C.E. I suggest that the survey of Common
Era rhetors which follows will bear this out.

Quintilian, in the course of his *Institutio Oratoria,* deals with epideictic
composition at two different points: in Book 3, chapter 7, is his discussion
of the function, topics, and arrangement of speeches of praise and blame,
while in Book 8, chapter 4, he treats the various methods of amplification.
Like the rhetoricians who preceded him, he regards amplification as basic
to encomia; "The proper function however of panegyric (*laudis*) is to
amplify (*amplificare*) and embellish (*ornare*) its themes" (3.7.6). Among
the various amplification techniques recommended by Quintilian are two
which have recurred throughout our historical sketch: comparison (*comparatio*) (8.4.3) and the description of the person's actions as unprecedented
(3.7.16).

Book 3 provides us with an understanding of how Quintilian believed an
encomium ought to be structured. When the speech extols a man (Quintilian admits the possibility of composing encomia on gods or on inanimate
objects, cf. 3.7.6) the man's ancestors and/or country are to be treated:

> . . . a theme which may be handled in two ways. For either it
> will be creditable to the objects of our praise not to have
> fallen short of the fair fame of their country and of their sires
> or to have ennobled a humble origin by the glory of their
> achievements (3.7.10).[290]

---

[289]Cf. Volkmann, *Die Rhetorik,* 315; Kennedy, *The Art of Rhetoric,*
615, 640.
[290]Cf. *Rhet. Her.* 3.7.13 for virtually the same interpretation of the
genealogy.

When he treats the proof of the speech, Quintilian proposes the same three-fold division advocated by Cicero and the *ad Herennium:* "The praise of the individual himself will be based on his character, his physical endowments and external circumstances" (3.7.12). And in structuring the main part of the speech, two options are open to the rhetor:

> It has sometimes proved the more effective course to trace a man's life and deeds in due chronological order, . . . At times on the other hand it is well to divide our praises, dealing separately with the various virtues, fortitude, justice, self-control and the rest of them and to assign to each virtue the deeds performed under its influence (3.7.15).

In the option which Quintilian presents here for his students he is recommending two methods which have come down from the fourth century: the chronological arrangement of Isocrates and the topical organization of Plato-Xenophon-Gorgias.

While Quintilian provides an idea of first century theory, one of his students, Tacitus (ca. 54-117 C.E.),[291] furnishes an example of how that theory appeared in practice. The *Agricola* of Tacitus, written in the year 98 in honor of his father-in-law, exhibits a number of features which appear to be encomiastic.[292] Tacitus opens the prooemium of the *Agricola* by contrasting the cynicism of the Domitian age with those days past when Romans gladly extolled the "works and ways of famous men" (*clarorum virorum facta moresque*) (*Agr.* 1). Since Agricola, by his conduct during the reign of Domitian, has provided an example of how great men can live in bad times, Tacitus wishes now to praise him so that he will be remembered. This task Tacitus undertakes ". . . albeit with unpractised

---

[291]For a summary of Tacitus' life, cf. H. W. Benario, *An Introduction to Tacitus* (Athens: University of Georgia, 1975), 12-21.

[292]For an analysis of the *Agricola* as an encomium, cf. A. Gudeman, *Tacitus: Agricola and Germania* (Boston: Allyn and Bacon, 1900) viii-xix. Rather than identifying it as an encomium or a *laudatio funebris,* some have wanted to classify it as belonging to the genre *exitus virorum illustrium.* Thus Benario, *Introduction to Tacitus,* 23-24. But Ronconi points out that Tacitus does not deal with the circumstances of Agricola's death, which he ought to have done if the *Agricola* was of this latter genre: "Agricola ist genau das Genteil von dem, was die Protagonisten der E(xitus) i(llustrium) v(irorum) sind." A. Ronconi, "Exitus illustrium virorum," *Reallexicon für Antike und Christentum: VI* (Theodor Klauser, ed.; Stuttgart: Anton Hiersemann, 1966) 1261-62.

and stammering tongue" ( *Agr.* 3). The genealogy follows (4), with reference to the titles and rank of Agricola's grandfathers and father, and the virtue of his mother. The description of his education and early military training (4-5) leads to a chronological recitation of his deeds (6-9, 18-42). The narration is interrupted at the point Agricola arrives in Britain as governor. Here Tacitus digresses into a description of the geography and ethnology of Britain (10-13), which is followed in turn by a list of the Roman governors who preceded Agricola. The purpose here seems to be one of syncrisis: Agricola's term of office and his military exploits in Britain will be seen to compare favorably with those of his predecessors.[293] Following this *Beispielreihe,* Tacitus resumes the narration of Agricola's term in Britain. The narration ends with the note that Agricola left "a peaceful and safe province to his successor" (40), and that upon his return to Rome, his conduct continued to be exemplary, even in the face of Domitian's suspicion and jealousy (41-42). The *Agricola* ends with an epilogue (42-46) in which Tacitus expresses the wish that "reverence" ( *admiratione*), "unending thankfulness" ( *immortalibus laudibus*), and "imitation" ( *similitudine*) will be the response of all men to his father-in-law's memory (46). In structure, in topics, and in commonplaces, then, the *Agricola* gives evidence of sharing a number of those features which we have come to recognize as standard in encomia.

With Quintilian and his student Tacitus we have arrived at the beginning of the second century of the Common Era, a time in which we meet the first of that series of Greek rhetoricians who compose the Second Sophistic. In this era epideictic assumes a far greater role in rhetorical theory and practice than it had among the Romans. The first rhetor to be considered here is Aelius Theon of Alexandria who, in the late first or early second century, produced a three-volume *Art of Rhetoric* and a *Progymnasmata.*[294] Although the former work is no longer extant, a large

---

[293]Cf. the example of the Roman governor Suetonius Paulinus, who was unable to capture the island of Mona because of a general rebellion in Britain (16), to whom Tacitus compares Agricola, who was able to take the same island peacefully, an act for which he "began to be regarded as a brilliant and a great man" (18). The translation of the *Agricola* here is that of W. Peterson, *Tacitus: Dialogus; Agricola; Germania* (Loeb Classical Library; New York: G. P. Putnam's Sons, 1932).

[294]Kennedy, *The Art of Rhetoric,* 615-16; Bryant, *Ancient Greek,* 97-98. The *Progymnasmata* of Theon were published by L. Spengel, *Rhetores graeci* (Leipzig, 1854) 2.60-130; and C. Walz, *Rhetores graeci* (London, 1832-36) 1.145-257.

part of the latter has been preserved. It comprises fifteen exercises designed for the student of rhetoric, one of which is the encomium. And within his discussion of the encomium, he presents a three-fold division of the grounds upon which a man may be praised that is virtually the same as the division given in Cicero, the *ad Herennium* and Quintilian. In Theon the three categories are those of "goods" or "excellences" (ἀγαθά): there are those of the mind, the body, and those which are exterior (τὰ περὶ ψυχήν τε καὶ ἦθος, τὰ δὲ περὶ σῶμα, τὰ δὲ ἔξωθεν).295 Arranged under each of these heads are the various specific attributes, qualities, virtues, and deeds which are not only listed in the comparable catalogues of the Roman rhetors, but which were listed by Anaximenes as well. Anaximenes, too, noted that a distinction should be made "between the goods (ἀγαθά) external to virtue (τὰ ἔξω τῆς ἀρετῆς) and those actually inherent in virtue (τὰ ἐν αὐτῇ τῇ ἀρετῇ)" (*Rhet. ad Alex.* 35.1440b.15). And just as "high birth" (εὐγένειαν) falls under the "external" heading in Anaximenes, so too "high birth" (εὐγένεια) is included at the same place in Theon's classification.296 By and large the breakdown in each of Theon's categories is the same as has appeared in the writings of previous rhetoricians: ancestry, education, and public service are external goods; beauty, strength, and health are listed as bodily excellences; and the four cardinal virtues, to which piety (ὅσιος), liberality (ἐλευθέριος), and high-mindedness (μεγαλόφρων) have been added, come under the heading of the goods pertaining to the mind.

Another *Progymnasmata,* which proved to be the most popular book of its type, was that of the important second century rhetor Hermogenes (b. ca. 161 C.E.) of Tarsus.297 In addition to his exercise book, he is known to have produced four other rhetorical treatises, one of which, his *On Staseis,* reveals his indebtedness to the theory of *stasis* advanced by Hermagoras in the second century B.C.E.298 Hermogenes was probably the most read and most influential Greek rhetorician in late antiquity.

As Theon had done in his *Progymnasmata,* Hermogenes included the

---

295Cf. Spengel, *Rhetores graeci,* 109, as cited by Burgess, "Epideictic Literature," 121. For a summary of Theon's outline of the distribution of the thirty-six qualities, attributes, and actions among the three categories, cf. Marrou, *History of Education,* 198-99.

296On the similarities between Theon and Anaximenes, cf. Burgess, "Epideictic Literature," 119, n. 1, 121, n. 2.

297On Hermogenes, his life and works, cf. Kennedy, *The Art of Rhetoric,* 619-24; and Bryant, *Ancient Greek,* 55-57.

298Kennedy, *The Art of Rhetoric,* 622.

encomium in his as one of twelve exercises he prescribed for students. After opening his discussion of the exercise with a statement of what an encomium is and isn't—"Encomium is the setting forth of the good qualities (ἔκθεσις τῶν προσόντων ἀγαθῶν) that belong to someone in general or in particular,"[299] encomia can be composed not only on men, but on things as well, and that "encomium differs from praise (ἔπαινου) in that the latter may be brief, . . . whereas encomium may be developed at some length"[300]—Hermogenes then lists the topics (τόποι) to be employed. They are the subject's race (ἔθνος), city (πόλις), family (γένος), birth, nurture (τροφή), and training (ἀγωγή). Then the nature (φύσις) of body and soul are to be set forth, and under each head will be listed the appropriate characteristics: beauty, stature, agility, and might under the former, while the four virtues will appear under the latter. Next come his pursuits (ἐπιτηδεύματα) which include mention of his profession and his deeds (πράξεις). After this Hermogenes writes that praise should be given for the category of external circumstances (τὰ δὲ ἐκτός): kin, friends, possessions, household, and fortune. Above all, he notes that amplification by means of comparison is basic to the task: ". . . the greatest opportunity (μεγίστη ἀφορμή) in encomia (ἐγκωμίοις) is through comparisons (συγκρίσεων), which you will draw as the occasion may suggest."

This pattern for the composition of encomia shared by Theon and Hermogenes, and taught through the use of their *Progymnasmata,* continued in rhetorical instruction for centuries to come. One indication of the persistence of these rules is to be seen in the corresponding section of the *Progymnasmata* of Aphthonius of Antioch, a full two or more centuries later.[301] In his section on the encomium, Aphthonius tells the student:

> Begin with an *exordium.* Then subjoin what stock the person is, divided as follows: of what people, of what country, of what ancestors, of what parents. Then explain his education under these heads: talents, arts, laws. Then introduce the chief of all the topics of praise, his deeds, which you will show to be the results of his excellences of mind, as fortitude or prudence; his excellences of body, as beauty, speed, vigor; his excellences of fortune, as his high position, his power, wealth, friends. Then

---

[299] For the Greek text, here and below, cf. Rabe, *Hermogenes Opera,* 14-18; the translation is that of Baldwin, *Medieval Rhetoric,* 30-33.
[300] Cf. above, 89-90.
[301] Aphthonius fl. ca. 400 C.E., cf. Bryant, *Ancient Greek,* 5.

bring in a comparison in which your praise may be heightened
to the utmost. Finally conclude with an epilog urging your
hearers to emulate him.[302]

In Aphthonius is represented an understanding of encomiastic theory
and practice which extends back over three-quarters of a millennium. The
topics and arrangement he recommends are those which had their roots in
Pindar, found development and expression in Isocrates, Xenophon, Plato,
Anaximenes, and Aristotle, and were handed down through hellenistic
times to Roman rhetors and the Greek rhetoricians of the Common Era.
At each point we have seen: (1) the necessity of amplification; (2) a
classification of the grounds for praise into those things which pertain to
virtue, physical gifts, and external circumstances; and (3) a basic outline
for the encomium that was standard over the centuries. That the same
arrangement should have been normative for so long is significant, given
the freedom that rhetoricians were permitted in terms of structure.[303]
Quintilian, for example, did not want his students to be enslaved by rules
regarding arrangement:

> Let no one however demand from me a rigid code of rules such
> as most authors of textbooks have laid down, or ask me to
> impose on students of rhetoric a system of laws immutable as
> fate, . . .
> . . . . . . . . . . . . . . . . . . . . . . . . . . . . . . . .
> . . . but more rules are liable to be altered by the nature of
> time and place, and by hard necessity itself. Consequently the
> all-important gift for an orator is a wise adaptability . . .
> (Quint. 2.12.1-2).

With such freedom permitted, the persistence of a certain scheme of
topics and arrangement over the years underscores the comment which
was made at the beginning of our survey relative to the conservatism of
ancient rhetoric.[304] And with that conservatism having preserved certain
methods of amplification and encouraged a standard τάξις to the encomium down to and beyond the second century B.C.E., we will want now to

---

[302]Aphthonius as translated by D. L. Clark, *Rhetoric in Greco-Roman
Education* (New York: Columbia University, 1957) 197. For an outline of
the topics of the encomium as they appear in the Greek text of Aphthonius, cf. Burgess, "Epideictic Literature," 120.

[303]Burgess, "Epideictic Literature," 121-22.

[304]Above, 104.

summarize these formal elements and make our own *syncrisis* with the form of Sirach 44-50.

Before we leave the final period in our historical summary, however, a word should be added about another rhetor of importance from the Second Sophistic, Menander of Laodicea (third century C.E.). Two discourses on epideictic bear his name, the διαίρεσις τῶν ἐπιδεικτικῶν and the περὶ ἐπιδεικτικῶν. In the former, Menander presents an extremely detailed breakdown of the various types of epideictic speeches.[305] The primary division is between speeches in honor of gods and those honoring mortal beings. The category of mortal beings is then divided into two groups: land and cities on the one hand, and persons and creatures on the other. The latter is subdivided further into rational beings and animals, with animals then broken down into land animals, birds, fish, etc. In the other work, περὶ ἐπιδεικτικῶν, however, Menander deals strictly with twenty three orations which are all variations of the encomium on a person: e.g., speeches offered on the occasion of marriage (περὶ ἐπιθαλαμίου), a birthday (περὶ γενεθλιακοῦ), and a funeral (περὶ ἐπιταφίου).[306] It is within this list that we find the introduction of the term λόγος βασιλι-κός,[307] which, as was noted in the terminology discussion, is properly an encomium of a king.[308] But setting that royal requirement aside, the rules given by Menander are identical to those we have already seen prescribed for the encomium in Theon, Hermogenes, and Aphthonius.[309]

Menander, however, does not seem to have been the author of the περὶ ἐπιδεικτικῶν.[310] Bursian argues that while Hermogenes wrote the διαί-ρεσις, the second treatise is by another hand. The manner in which various epideictic speeches are classified differs between the two works, and with the frequent mention of Troas in the second book, it points to its origins there by an anonymous author.[311] Be that as it may, the περὶ

---

[305]For a summary of Menander's divisions of epideictic oratory, cf. Bursian, *Der Rhetor Menandros*, 18. Bursian's publication of the Greek text of the διαιρεσις is on 30-68.

[306]Ibid., 69-142, for the Greek text of the περι ἐπιδεικτικῶν.

[307]Ibid., 95.

[308]Above, 84, 99.

[309]Cf., e.g., the comparison Baldwin mades between the τάξις of Aphthonius and that of Menander. Baldwin, *Medieval Rhetoric*, 31, n. 60.

[310]Kennedy, *The Art of Rhetoric*, 637.

[311]Cf. Bursian, *Der Rhetor Menandros*, 17-18, where he notes that while nearly all the speeches treated in the περὶ ἐπιδεικτικῶν would come under the heading of encomia of persons in the διαίρεσις, two resist that classification: the ἐπιβατήριος (which is an encomium of a god), and the Σμινθιακος (an encomium of Apollo, the Sminthian).

ἐπιδεικτικῶν continues to serve as a witness to the encomiastic theory advocated in the Second Sophistic.

## 4. The Shape of the Greek Encomium

In the course of the foregoing survey the features of the encomium which have been repeatedly in evidence and which appear to be the basic marks of the εἶδος are: (1) the use of amplification (αὔξησις), and (2), a distinct arrangement (τάξις) or outline that has remained relatively standard throughout the periods discussed. I would like to summarize these two characteristics as a basis for our subsequent analysis of Sirach 44-50 as an encomium.

### a. Proof by Amplification

Amplification is basic to the task of praising a man.[312] Inasmuch as the encomiast seeks to portray his subject as an ideal figure, he uses techniques of amplification in order to describe his subject's character and achievements in the best possible light,[313] as well as to present him as someone who surpasses all others in virtue.[314] To this end the encomiast regards himself as free to take liberties with what is known about his subject's life: ". . . everyone knows that those who wish to praise a person must attribute to him a larger number of good qualities than he really possesses, . . . (Bus. 4).[315] Such license enables Isocrates to avoid any mention of the assassination of Evagoras in his encomium of the Cypriot king.[316] And Xenophon, though as a historian he mentions Agesilaus' lameness in the Hellenica, as an encomiast he is completely silent

---

[312]Volkmann, Die Rhetorik, 321-23.

[313]Dihle, Studien, 10.

[314]". . . those who undertake to praise any people . . . must show . . . that they excelled in all the virtues . . . ," Isocrates, Panathen. 123.

[315]But cf. Bus. 32 where Isocrates draws a distinction between the type of amplification he practiced and, evidently, a more extreme form of exaggeration employed by the sophist Polycrates: "Nay, your account is far less credible than mine, since I attribute to him (viz., Busiris) no impossible deed."

[316]Stuart, Epochs, 62. On Isocrates' omission of the circumstances surrounding Evagoras' death, cf. van Hook, Isocrates: III, 2.

about his hero's physical handicap.[317] It was the license taken by encomiasts in their use of amplification that prompted Plato's criticism in the *Symposium* (cf. 198c-198e).[318] Nevertheless, amplification continued as the most distinctive mark of the encomium from the fourth century works of Isocrates, Xenophon, and Plato down to the rhetors of the Common Era; throughout the period covered by our survey it is considered fundamental to the idea of the encomium by various teachers of rhetorical theory (cf., e.g., Aristotle, *Rh.* 1.9.40, 2.18.5, 3.17.3; Quint. 3.7.6; Hermogenes, *Progym.*;[319] Menander, *On Epideictic*[320]).

All during the near-millennium of our survey, amplification was accomplished by means of a variety of techniques, commonplaces, and stylistic devices. The principal ones we have seen are as follows:

(i) Comparison

Perhaps the most-used technique is that of syncrisis or comparison.[321] Its use is attested in the lyric poets, in fourth century prose and third century poetic encomia, and it is enjoined by the handbooks from that of Anaximenes to those of the Common Era. Although σύγκρισις/ συγκρίνω are the preferred terms employed to designate the technique, others are also used: e.g., παραδείκνυμι (Isocrates, *Panathen.* 39); παραβάλλω (*Evag.* 33); ὑπερβάλλω (*Evag.* 65); ἀντιπαραβάλλω (*Rhet. ad Alex.* 3.1426a28-29; Aristotle, *Rh.* 1.9.38); παρίστημι (*Panathen.* 39; *Rhet. ad Alex.* 35.1441a.25); and εἰκάζω (*Rhet. ad Alex.* 3.1426b.3).[322]

The encomiast may choose to compare his subject with the example (παράδειγμα) of another worthy person (cf. Aristotle, *Rhet.* 1.9.38; Cicero, *de Oratore* 2.348). This type of comparison was discussed earlier in our consideration of the *Beispielreihe* as a subordinate genre in the

---

[317]Stuart, *Epochs,* 64.

[318]Cf. the discussion of Plato's criticism of excesses in amplification, above, 153.

[319]Cf. the quote from Hermogenes, above, 175.

[320]Cf. the quote from Menander, above, 99.

[321]For a discussion of the use of comparison in the encomium, cf. F. Focke, "Synkrisis," *Hermes* 58 (1923) 335-39.

[322]συγκρίνω and σύγκρισις are present in theoretical discussion from as early as Aristotle (*Rh.* 1.9.38) to Hermogenes and Aphthonius, cf. above, 175-76, and Burgess, "Epideictic Literature," 120-125.

encomium.[323] And encomiasts who have made use of it include Pindar (cf. the victory of Pytheas//the victory of his uncle, Euthymenes, Nem. 5.41-43; Chromius//Hector, Nem. 9.39-43); Isocrates (Evagoras//Cyrus, Evag. 37-39; Evagoras//heroes of Trojan War, Evag. 65; Theseus// Heracles, Helen 23; Helen//Alcmena, Danaë, Nemesis and Leda, Helen 61; Timotheus//Pericles, Antidosis 111); and Theocritus (Ptolemy//the house of Atreus, Id. 17.118-120; Ptolemy and Arsinoe//Zeus and Hera, 17.130-132; Hiero//those heroes extolled by Homer and Simonides, Id. 16.34-75). The syncrisis may be of a more general nature where the encomiast compares his subject with an indefinite person or persons rather than with a specific historical or mythical example. Thus Isocrates contrasts Evagoras with "other exiles from royal power" who have become "humbled in spirit because of their misfortunes" (Evag. 27). In like manner, he writes that Theseus did not do as other rulers in general do, viz., "impose the labours upon the citizens and himself alone enjoy the pleasures . . ." (Helen 36). Negative comparisons with specific examples also appear. In the Busiris Isocrates describes how among all those who have borrowed political customs from the Egyptians, the Spartans have made poor use of them (Bus. 19), and Plato, in the Menexenus, contrasts the Athenians, who are "pure Greeks", with the barbarian, only nominally Greek descendents of "Pelops, Cadmus, Aegyptus or Danaus" (Menex. 245d).

In pre-Aristotelian rhetoric comparison meant not only the parallel drawn between the subject and historical or mythical παραδείγματα, but it included the use of what we would call simile.[324] The similes of Bacchylides (Automedes = "the brilliant moon of the mid-month," 36.21-32), Pindar (Phylacidas = the whetstones of Naxos, Isth. 6.72-73; Melesias = the dolphin, Nem. 6.66-69), as well as Plato's use of similes in the praise of Socrates given by Alcibiades in the Symposium would all come under the heading of comparison. In the lattermost instance, Alcibiades introduces his speech by stating, "The way I shall take, gentlemen, in my praise (ἐπαινεῖν) of Socrates, is by similitudes (δι' εἰκόνων)" (Symp. 215a). The use of two similes follows: "I say he is most like (ὁμοιότατον) the Silenus-figures . . ." (215a), and "I further suggest that he resembles (ἐοικέναι) the satyr Marsyas . . ."[325]

As a technique of amplification, comparison was employed throughout

---

[323]Cf. the discussion of σύγκρισις and παραδείγματα, above, 99-103.

[324]McCall, Ancient Rhetorical Theories, 17, 259, notes that ancient usage does not mark simile off as a distinct form of composition.

[325]Cf. Ibid., 14.

the various parts of the arrangement, although it was especially suited to the purposes of the main body of the speech where the subject's virtues, physical appearance, and achievements were narrated. It also found use in the γένος of the encomium where a comparison was set up between the subject and praiseworthy acts of his ancestors. Thus Isocrates writes that he desires to narrate the deeds of Evagoras' legendary ancestors so that ". . . all may know that he proved himself not inferior to the noblest (καλλίστων) and greatest (μεγίστων) examples (παραδειγμάτων) of excellence which were of his inheritance" (*Evag.* 12). In a similar fashion, Plato describes the noble deeds of the ancestors of the heroes who were being praised in Aspasia's funeral oration (cf. *Menex.* 239b).

And in addition to its use at various points in the encomium, comparison became one of the fixed topics in the structure. Placed generally between the recitation of the subject's achievements and the epilogue, it is employed in Xenophon, where he contrasts the life-styles of Agesilaus and Artaxerxes II (*Ages.* 9.1-7): "I will next point out the contrast (ὑπεστήσατο) between his behaviour and the imposture of the Persian king" (9.1). As a separate topic, its use is enjoined by the Common Era rhetors, Hermogenes, Menander, and Aphthonius.[326]

## (ii) Inadequacy of the Encomiast

A second method of amplification that was evident in our historical survey is the commonplace of inadequacy. This may take the form of a statement that the deeds and/or virtues of the subject are too great or too numerous for them to be adequately treated in the course of an encomium. Or the emphasis may be shifted to the speaker: there is so much material that the orator or poet feels incapable of the task. This theme is found as early as Pindar who, for example, feels that just as it is impossible to number all the grains of sand, so too he would be unable to count up all the benefits which Theron had bestowed upon others (*Oly.* 2.98-100).[327] Isocrates uses this commonplace frequently (cf. *Concerning the Team* 21, 39; *Helen* 29; *Evag.* 40, 48-49; *Antidosis* 8, 114; *Panthen.* 74; *Oration 5: To Philip* 110; *Letter to Archidamus* 4). Xenophon begins the *Agesilaus* with one, viz., "I know how difficult it is to write an appreciation of Agesilaus that shall be worthy of his virtue and glory" (1.1), while

---

[326]Cf. above, n. 322, and Baldwin, *Medieval Rhetoric*, 31, n. 60.

[327]Cf. above, 112-13, for other examples of this commonplace in Pindar.

Plato employs it in the Aspasia speech of the *Menexenus* (246ab) and in
the speech of Agathon (*Symp.* 196b): ". . . yet there remains much more
which I might say . . ."). Theocritus, too, in Idyll 17—the encomium of
Ptolemy— writes of his inadequacy: "Of what am I to make mention first,
for countless to tell are the blessings wherewith heaven has honoured the
best of kings" (11-12).[328] And, as was noted in our consideration of the *ad
Herennium*, the author recommends its use as a means of amplification
(3.6.11).[329]

Although the commonplace of inadequacy seems to have been especially suited to the purposes of the prooemium, it could appear at other
points within the arrangement of an encomium. For example, in Isocrates'
*Helen* (29) and *Evagoras* (40, 48-49), the commonplace is utilized within
the narration of the πράξεις as a device whose purpose is perhaps to
relieve the monotony of the continuous recitation of deeds.

(iii)  Actions as Unique or Unprecedented

Another commonplace whose use in encomia extends from the lyric
poets to the rhetoricians of the Common Era is for the encomiast to
portray his subject's actions as unique or unprecedented. Both Anaximenes
and Aristotle recommend it:

> Another possible way of magnifying (μεγάλα ποιεῖν) good or
> bad actions is if you prove (ἀποφαίνῃς) that . . . no one else
> had attempted them (viz., the actions) before, . . . (*Rhet. ad
> Alex.* 3.1426a.36-39).

> We must also employ many of the means of amplification
> (αὐξητικῶν); for instance, if a man has done anything alone
> (μόνος), or first (πρῶτος), or with a few (μετ' ὀλίγων), or has
> been chiefly (μάλιστα) responsible for it; all of these circum-
> stances render an action noble (*Rh.* 1.9.38).

In like manner, it is enjoined by both Cicero (*de Oratore* 2.347) and Quintilian (3.7.16), whose comments we had occasion to cite earlier.[330]

Encomiasts mentioned in our survey, whose utilization of this common-

---

[328]On this commonplace in Theocritus and Callimachus, cf. above,
159, 161-62.
[329]Above, 168-69.
[330]Above, 167, 171.

place has been noted, are the lyric poets Simonides, Bacchylides, and Pindar.[331] Isocrates makes copious use of it. In his encomium on Timotheus in the *Antidosis,* he employs it repeatedly in amplifying the actions of the general:

> . . . he has taken more cities by storm than any other man has ever done, . . . (*Antidosis* 107).

> And if you can point to any other man who has done a like thing, I stand ready to admit my folly . . . (112)

> . . . in this kind of sagacity there has never been anyone like him or even comparable with him, . . . (118; cf. also 125, 127).

Other encomia of Isocrates where it appears include the *Evagoras* (13), *Helen* (43), *Letter to Archidamus* (3) and *Panathenaicus* (73, 76, 78). Xenophon employs it in the *Agesilaus* (cf. 7.1 and 9.7), and we have already observed it in Theocritus' encomium of Ptolemy (Id. 17.95, 121-123) and in the hymns of Callimachus (2.42).[332]

(iv) Actions That Produced Good or Desirable Results

A method that is singled out for consideration by Anaximenes, examples of which are attested in Isocrates and Xenophon, is where the encomiast makes explicit that the actions of his subject were beneficial for his city and its citizens: "First you must show, . . . that the actions of the persons in question have produced many bad (viz., in the case of vituperative oratory), or good (ἀγαθά) results. This is one method of amplification (τρόπος τῆς αὐξήσεως) (*Rhet. ad Alex.* 3.1426a.20).[333] In Isocrates' encomia this method is utilized in *Evagoras* 47 where, after he recounts how Evagoras took the throne, Isocrates praises him for rehabilitating Salamis, "which had been reduced to a state of barbarism:"

---

[331] For examples in Simonides, Bacchylides, and Pindar, cf. above, 107-08, 117-18.

[332] Translation of the lines of Theocritus and Callimachus are given above, 162.

[333] Cf. Quint. 3.7.16: ". . . emphasizing what was done for the sake of others . . ."

Evagoras remedied all these defects . . . acquired much additional territory, surrounded it with new walls and built triremes, and with other construction so increased the city that it was inferior to none of the cities of Greece (47).

And in the *Antidosis*, Isocrates presents Timotheus' deeds in such a way in order to point out that all the cities the general has won for Athens came at no cost to the citizenry. Rather, the cost of his campaigns was borne largely by Timotheus himself (*Antidosis* 108, 113). Also because of his exemplary behavior he was able to win for Athens the good will of those Greeks who heretofore had had no love for her (*Antidosis* 124, 126). And Isocrates extends his use of this mode of amplification to encomia celebrating legendary figures: in the *Helen*, Theseus' victories over the bull of Poseidon, the Centaurs, and the Minotaur (25-28, 35) are presented as having set free those whom they had terrorized. Also, in the encomium of Agamemnon, Isocrates emphasizes that his hero ". . . did not give up fighting . . . before reducing to slavery the city of him who had offended against Hellas and putting to an end the insolence of the barbarians" (*Panathen.* 83).

Xenophon, too, praises the favorable consequences of Agesilaus' rule. After the collapse of the Athenian empire and the turmoil that followed, it was the Spartan king who brought about "harmony and prosperity" (*Ages.* 1.37-38). Moreover, the benefits of his reign even outlived him:

So complete was the record of his service to his fatherland that it did not end even when he died: he was still a bountiful benefactor of the state when he was brought home to be laid in his eternal resting place, . . . (*Ages.* 11.16).

(v) Other Commonplaces of Amplification

Rhetors were encouraged to describe their subject's actions in terms that would make it clear that their accomplishments were not the result of mere chance, but were due to the character of the man. This could be done by either suggesting that the subject acted intentionally or by showing that he acted in the same way on numerous occasions. Both Anaximenes and Aristotle call attention to such possibilities for amplification:

Another possible way of magnifying good or bad actions is if you prove that the agent acted intentionally, arguing that he had long premeditated doing the acts, that he repeatedly set

about doing them, that he went on doing them a long time, . . .
(*Rhet. ad Alex.* 3.1426a.36-39).

Also, if a man has often been successful in the same thing; for
this is of importance and would appear to be due to the man
himself, and not the result of chance (*Rh.* 1.9.38).

Thus Isocrates seeks to portray Evagoras as a king who only acted after
careful deliberation: ". . . he judged that he should not . . . act on the spur
of the moment; nay, he spent most of his time in inquiring, in deliberation
and in taking counsel . . ." (*Evag.* 41-42; cf. also *Panathen.* 80). Agesilaus
as well is pictured by Xenophon as one who gave forethought to the
demands that would be placed on his troops, seeing to it that they would
be "capable of meeting all calls on their endurance; . . ." (*Ages.* 2.8). And
that the military and political achievements of Theseus, Timotheus,
Evagoras, et al., were not a consequence of mere fortune is brought home
by Isocrates through his use of a series of examples which illustrate how
his heroes repeatedly demonstrated their skill. Mention was made already
of Theseus' victories not only over the bull of Poseidon, but over the
Centaurs and the Minotaur as well (*Helen* 25-28). So too Evagoras' skill as
a commander was demonstrated not once, but repeatedly: in his ability to
return from exile, storm the palace, and regain the palace with a force of
only fifty men (*Evag.* 27-30); in the strategic advice which Isocrates says
Evagoras gave that helped bring about the victory of Conon and the
Persian fleet at Cnidus (*Evag.* 54-56); and Isocrates' report that ". . . he
almost subdued the whole of Cyprus, ravaged Phoenicia, took Tyre by
storm, caused Cilicia to revolt from the king (viz., Artaxerxes II), and
slew so many of his enemies that many of the Persians, when they mourn
over their sorrows, recall the valour of Evagoras" (*Evag.* 62-63).

In addition to the commonplace of actions done repeatedly, the fourth
century rhetors often described the ease with which their subjects were
able to act. Tasks which required great courage they were able to do
singlehandedly, as in the case of Theseus (*Helen* 31), or they only needed a
small force, as Evagoras did when he regained the throne in Salamis
(*Evag.* 28-29, 64). Evagoras, although outnumbered by the Persians, was
able to make peace with Artaxerxes (*Evag.* 61), while Timotheus required
only a small contingent to take Corcyra (*Antidosis* 109).[334] And Agesilaus,

---

[334]Cf. also *Antidosis* 113 where, out of his personal resources, Timotheus was able to take Potidaea—upon whose recapture Athens had
already spent 2400 talents.

After crossing the Hellespont, he passed through the very
same tribes as the Persian king with his mighty host; and the
distance that had been traversed by the barbarian in a year
was covered by Agesilaus in less than a month ( *Ages.* 2.1).

(vi) Stylistic Factors in Amplification

In the work *On Style*, attributed to Demetrius of Phaleron, the author
refers to the rhetorician Polycrates as having employed "antitheses,
metaphors, and every trick and turn of eulogy" (2.120).[335] Behind this
comment is a recognition of the fact that amplification may be effected
in epideictic oratory not only through the techniques and commonplaces
reviewed thus far, but by the particular choice of words and the various
stylistic devices utilized by the encomiast. *Synonymenwahl* was one of the
concerns in Quintilian's theory of amplification: "The first method of
amplification or attenuation is to be found in the actual word employed to
describe a thing . . ." (8.4.1-2).[336] Long before Quintilian's theoretical
expression of it, however, authors had recognized the importance of the
effective use of words in encomia. Thus Simonides, it will be recalled,
when asked to compose an ode in honor of the winner in a mule-car race,
chose to speak of the victorious team not as mules, but as ". . . daughters
of storm-footed steeds."[337] And to Isocrates the choice of the right word
or phrase is an aspect of amplification; in the *Helen* he comments on his
use of hyperbole: ". . . I, for my part, am justified in employing extrava-
gant language (τηλικαύταις ὑπερβολαῖς) in speaking of Helen; . . ."
(*Helen* 54).

One type of hyperbole of which encomiasts were fond is the super-
lative. Gorgias, in his *Helen*, speaks of Helen as "the fairest flower,"
Tyndareüs "the greatest of humanity," and Zeus "the lordliest of divinity"
(Gorgias, *Helen* 3-4).[338] Isocrates makes frequent use of superlatives:
Alcibiades was the ward of the Pericles who was "most moderate" (σωφρο-
νέστατον), "most just" (δικαιότατον), and "wisest" (σοφώτατον) of all

---

[335]Cf. our reference to this text and its possible dates, above, 98.

[336]For a discussion of *Synonymenwahl* in rhetorical theory, cf.
Lausberg, *Elemente*, 36-37.

[337]The incident is described by Aristotle in his *Rhetoric*, cf. above,
108.

[338]Cf. the translation of Gorgias' *Helen* in van Hook *Isocrates: III*, 55.
The paragraph numbering, again, is that of Freeman, *Ancilla*, cf. above,
125, n. 126.

Athenian citizens (*Concerning the Team* 28); Evagoras is compared to his ancestors who were the "noblest" (καλλίστων) and "greatest" (μεγίστων) and "most renowned" (ὀνομαστότατοι) among their contemporaries (*Evag.* 12-13); Isocrates is hard pressed to decide which of Evagoras' achievements is "the greatest" (μεγίστον) (*Evag.* 69); the land and people ruled by Busiris are the "fairest" (κάλλιστον), "healthiest" (ὑγιεινοτάτους), and "most-long-lived" (μακροβιωτάτους) respectively (*Bus.* 15, 22); and like Gorgias' Helen, Isocrates' Helen is portrayed in superlatives:

> . . . for beauty she possessed in the highest (πλεῖστον) degree, and beauty is of all things the most venerated, the most precious, and the most divine (σεμνότατον καὶ τιμώτατον καὶ θειότατον) (*Helen* 54).

In Agathon's encomium on Love, Eros is described as "most blessed, fairest and best, and youngest" of the gods (*Symp.* 195a), while in the Aspasia speech, Plato has Socrates relate that among all the victories won by Athens' heroes, it was the battle of Salamis that was the "noblest" (κάλλιστον) (*Menex.* 241a). And in Theocritus' Idyll 17, Ptolemy is regarded as "the most excellent" (προφερέστατος) of men and "the best of kings" (ἄριστον βασιλήων) (17.4, 12).

A stylistic device of which ample use was made in the Isocratean and Xenophontic encomia is that of the rhetorical question. Frequently it is the syntatic feature by which the commonplace regarding uniqueness is introduced. We saw it in Simonides, "Who among those of our time ever bound upon him so many victories . . .?"[339] And among the rhetorical questions employed by Isocrates are:

> What man (τίς) would have rejected marriage with Helen, . . . (*Helen* 49).

> . . . who (τίς) of the men who were with him (viz., Timotheus) in the field would not pronounce him incomparable? (*Antidosis* 120).

> For what (τί γάρ) element of glory did he lack who won a position of such exalted honour that, were all the world to unite on the search for a greater, no greater could be found? (*Panathen.* 76; for additional use of the rhetorical question in

---

[339]Above, 107.

Isocrates, cf. *Evag.* 66; *Busiris* 10; *Antidosis* 108, 118; *Pana-then.* 80).

And Xenophon utilizes the device in the *Agesilaus:*

> . . . who except Agesilaus has ever striven either to bring about the revolt of a tribe from the Persian, or to save a revolting tribe from destruction, or by some means or other to involve the Great King in trouble so that he will be unable to annoy the Greeks? (7.7).

> For who (τίς μὲν γάρ) in his prime was so formidable to his foes as Agesilaus at the very limit of human life?

> Whose (τίνος) removal brought such welcome relief to the enemy as the death of Agesilaus, . . .?

> Who gave (τίς) such confidence to allies as Agesilaus, though now on the threshold of death?

> What (τίνα) young man was more regretted by his friends than Agesilaus, though he died full of years? (all *Ages.* 11.15; cf. also 4.1, 3, 5; 5.1; 7.4).

## b. The Arrangement (τάξις) of the Encomium

In the course of our survey we have observed two contrasting tendencies in the arrangement of topics in the encomium: on the one hand there appears to have been a basic outline or structure in use from the time of the lyric poets to the rhetors of the Common Era,[340] while on the other hand there is at the same time a great deal of freedom accorded the encomiast in the organization of his topics.[341] This freedom, moreover, is

---

[340]Cf. my comments on the conservatism of rhetoric, above, 104, 176. Moreover, Stuart, *Epochs,* 66, states that ". . . parallelism both in method of arrangement and range of ideas is likely to exist between encomia that have no atavistic connection. The most patent variation in framework is achieved in proportion as the encomiast adheres to a severe classification of his data under the virtues as captions, or declares for a freer method." Also cf. the reference in Burgess, of which we've made mention before, "Epideictic Literature," 119-20.

[341]Cf. the discussion, above, 176, where mention is made of the flexibility permitted the rhetor by Quintilian (2.13.1-2). Also, Prof.

seen even within the works of a single author. Leo, for example, remarks that Isocrates would vary his arrangement from encomium to encomium.[342]

The basic pattern common to all types of speeches goes back to the three and four part outlines of Corax and Tisias.[343] And as the four part structure of Tisias was adapted to the needs of epideictic oratory, the topics organized under the four heads appear to have been the prooemium, the γένος, the πράξεις, and the epilogue. All four have become familiar to us from the encomiastic material we have reviewed from the time of Gorgias and Isocrates down to that of Aphthonius. Moreover, the same four topics appear with sufficient frequency in the epinicia that we chose to inventory the encomiastic features in Pindar under these four headings.[344] Although there were additions made to this basic structure from Isocrates on, I suggest that these additions were merely modifications of the four-part τάξις, rather than being substantive changes.

Aristotle, on the one hand, represents someone who attempted to alter the arrangement of oratory by seeking to keep it as simple as possible. Reference has been made to his recommendation that a speech need have only two parts, the statement of the case (πρόθεσις) and the proof (πίστις), and at the most four, with the addition of a prooemium and an epilogue.[345]

In the case of epideictic, however, he admitted a fifth part, the narrative (διήγησις).[346] By the narrative in epideictic Aristotle appears to signify a chronological recitation of the subject's deeds,[347] while the

---

George Kustas, Classics Department, SUNY, Buffalo, in a private conversation while he was Visiting Professor of Rhetoric at the University of California, Berkeley, November 1975, noted that the encomium does not possess an absolutely fixed structure. We should expect to find, rather, a great deal of variation within a general outline. Thus any given encomium will not follow precisely the τάξις recommended by a particular handbook.

[342]Leo, *Die griechisch-römische,* 92.

[343]Above, 122-23.

[344]Above, 111-20.

[345]*Rh.* 3.13.1-3, and above, 157.

[346]*Rh.* 3.16.1, and above, 157.

[347]Cf. *Rh.* 3.16.1: : ". . . for it is necessary to go through the actions which form the subject of the speech:" and 3.16.3: "It is only necessary to recall famous actions; . . ."

proof consists of amplifications.[348] In other words, that which Aristotle would treat in two parts—διήγησις and πίστις—our basic outline regards as but one topic, viz., the recitation of the πράξεις within which amplification is employed.

On the other hand, in contrast to Aristotle's concern for simplicity, there was the tendency for all types of speeches to add topics. Hermagoras, it was noted, expanded the τάξις of forensic oratory to six parts,[349] and the author of the ad Herennium attempted to specify those topics in an epideictic speech which would correspond to Hermagoras' added partition and refutation.[350] Perhaps it was under this type of stimulus that elements which had appeared within one of the four traditional topics of the epideictic τάξις were elevated to the status of separate topics themselves. Thus σύγκρισις, which we discussed as a method of amplification within the πράξεις and/or γένος of the encomium, became an independent topic as well. As such it appears as early as the Agesilaus of Xenophon where, in section 9, the life styles of the Spartan king and Artaxerxes are contrasted.[351] Later on it was listed as a fixed topic in the exercises on the encomium prescribed in the Progymnasmata of Hermogenes and Aphthonius.[352] These Common Era rhetors recommended that the formal σύγκρισις be located between the πράξεις and the epilogue—where Xenophon had placed it in the Agesilaus.

One element which may have originated as a part of the γένος that, in turn, became a separate topic in some encomia is the γένεσις, which deals with the circumstances of the subject's birth. It appears to be a separate item in Isocrates' Evagoras where it is clearly marked off from the preceding γένος ("Such was [οὕτω δε] the state of affairs in Salamis . . . when Evagoras was born" [21]), and from the section that follows ("And I shall begin my account of him with the generally accepted facts" [21]). The γένεσις usually referred to ". . . any noteworthy fact preceding or attending the birth—an omen or a dream."[353] Isocrates, however, writes that "I prefer to say nothing of portents, the oracles, the visions . . . not because I disbelieve the reports, but that I make it clear to all

---

[348]Cf. within Aristotle's discussion of Proof (3.17): "In epideictic speeches, amplification is employed, as a rule, to prove (πιστεύεσθαι) that things are honourable or useful" (3.17.3).

[349]Above, 164-65.

[350]Above, 168.

[351]Above, 140-41, 181.

[352]Cf. above, 175-76, and Burgess, "Epideictic Literature," 125-26.

[353]Burgess, "Epideictic Literature," 122.

that I am so far from resorting to invention . . ." (21). Evidently, Isocrates
believed that the convention of including a γένεσις was called for, even
though he did not want to employ it in the traditional manner. A comparable γένεσις is included by Theocritus in Idyll 17 (56-76) where he writes
of Ptolemy's birth, the joy with which the people of Cos greeted his birth,
and the sign of Zeus's eagle that accompanied it. Yet this γένεσις appears
to flow directly from the γένος that precedes it, such that it may not
have been considered as a separate topic by the poet. Outside of these
two instances—Idyll 17 and the *Evagoras*—there does not seem to be any
further use of the γένεσις in the pre-Common Era materials we have
examined. In the first century C.E., however, Quintilian refers to the use
in encomia of the omens or prophecies which foretold the greatness of
one's subject (3.7.11), and in the second century, Hermogenes directs the
student of rhetoric that "You will say what marvelous things befell at the
birth, as dreams or signs or the like."[354] But it is omitted in the other
encomia of Isocrates—both those of historical and mythical personages—
and in Xenophon's *Agesilaus*. Moreover, at the point in the *Rhetorica ad
Alexandrum* where we would expect the γένεσις to be treated, Anaximenes makes no mention of it (35.1441a.15).[355]

Later rhetorical theory added the topic of ἀνατροφή directly after the
γένεσις. According to Hermogenes the encomiast would here want to
treat both the subject's nurture and education:

Next, the nurture, as, in the case of Achilles, that he was
reared on lions' marrow and by Chiron. Then the training, how
he was trained and how educated.[356]

Aphthonius seems to restrict the topic to education alone: "Then explain
his education under these heads: talents, arts, laws."[357] While earlier
handbooks specified that the subject's education and youth ought to be
mentioned, they give the impression that this was to be done not so much
as a separate topic, but that these elements were but aspects of either
the subject's γένος or πράξεις. In the case of the *ad Herennium*, the
author recommends treatment of "Education—in praise: that he was well

---

[354]Hermogenes as translated by Baldwin, *Medieval Rhetoric*, 31.

[355]At 35.1441a.15 there is a lacuna. But, to judge from the conjectural
restoration in Rackham's text, the gap would not have been of sufficient
size to include any treatment of the γένεσις.

[356]Baldwin, *Medieval Rhetoric*, 31-32.

[357]Clark, *Greco-Roman Education*, 197.

and honourably trained in worthy studies throughout his boyhood" (3.7.13).
Yet this recommendation is a part of the discussion of genealogy. One
example of an epideictic speech where the ἀνατροφή seems to be but a
part of the γένος is the *Menexenus* where the praise of the ancestors, and
the city that gave birth to the heroes, blends into the description of the
nurture and education Athens provided for them (*Menex.* 238ab). Following this ἀνατροφή, the γένος continues through 239c.

In Anaximenes, the ἀνατροφή is set off as a separate topic
(35.1441a.15-35). Yet his emphasis is on having the encomiast praise the
subject's actions while a young man. The only difference between Anaximenes' suggestion here and his treatment of the πράξεις itself is in terms
of the difference in age: e.g., in the ἀνατροφή the encomiast is urged to
amplify actions by means of comparison ("You must also compare the
distinguished achievements of other young men . . ." [35.1441a.27-32]).
Thus it would appear that there is virtually no difference between the
ἀνατροφή and the πράξεις in Anaximenes. Both involve the recitation and
amplification of the subject's deeds. Isocrates seems to regard the ἀνατροφή in this way in the *Evagoras* where, while it is set off from the
preceding γένεσις by the phrase, "And I shall begin (ἄρξομαι δ') my
account of him . . ."(21), it blends into the narration of circumstances that
led Evagoras into exile (26), the return from which was the first of his
deeds (27-32). The only other encomium of Isocrates that devotes any
attention to a person's youth or education is the praise of Alcibiades in
*Concerning the Team*. There Isocrates mentions the fact that the elder
Alcibiades was an orphan who became a ward of Pericles (*Concerning the
Team* 28). At the point in the *Helen* where we might expect to find the
topic of ἀνατροφή, sec. 18, where she is described as "not . . . yet in the
full bloom of her beauty, but already surpassing other maidens, . . .,"
Isocrates inserts his encomium of the Theseus who abducted her. The
topic is absent in the *Busiris,* and in the encomia of Timotheus and Agamemnon in the *Antidosis* and *Panathenaicus* respectively, nor does it
appear in Theocritus' Idyll 17.

A third element that became a separate topic in the τάξις outlined by
the *Progymnasmata* is the ἐπιτηδεύματα or description of the subject's
life pursuits. Hermogenes, for example, recommends it: "Next his pursuits, what sort of life he pursued, that of philosopher, orator or soldier,
. . ."³⁵⁸ But even among the Common Era rhetors there was considerable

---

³⁵⁸Baldwin, *Medieval Rhetoric,* 32.

variety in its use and definition.[359] From the discussion given in
Menander, Burgess is of the opinion that in practice the ἐπιτηδεύματα
were generally intermingled with the πράξεις.[360] This was certainly the
case in earlier encomia where there is no separate statement of the
subject's pursuits apart from the recitation of his virtues and deeds. A
distinct topic of ἐπιτηδεύματα is not in evidence in the encomia of Isocrates, Xenophon, and Theocritus, nor is there any theoretical consideration of it in Aristotle, Anaximenes, the ad Herennium, and Quintilian.

Given the fact that the elements of γένεσις, and ἀνατροφή, ἐπιτηδεύματα, and σύγκρισις are either later additions to the τάξις of the
encomium, or that they do not appear in encomia to the degree that the
standard four topics do, together with the observation that these additional elements may be subsumed under one of the traditional topics, I
choose to define the basic form of the encomium in terms of the
arrangement of prooemium, γένος, πράξεις, and epilogue.

(i) The Prooemium

Despite Aristotle's comment that a speech need not have a prooemium,
all the independent encomia which were examined in the course of this
study have opened with one.[361] The encomium, then, throughout its
history, began with a prooemium.[362] But even though it was a fixed topic,
the encomiast was permitted a great deal of freedom in developing it;
anything which the subject suggests could be shaped into an appropriate
introduction to an epideictic speech.[363] Aristotle acknowledges the
freedom taken in the prooemia of his day by drawing the analogy between
writing an epideictic speech and playing a piece of music:

> The prelude resembles the exordium (προοιμίῳ) of epideictic
> speeches; for as flute-players begin by playing whatever they

---

[359]Burgess, "Epideictic Literature," 122.
[360]Ibid., 123.
[361]The exceptions are those encomia that are not independent works,
but were incorporated into other compositions, e.g., the encomia of
Timotheus, Alcibiades, and Agamemnon which are subordinate parts of
Isocrates' speeches Antidosis, Concerning the Team, and Panathenaicus
respectively.
[362]Volkmann, Die Rhetorik, 319.
[363]Burgess, "Epideictic Literature," 122.

can execute skillfully and attach it to the key-note, so also in
epideictic speeches should be the composition of the exordium;
the speaker should say at once whatever he likes, give the key-
note and then attach the main subject. And all do this, an
example being the exordium (προοίμιον) of the *Helen* of
Isocrates; for the eristics (viz., the sophists whom Isocrates
attacked in the prooemium) and Helen have nothing in common. (Aris., *Rh.* 3.14.1)

Given such latitude in invention with respect to the prooemium there
are, however, some elements and commonplaces which tend to recur. One
is for the introduction to contain a summary of the speech as a whole. In
the theory laid down by Anaximenes, he recommends that the prooemium
of an epideictic speech be arranged in the same way as in speeches of
exhortation and dissuasion (*Rhet. ad Alex.* 35.1440b.15), and the prooemia
of the latter are to contain a summary of the argument:

> In general terms, the introduction (προοίμιον) is a preparation
> of the hearers and a summary explanation of the business (τοῦ
> πράγματος ἐν κεφαλαίῳ) to persons who are not acquainted
> with it, in order to inform them what the speech is about and
> enable them to follow the line of arguments, . . . (*Rhet. ad
> Alex.* 29.1436a.34-36).

Plato, in the *Menexenus,* does this with the introduction in the oration of
Aspasia, where right after Socrates recalls her initial statement that the
heroes deserve praise, he goes on to relate:

> And the speech required is one which will adequately eulogize
> (ἐπαινέσεται) the dead and give kindly exhortation (παραινέ-
> σεται) to the living, appealing to their children and their
> brethren to copy the virtues of these heroes, and to their
> fathers and mothers . . . offering consolation. Where then
> could we discover a speech like that? . . . We ought in my
> judgement, to adopt the natural order in our praise, . . .
> Firstly, then, let us eulogize (ἐγκωμιάζωμεν) their nobility of
> birth, and secondly their nurture and training: thereafter we
> shall exhibit the character of their exploits, how nobly and
> worthily they wrought them" (*Menex.* 236e-237a).

A second commonplace employed in epideictic prooemia is the one
wherein the encomiast speaks of his inadequacy in treating the subject.
We have treated it already as a means of amplification, where a number

of illustrations were listed.[364] Its appearance as a commonplace was noted as early as the lyric poets,[365] and, to judge from his comments in the *Panegyricus*, it had become an accepted part of Sophistic practice by Isocrates' time:

> For I observe that the other orators in their introductions seek to conciliate their hearers and make excuses for the speeches which they are about to deliver, sometimes alleging that their preparation has been on the spur of the moment, sometimes urging that it is difficult to find words to match the greatness of their theme. (13).

In addition to employing it in the body of an oration, Isocrates—as did Xenophon and Theocritus—utilized it in prooemia. His comment on the difficulty of using prose in eulogizing (ἐγκωμιάζειν) a man (*Evag*. 8) would seem to be a form of this commonplace. A theoretical statement regarding its use in prooemia is given in the *ad Herennium* where, as a part of the author's attempt to systematize the types of commonplaces from which an encomiast may choose, depending on the perspective from which he composes his introduction (viz., that of the speaker, the subject, or the audience), he states that the theme of inadequacy should be employed if one is starting one's speech with respect to the subject and the magnitude of his deeds (3.7.11).

That it continued to be utilized as a part of the introduction in later encomia may be seen in Tacitus' introduction to the *Agricola* where he concludes his prooemium with: ". . . I shall not regret the task of recording our former slavery and testifying to our present blessings, albeit with unpractised and stammering tongue" (3). The persistence of this commonplace, particularly in the prooemium, led the eleventh-century rhetorician John Doxopater to comment that "It is the law of encomiasts to agree always that the subject is greater than words can match," and Burgess to conclude that this commonplace was one of the principal marks of the encomiastic prooemium.[366]

Another commonplace whose frequency of use in the prooemium ranks with that of inadequacy is the orator's statement that he and his audience have an obligation to praise the subject. In discussing invention in the exordium to an epideitic speech, Aristotle lists this as a possible approach

---

[364]Above, 181-182.

[365]Cf. above, 106 (Ibycus), 112-13 (Pindar).

[366]Burgess, "Epideictic Literature," 122.

to developing a prooemium: "Exordia may also be derived from advice (συμβουλῆς), for instance, 'one should honour the good,' wherefore the speaker praises Aristides, . . ." (3.14.3). And the author of the *ad Herennium* sees this commonplace as appropriate when the orator begins his encomium from the perspective of his own self:

> From our own person: if we speak in praise, we shall say that we are doing so from a sense of duty, . . . or from goodwill, because such is the virtue of the person under discussion that every one should wish to call it to mind; . . . (3.6.11)

This theme that the subject's virtues or achievements are such that the encomiast must honor them was seen in Pindar,[367] in Gorgias' *Helen*,[368] and it is employed by Isocrates, both in the *Evagoras* and his *Helen:*

> Men of intelligence, . . . should ignore such as these (viz., those who would rather listen to the praise of legendary figures rather than that of their own benefactors) and accustom their fellows to hear about those whom we are in duty bound to praise (λέγειν δίκαιόν ἐστιν), . . . (*Evag.* 7).[369]

> As for Helen, daughter of Zeus, who established her power over such excellence and sobriety, should she not be praised and honoured, and regarded (πῶς οὐκ ἐπαινεῖν χρὴ καὶ τιμᾶν καὶ νομίζειν) as far superior to all the women who ever have lived? (*Helen* 38).

And Xenophon speaks of his obligation to praise Agesilaus, as does Aspasia of her duty toward the heroes of Athens in Socrates' report of her oration in the *Menexenus:*

> I know how difficult it is to write an appreciation of Agesilaus . . . Nevertheless the attempt must be made. For it would not be seemly that so good a man, just because of his perfection, should receive no tributes of praise, however inadequate" (*Ages.* 1.1).

---

[367]Above, 111.
[368]Above, 126-27.
[369]Emphasis mine.

> But in respect of words, the honour that remains still due to these heroes the law enjoins (προστάττει) us, and it is right, to pay in full (ἀποδοῦναι). For it is by means of speech finely spoken that deeds nobly done gain for their doers from the hearers the meed of memory and reknown" (*Menex.* 236de).

The sense of duty felt by the orator comes from the conviction that without the medium of the encomium, the subject, together with his virtues and deeds, would not be remembered in generations to come. Isocrates expresses this with respect to Evagoras:

> . . . men of ambition and greatness of soul . . . prefer a glorious death to life, zealously seeking glory rather than existence, and doing all that lies in their power to leave behind a memory of themselves that shall never die (ἀθάνατον).
> . . . . . . . . . . . . . . . . . . . . . . . . . . . . . .
> But the spoken words which should adequately recount the deeds of Evagoras would make his virtues never to be forgotten (ἀείμνηστον) among all mankind. (*Evag.* 3-4).

Not only does Isocrates see his encomium as the means by which Evagoras might be immortalized, but in the *Antidosis* he relates how he once chided Timotheus for not taking advantage of this opportunity for eternal remembrance which the encomiast can provide:

> And yet I wonder if you realize how many men have either come to grief or failed of honour because of the misrepresentation of these orators; how many in the generations that are past have left no name, although they were far better and worthier men than those who are celebrated in song and on the tragic stage. But the latter, you see, found their poets and historians, while the others secured no one to hymn their praises. Therefore, if you will only heed me and be sensible, you will not despise these men whom the multitude are wont to believe, . . . (*Antidosis,* 136-37).

And it will be recalled, moreover, from our earlier discussion of Theocritus, that the purpose of his Idyll 16 was to secure Hieron's patronage so that the poet might be in a position to immortalize the king in verse as Homer and Simonides had done for the heroes of past ages.[370]

---

[370]Cf. above, 160-61.

Besides the sense of obligation to the subject which the encomiast expressed in the prooemium, he also felt it necessary to appeal to his audience. As Aristotle envisioned it:

> In epideictic oratory, one must make the hearer believe that he shares the praise, either himself, or his family, or his pursuits, or at any rate in some way or another (Rh. 3.14.11).

Anaximenes, too, says that the audience must be taken into account where, while treating epideictic prooemia in common with those in speeches of exhortation and dissuasion, which we mentioned above (Rhet. ad Alex. 35.1440b.15), he advises—in addition to recommending the use of the summary statement—that the orator ought to exhort his audience to attend and "make them well-disposed towards us" (εὔνους ἡμῖν αὐτοὺς ποιῆσαι) (29.1436a.37). Attempts to conciliate the audience may be seen in Pindar, who praises not only the winners of the games, but their cities as well,[371] and in Isocrates who, as the younger Alcibiades begins the praise of the elder, has the younger say that he will include in his account of the πράξεις events from an earlier time "for the benefit of the younger men" (Concerning the Team 4).

Two final elements which may appear in the prooemium of an encomium are, first of all, some mention by the orator or poet of the method he will use in his praise, especially if it is novel, and second, he will often contrast his encomium with the attempts others have made to treat the same theme. In regard to the former, we observed it in Pindar —who speaks of the novelty of setting his epinicia to both flute and lyre[372]—and in Isocrates, who regarded his use of prose in the Evagoras as a new technique (Evag. 8-10).[373] And in terms of the latter, judgments upon the efforts of other encomiasts are included in Isocrates (Evag. 11, Helen 14, Bus. 4, Oration V: To Philip 109) and in the Agathon speech of the Symposium (194e).[374]

---

[371] Above, 111-12.

[372] Above, 112.

[373] Above, 132-133.

[374] Criticism of other encomia or encomiasts is also expressed outside the prooemium; cf. Pindar, above, 121-22; Plato in the Menexenus, 239c; and in the defense Isocrates makes of his work, Antidosis 166.

(ii) The γένος

The second fixed topic which appeared in encomia throughout the course of our survey is that of the γένος. Treating both the immediate and remote ancestry of the subject,[375] it is of sufficient importance that it is covered in rhetorical handbooks out of every period, from Anaximenes to Aphthonius. Anaximenes recommends an enumeration of ancestors "from the beginning down," and with each one named, "mentioning something to his credit" (*Rhet. ad Alex.* 35.1440b.30).[376] Aristotle, although he did not name γένος as a separate topic in his proposal on arrangement, appears to look favorably on the way it was used by Isocrates and Gorgias:

> Epideictic speeches should be varied with laudatory episodes, after the manner of Isocrates, who is always bringing somebody in. This is what Gorgias meant when he said that he was never at a loss for something to say; for, if he is speaking of Peleus, he praises Achilles, then Aeacus, then the god; . . . (*Rh.* 3.17.11)

In the theory taught by the *ad Herennium* and Quintilian, it is clear that the γένος served a syncritistic purpose: to honor the ancestors was a form of praise for the subject of the encomium. We observed that the *auctor* of the *ad Herennium* wanted the encomiast to demonstrate that the person being praised was either the peer of or superior to his ancestors (*Rhet. Her.* 3.7.13),[377] and Quintilian remarks that ". . . it will be creditable to the objects of our praise not to have fallen short of the fair fame of their country and of their sires . . ." (Quint. 3.7.10).[378] The γένος is also enjoined in the *Progymnasmata* of the Second Sophistic rhetors, Hermogenes and Aphthonius, as we've had occasion to note above.[379]

Two aspects of genealogical theory merit further comment. The first is that both the immediate and remote ancestors of the person are extolled. To be sure, this is not a striking feature when the encomium is of a mythical figure, but it becomes quite evident when the encomiast is working

---

[375]Burgess, "Epideictic Literature," 122; Volkmann, *Die Rhetorik,* 324-25.
[376]Above, 102-03.
[377]Above, 169.
[378]Above, 171.
[379]Cf. above, 174-75, for Hermogenes, and 175-76 for Aphthonius.

with historical personages. In such cases the γένος covers both historical
and legendary ancestors. Isocrates, for example, in his genealogy of
Evagoras, traces the latter's forebearers back from Teucer, the founder of
Salamis, to Aeacus and Zeus (*Evag.* 13-18). Moreover, Xenophon views
Agesilaus as a descendant of Heracles (*Ages.* 1.2), and likewise the son
Archidamus III is honored by Isocrates as of the line of Heracles and Zeus
(*Letter 9: To Archidamus* 3). The same mythical parentage is attributed to
Ptolemy Philadelphus by Theocritus (Id. 17.15-33).[380]

The other aspect that should be noted is the element of syncrisis which
the γένος introduces. Alongside the theoretical statements in the *ad
Herennium* and Quintilian, there are a number of passages in encomia
where it becomes clear that the genealogy has a syncritistic purpose. The
example that makes it most explicit is, again, that of *Evagoras* 12:

> I believe it is fitting that I should also recount them (viz.,
> Evagoras' ancestors) . . . that all may know that he proved
> himself not inferior to the noblest and greatest examples
> (παραδειγμάτων) of excellence which were of his inheri-
> tance.[381]

To this we may add Isocrates' *Concerning the Team* where the comparison
with ancestors is also apparent. The γένος of the elder Alcibiades is
introduced by his son with:

> . . . I desire very much to recount to you my father's private
> pursuits, going back a little to make mention of his ancestors,
> that you may know that from early times our standing and
> services have been the greatest and most honourable among
> the citizens of Athens (24).

The γένος then follows with its narration of the deeds of the Alcmeonidae, and once the younger Alcibiades begins the πράξεις of his father,
he makes it explicit that the deeds he is now relating are to be compared
with those of the ancestors:

---

[380]In the genealogy of Alcibiades, while Isocrates does not include
mythical figures, he does trace it back to the earliest times of Athens,
viz., Alcibiades' father was of the Eupatrids and his mother a member of
the Alcmeonidae. Cf. *Concerning the Team* 25.

[381]Cf. above, 102, 181.

> When he was admitted to citizenship, he (Alcibiades) showed
> himself not inferior to those whom I have mentioned, . . . from
> the beginning he was so fired with ambition that he thought
> that even their great deeds should be held in remembrance
> through his own (29).

The syncrisis effected through the use of genealogy need not always be
that of the positive examples provided by the ancestors. The comparison
may also be with a negative example which, in turn, will make the subject's deeds appear all the better. This seems to be the case in *Evagoras*
19-20 when, at the close of the γένος, Isocrates introduces the story of
the Phoenician who usurped the throne of Salamis from Evagoras' fathers.
This incident is understood by Isocrates to be part of the γένος in that
Evagoras' γένεσις does not begin until the following section (21), with the
ἀνατροφή and πράξεις following respectively.

(iii)  The πράξεις

In encomiastic theory the πράξεις was regarded as the chief topic.[382]
Both Hermogenes (τὸ δὲ κυριώτατον αἱ πράξεις) and Aphthonius explicitly identify it as such,[383] and it is discussed in all of the extant rhetorical treatises from Anaximenes to Quintilian.

First of all, in outlining how the πράξεις should be developed,
Anaximenes appears to favor the topical approach taken by Gorgias,
Xenophon and Plato in his speech of Agathon:[384]

> . . . we shall next set out the achievements of the person we
> are praising when an adult. We shall put first his justice
> (δικαιοσύνην), and after having magnified (αὐξήσαντες) this in
> a manner similar to what has been said already, we shall come
> to his wisdom (σοφίαν), . . . and after going through this in the
> same way, we shall set out his courage (ἀνδρείαν) . . . (*Rhet.
> ad Alex.* 35.1441b.5-10).

---

[382]Burgess, "Epideictic Literature," 123.
[383]For Hermogenes, cf. Rabe, *Hermogenis Opera*, 16; and cf. the
passage from Aphthonius' *Progymnasmata* in Clark, *Greco-Roman Education*, 197, quoted above, 175-76.
[384]Above, 140-41, 152.

Aristotle, too, seems to recommend an arrangement organized around the several categories of virtue:

In the epideictic style the narrative (διήγησις) should not be consecutive, but disjointed;

. . . . . . . . . . . . . . . . . . . . . . . . . . . . .

From some facts a man may be shown to be courageous (ἀνδρεῖος), from others wise (σοφός) or just (δίκαιος) (Rh. 3.16.1-2).

Similar treaments of this method were seen in our earlier discussions of the ad Herennium and Quintilian.[385] Quintilian, however, as was noted, also recommends the alternate method of arranging the topic (3.7.15): the chronological schema practiced by Isocrates in the Evagoras and else-where.[386] In addition to Isocrates' use of the method, it was employed by Plato in the Menexenus (239d-246a) where his recitation from time-to-time makes it clear that the deeds reported are evidences of the heroes' virtue (e.g., 241cd, 243a).[387] Thus the chronological πράξεις—witnessed in Isocrates, the Menexenus, and Quintilian—continued as a viable alternative to the topical πράξεις preferred by other rhetoricians.

Apart from the major division of the πράξεις into virtues and deeds, there is evidence that encomiasts often would classify deeds according to type, with the primary categories being deeds of war and those of peace.[388] Already in Pindar we saw an attempt to include achievements other than simply the victories in the games. Pythian II, for example, praised Hieron for his military exploits and his wise counsel.[389] Isocrates extolled Evagoras not only for his regaining the throne of Salamis and other military exploits, but for his public works—building a harbor, forti-fying the city, supplying it with new triremes, and introducing the arts (Evag. 47). Likewise, Busiris is celebrated for his skill as an administrator, which made the Egyptian political system one to be emulated, and as one who patronized philosophy and religion (Bus. 15-29). And Isocrates first

---

[385]Above, 169-70, 172.

[386]On the chronological arrangement of the πράξεις in Isocrates, cf. above, 137-39.

[387]Cf. Isocrates' attempt to punctuate the chronological recitation of Evagoras's deeds with reference to how his achievements manifest his virtues, above, 137-38.

[388]Burgess, "Epideictic Literature," 123-24.

[389]Cf. above, 117.

treats the military achievements of Alcibiades (*Concerning the Team* 29-30), after which he describes his victories in the chariot races (32-35), and finally, the manner in which he discharged his civic responsibilities (35-38).

Finally, it should be noted that the πράξεις was the topic within which the encomiast employed most of the commonplaces we described earlier under the heading of amplification.[390] As the deeds of the subject were recounted—either in chronological sequence or grouped according to the virtue they illustrated—the orator sought to magnify them by stressing the sheer number of them, the ease and frequency with which they were done, and the good and noble consequences they had.

(iv) Epilogue

The fourth and last of the topics employed in encomia of all periods is the epilogue. On the one hand, we have observed elements proper to the epilogue in the lyric poets,[391] while at the other extreme, it appears as one of the topics listed in Aphthonius' τάξις.[392] Although it was felt to be a required topic, considerable freedom was given to the encomiast in developing his epilogue:

> Like the προοίμιον its form depends upon what the subject or the circumstances suggest. It is often a brief summing up of the results of the life under discussion and an appeal to others to imitate his virtues. It ends most appropriately with a prayer.[393]

The freedom with respect to invention in the epilogue may account for the only brief attention given to it by Anaximenes and the *auctor* of the *ad Herennium*. All they recommend is that the epilogue include a summary or recapitulation of what has been said. To this amplifications, enthymenes, or maxims may be added, viz., the encomiast may make use of whatever commonplaces he deems relevant.

---

[390]Cf. above, 179-85.
[391]Cf. above, 109, 118-20.
[392]Cf. the list of topics in Aphthonius' *Progymnasmata* in Burgess, "Epideictic Literature," 120.
[393]Ibid., 126.

. . . when we have reached the conclusion of this section (viz., the πράξεις) and we have gone through all the species of virtue, we shall recapitulate (παλιλλογήσαντες) what we have said before in a summary (κεφαλαίῳ), and then affix either a maxim (γνώμην) or else a consideration (ἐνθύμημα) as a conclusion (τελευτήν) to the whole speech (Rhet. ad Alex. 35.1441b.10).

Our conclusions (conclusionibus) will be brief, in the form of a summary (enumeratione) at the end of the discourse; in the discourse itself we shall by means of commonplaces (locos communes) frequently insert brief amplifications (breves amplificationes) (Rhet. Her. 3.7.15).

In contrast to these simple prescriptions for a summary and amplifications, Aristotle—who it will be remembered once wrote that an epilogue was not essential—presents a more extensive theory for the conclusion to a speech. And since his recommendations are for speeches of all types, they would in general apply to the epideictic epilogue as well.

The epilogue (ἐπίλογος) is composed of four parts: to dispose the hearer favourably (κατασκευάσαι εὖ) towards oneself . . .; to amplify . . .; to excite the emotions of the hearer; to recapitulate (ἀναμνήσεως) (Rh. 3.19.1).

Aristotle adds, then, to the elements outlined by Anaximenes and the auctor one part designed to put the orator in the best light and an exhortation or an appeal to the audience's emotions. The first of these additions, however, seems to be designed primarily for forensic speeches where the speaker desires at the close of his oration to praise himself and blame his adversary. Consequently, it does not appear in the epilogues of encomia—for there we are not trying to win the audience's approval vis-à-vis an opponent. The other added element, though, coupled with the two Aristotle recommends in common with the ad Herennium and Anaximenes, may be seen in the conclusions to the encomia reviewed in the course of this study.

Thus recapitulation is employed in the epilogues to Isocrates' encomium of Timotheus and Xenophon's Agesilaus:

And now to sum up (κεφάλαιον) all this: In other times many calamities were wont to be visited upon the Hellenes, but under his leadership, no one can point to cities devastated, governments overthrown, men murdered or driven into exile, or any other of those ills that are irreparable (*Antidosis* 127).

I propose to go through the story of his virtue again, and to summarize it (ἐν κεφαλαίοις ἐπανελθεῖν τὴν ἀρετὴν αὐτοῦ), in order that the praise of it may be more easily remembered (*Ages.* 11.1).

The other element, whose place in the epilogue is recommended jointly by Anaximenes, Aristotle, and the *ad Herennium*, is the use of amplification. Here the usual commonplaces are utilized, as in the *Evagoras* (73) and the *Menexenus* (246ab) where Isocrates and Socrates/Aspasia respectively note that much more could be said concerning the deeds of their heroes, but time and space will not permit.

Aristotle's requirement that the epilogue include an appeal to the hearers' emotions is one of which abundant use was made in the encomia considered thus far. In fact, it gives every appearance of being the feature that is most characteristic of the epilogue. The purpose of the appeal is to exhort the hearer to join in the praise of the person being extolled, and/or to emulate his deeds and virtues. Employment of hortatory elements was seen above in Bacchylides and Pindar,[394] in Plato's speech of Agathon (*Symp.* 197e) and his *Menexenus* (248e),[395] and in Tacitus' *Agricola* (46).[396] Isocrates, too, concludes his encomia with similar appeals to the emotions: Nicocles is urged to follow the example of his father (*Evag.* 77); those who have the means are called on to honor Helen with sacrifices and thank-offerings, and philosophers "should speak of her in a manner worthy of her merits" (*Helen* 66); and Philip is exhorted to follow the example offered by Heracles, whom Isocrates has just eulogized (*Oration V: To Philip* 113-14). And Xenophon, alongside his extensive summary of Agesilaus' virtues in the epilogue, offers the Spartan king as a paradigm of virtue for all men to imitate:

. . . I think that the virtue of Agesilaus may well stand as a noble example (παράδειγμα) for those to follow (ἀσκεῖν) who wish to make moral goodness a habit (*Ages.* 10.2).

Moreover, it is under the heading of the appeal to emotions that we would

---

[394]Above, 109, 118-20.
[395]Above, 152 (speech of Agathon), p. 154 (*Menexenus*).
[396]Above, 173.

want to treat the prayer-element with which some encomia conclude. Pindar's epinicia often close with a prayer to Zeus for the continued well-being of the subject,[397] and we saw that Theocritus ends Idyll 17 by exhorting Ptolemy to pray for ἀρετή. [398]

A final item which is present in the epilogues of the *Evagoras* and the *Agesilaus,* but which is not integral to encomiastic epilogues in the theory of the handbooks, is the catalogue of blessings which was mentioned in our discussions of Isocrates and Xenophon.[399] Presumably, given the freedom accorded the encomiast, the presence of this element in the epilogues of these two works was the choice of the respective authors. There does not seem to be evidence of its presence in epilogues of the other encomia we have examined.

## E. THE FORM OF THE ENCOMIUM AND SIRACH 44-50

### 1. Proof by Amplification

Amplification, as has been seen, is the basic mark of the encomium; by the omission or suppression of discreditable incidents, by the attribution of qualities that do not exist, and by tailoring his narration, the encomiast seeks to portray his subject in the best possible light. I suggest that this is what Ben Sira is engaged in as he praises Simon II and the fathers of old in chaps. 44-50.

Earlier, in the discussion of Sirach 44-50 as an example of pre-rabbinic midrash, attention was called to Sirach's use of scripture.[400] There it was noted that he did not merely quote materials from "the Law, the Prophets and the other books of our fathers" (cf. Prologue to Sirach), but that he dealt freely with them, offering interpretations to suit his purposes. While he draws upon 1 Chronicles for his picture of David who ". . . placed singers before the altar," and ". . . gave beauty to the feasts, and arranged their times throughout the year, . . ." (47:9-10, RSV; cf. 1 Chr. 25:1-8, 23:24-32), he makes no mention of David's provisions for the building of the temple (cf. 1 Chr. 28). In this regard, then, Snaith calls attention to

---

[397] Above, 118-120.
[398] Above, 159-60.
[399] Above, 131-32, 142.
[400] Above, 48-50.

Ben Sira's uncritical use of biblical material.[401] But such uncritical use is quite in keeping with the goal of amplification. Evidently it suits Sirach's purpose to emphasize David's cultic role solely in terms of organizing Levites and musicians, thereby giving Solomon full responsibility for building the temple. Thus both figures are described as having innovated elements of the cultus alongside of their political or military achievements. Similarly, Ben Sira shifts emphases from those evident in the received tradition. While Moses is the dominant figure in the Pentateuch, he is subordinated to Aaron in the course of the Praise of the Fathers: Sirach devotes five verses to the former (45:1-5), but seventeen verses to the latter (45:6-22).[402] This subordination ought not be surprising, given the parallels, seen earlier, which he wants to establish between the priestly figures in the tradition and Simon II.[403]

Such a selective use of material will mean that the encomiast, in addition to altering his sources, will use them selectively, viz., he will omit those incidents which fail to bring credit to his subject. This procedure is certainly not new with Ben Sira, for in Hebrew literature it is obvious that the Chronicler did the same with his sources in Samuel-Kings. But as Ben Sira fails to mention certain persons in his *Beispielreihe* and suppresses discreditable details about others, his method is certainly in harmony with the practice of the encomiast.[404] Examples of amplification by omission in 44-50 include, first of all, the failure to mention the negative elements in the story of Jacob. There is no reference to Jacob's deceit in gaining the birthright (Gen 25:29-34) or stealing the blessing (Gen 27:1-45) away from Esau. Rather there is only a simple statement that the Most High made the blessing rest upon the head of Jacob (44:23), without calling any attention whatsoever to the circumstances under which Jacob obtained it. Another illustration of the suppression of less pleasing incidents may be in Sirach's failure to mention the details of the event in which Phinehas demonstrated his zeal for the Lord (45:23), viz., his murder of the Israelite and the Midianite woman whom he caught in an act of adultery (Num 25:6-9). While Ben Sira makes explicit that Phinehas' action had a positive consequence—that of atonement for Israel—perhaps

---

[401]Snaith, *Ecclesiasticus*, 235.

[402]Cf. Oesterley and Box, in Charles, *Apocrypha*, 479; te Stroete, "Van Henoch," 127.

[403]Cf. above, 12-17.

[404]Cf. Janssen, *Das Gottesvolk*, 17: "Er lässt alles Negative aus. . . ."

the circumstances of the incident, if related, would detract from the picture he sought to paint.

The most striking omissions in Sirach 44-50, however, are not in terms of the suppression of details and incidents, but of the failure to mention certain individuals altogether. Here the names of Joseph, Saul, and Ezra come to mind. Now while Joseph is, to be sure, mentioned at 49:15, it seems out of place. The context there is that of a catalogue of antediluvian figures—Enoch, Shem, Seth and Adam (plus Enosh in MS B)—where Joseph does not logically fit. We should expect to find him included, rather, back between 44:23 and 45:1, but Sirach instead passes directly from Jacob to Moses. Why? One possible answer is that the Joseph traditions were associated with the old Northern Kingdom of Israel, and hence with the Samaritans. Mention of Joseph in the sequence between Jacob and Moses might bring to mind the story of Jacob's adoption and blessing of Joseph's two sons, Ephraim and Manasseh (Gen 48). Moreover, the name of Joseph itself was used at times to identify the tribes of Ephraim and Manasseh (cf. Num 1:32, 36:1), as well as the Northern Kingdom as a whole (cf. the parallelism, Joseph//Ephraim, Manasseh, Benjamin, Ps 80:1-2 E.V. , 2-3 MT ). But Sirach has no love for the Samaritans, the remnant of the Joseph tribes, those "foolish people who live in Shechem" (50:26). His antipathy may have been occasioned, as Purvis has argued, by an active campaign waged by the Samaritans and the Transjordanian Tobiads against the policies of Simon II and the Jerusalem Tobiads.[405] Another possibility is suggested by Middendorp who says that Sirach may have pulled Joseph's name out of sequence to avoid the remembrance of the role he played as vizier to the Pharaoh.[406] If, as we are assuming, the Praise of the Fathers was written after Simon's death and during the high-priesthood of his son Onias III, Ben Sira may have wanted to avoid the appearance of approving Onias' switch from the pro-Seleucid sympathies of his father to adopting a pro-Ptolemaic stance by including the example of Joseph who served as an Egyptian official.[407] There is, however, still the problem of Joseph in 49:15. But I hope to show, when the *Beispielreihe*

---

[405] J. D. Purvis, "Ben Sira and the Foolish People of Shechem," *JNES* 24 (1965) 88-94. Qualified approval of Purvis's thesis is given by R. J. Coggins, *Samaritans and Jews: The Origins of Samaritanism Reconsidered* (Atlanta: John Knox, 1975) 84.

[406] Middendorp, *Die Stellung,* 56.

[407] On the transfer of allegiances by Onias III, cf. V. Tcherikover, *Hellenistic Civilization and the Jews* (Philadelphia: The Jewish Publication Society, 1966) 156.

is presented as the γένος of Ben Sira's encomium, that Joseph is an object of comparison here rather than an object of praise.

The omission of Saul in Sirach's list of heroes is not surprising, especially when we consider his glorification of David, his antipathy toward the Samaritans, his knowledge that Saul did not provide the example of piety he desired (cf., e.g., 1 Sam 15:1-35; 28:3-19; 1 Chr 10:13-14), and the fact that similar concerns had years before led the Chronicler to minimize the role of Saul. The omission of Ezra, however, is hard to understand. For how could Ben Sira—who honors the scribe (38:24; 39:1-11) and holds the Law of Moses (cf., e.g., 17:11-12; 23:23; 24:23; 41:8; 42:2; 45:5; 49:4) in such high regard—fail to mention Ezra, "a scribe skilled in the law of Moses which the Lord the God of Israel had given" (Ezra 7:6, RSV)? Commentators have advanced three proposals in explanation. The first, that of Smend, Rudolf, and Galling,[408] is that Ben Sira found Ezra's legislation on mixed marriages too severe; in the Jerusalem of the third and early second centuries, intermarriage was a matter of indifference. Thus embarrassment, over Ezra's command to those involved to repent and divorce their foreign wives (Ezra 9-10), led Sirach to omit him from his list of heroes. A second suggestion, offered by Herford, Oesterley, and Box,[409] concerns the difference between what the scribe was in Ezra's time and in Ben Sira's day. Ezra was not an important figure to Sirach in that the former's concern was narrowly and exclusively focused on the Mosaic law. But the scribes whom Ben Sira extols, and whom he teaches in his school, are not the priestly interpreters of the law like Ezra. Rather they are "secular" scribes, skilled not only in the Mosaic code, but in the breadth of the wisdom tradition as well (cf. 39:1b, ". . . seek out the wisdom [σοφίαν] of all the ancients, . . ."; 39:2-4).[410] The distinction, then, between the priest-scribe Ezra and the scribe of Ben Sira's day, coupled with a lack of references to Ezra in other materials until Josephus,[411] indicate that he was not an important figure either to

---

[408]Smend, *Commentary*, 474; W. Rudolph, *Chronikbücher* (HzAT: I, 21; Tübingen: J. C. B. Mohr (Paul Siebeck), 1955) x; and Galling, *Studien zur Geschichte Israels*, 129, n. 3.

[409]R. T. Herford, *Talmud and Apocrypha* (reprinted from the 1st ed. of 1933; New York: Ktav, 1971) 201-2; Oesterley and Box, in Charles, *Apocrypha*, 506.

[410]Cf. E. Bickermann, *From Ezra to the Last of the Maccabees* (New York: Schocken Books, 1962) 68-71.

[411]Cf. J. Myers, *Ezra-Nehemiah*, lxxii. Josephus' use of Ezra traditions is based upon 1 Esdras, the translating and editing of which most likely

Ben Sira or his time. Thus he was not included at Sir 49:13.[412]

While there may be truth to either or both of the above, the third proposal that has been made seems to me to relate more directly with the intention of the Praise of the Fathers. Ulrich Kellermann has argued that Ben Sira's purpose in extolling Simon II is for the benefit of Simon's son and successor Onias III.[413] Onias is not the high priest that his father was; to Sirach, while Onias may have been a pious man (cf. 2 Macc 3:1), he was not the strong political leader Simon had been. Rather Onias seemed to exemplify the political quietism once seen in Ezra.[414] Thus, according to Kellermann, Ezra represents a figure with whom Ben Sira would neither want to compare Simon nor want to offer as an example for Onias III to emulate.

Isocrates, it will be recalled, acknowledges in his *Busiris* that the encomiast will want to attribute qualities to his subject that do not exist. I submit that although once again there is biblical precedent here (e.g., the Chronicler attributing the plans for the temple to David, cf. 1 Chronicles 22), Sirach's act of supplementing his reports on various figures is an example of αὔξησις. Amplification of this type would appear to be behind Ben Sira's description of Moses' ordination of Aaron. In the narrative of Exodus 29, the bestowal of the priesthood upon Aaron and his sons is by a perpetual statute, חק עולם (29:9). The same phrase is used of Aaron by Sirach at 45:7, וישימהו לחק עולם. But later on in his narration of Aaron, he writes that Aaron's ordination was an everlasting covenant for him, ותהי לו ברית עולם (45:15). The notion of the priesthood being established as an everlasting ברית does not appear until the story of Phinehas, who

---

post-dates the book of Daniel. 1 Esdras 4:40a and 4:59-60 seem to be dependent on Dan 2:37 and 2:22-23 respectively. Cf. Eissfeldt, *Old Testament,* 576.

[412]Galling, *Studien zur Geschichte Israels,* suggests—in addition to his proposal regarding embarrassment over Ezra's stand on mixed marriages —that omission of Ezra at 49:13, and taking the *Rückblick* of 49:14-16 to be secondary, would place the narration of Nehemiah's and Simon's engineering achievements side-by-side. Although that comparison is intended, as we have shown, it is not dependent on the two figures being juxtaposed. Moreover, I will argue below that 49:14-16 is not secondary, but is an integral part of the γένος of Simon II.

[413]U. Kellermann, *Nehemiah: Quellen, Ueberlieferung und Geschichte* (BZAW 102; Berlin: Alfred Töpelmann, 1967) 112-15.

[414]Cf. Myers, *Ezra-Nehemiah,* lxii, lxxiv, regarding the lack of political activity attributed to Ezra.

was granted "the covenant of a perpetual priesthood" (ברית כהנת עולם)
(Num 25:13) because of his zeal for Yahweh. Thus Sirach extends the idea
of the priestly ברית to Aaron and thereby it becomes a *Stichwort* to link
together the priesthoods of Aaron (45:15), Phinehas ( . . . ברית שלום,
כהונה גדולה עד עולם, 45:24), and Simon II (ויקם לו ברית פינחס,
50:24).[415]

An honor attributed to Phinehas which is of Sirach's creation appears at
45:23 where the grandson of Aaron is called "the third in glory" (τρίτος
εἰς δόξαν).[416] The reference here seems to be to the trinity of Moses,
Aaron, and Phinehas, who alone make up the subject of chap. 45. Ben Sira,
then, puts Phinehas—who plays a relatively minor role in MT (in addition
to Num 25:6-13, cf. 31:6; Josh 22:13-34; Judg 20:27-28; Ps 106:30-31)—on
a par with Moses and Aaron. In addition to the rank given him by Sirach,
he has attributed to him the responsibility of managing the sanctuary
(לכלכל מקדש, 45:24) as a consequence of the covenant with him. Yet the
closest the MT comes to providing details of Phinehas' priestly duties is in
Num 31:6, where he carries the vessels of the sanctuary (כלי הקדש) into
the battle with Midian, and in Judg 20:28 where the Deuteronomistic
historian notes that Phinehas ministered (עמד) before the ark of the covenant at Bethel. Here again it appears that Ben Sira wants to magnify
Phinehas' role as a priest so that, in turn, he will be able to use him in
amplifying Simon II.

Other figures in the *Beispielreihe* of 44:16-49:16 to whom Sirach attributes actions not listed in MT include Elijah and Isaiah. After reporting on
a series of Elijah's achievements, which include both the miraculous
(48:3,5,9) and the political (48:6,8), the narration turns to the eschatological deeds which Elijah was expected to perform (48:10). Here Ben Sira

---

[415]The reference to the covenant of Phinehas in 50:24 appears only in
MS B. Since the Zadokite priesthood had long since been replaced by the
Hasmoneans by the time of the Greek translation (132 B.C.E.), the grandson omitted the reference to Simon and Phinehas in his translation of the
closing doxology. Cf. Smend, *Commentary*, 490.

[416]This line is partially destroyed in MS B. Smend, *Commentary*, 436,
who was followed by Oesterley and Box, 489, restored it to "[was glorious]
in might [as a third]," בגבורה נה[דר שליש]י. Vattioni's text, after Lévi,
proposes בגבורה נחל שלישי בהוד. But, if Smend, *Text*, 51, is correct,
there is not sufficient space in MS B for that long a restoration since it
appears to be as long as Peters' נחל כבוד שלישי, which he regards as
impossible.

employs the expectation from Mal. 4:5-6 [EV] (=3:23-24 [MT]), that Elijah
"will turn the hearts of fathers to their children . . ." But to that he adds
the prospect that Elijah will restore the tribes of Jacob (בט]‎ להכין‎
‎ל[ארש]י [48:10], cf. Greek καταστῆσαι φυλὰς Ἰακωβ). This interpretation
that the Malachi passage refers to the restoration of the tribes is new
with Sirach.[417] After Sirach's time it became a part of the rabbinical
exegesis of Malachi (cf. *Ed* 8:7 in the Mishnah). Restoration of the tribes
by Elijah may be Sirach's attempt to attribute a future "political" deed to
the prophet to go along with those he has already accomplished.

One of the incidents from the reign of Hezekiah that is utilized by Ben
Sira is the story of how, during the former's illness, Isaiah was able to
make the shadow recede ten steps on the sundial of Ahaz as a sign he
would be healed (2 Kgs 20:8-11). But in Sir 48:23 it is not the shadow
whose movement is affected by Isaiah's cry to Yahweh. Rather it is Isaiah
himself who brings about a movement of the sun and who lengthened the
life of the king. Although 48:23 is not extant in MS B, it is clear that it is
the sun which was mentioned, not the shadow (cf. Greek ἥλιος; Syriac
ܫܡܫܐ ). The intent here seems to be clearly one of amplification; it
serves to make Isaiah appear to be all the more a miracle-worker. And the
miraculous element is one that Ben Sira repeatedly stresses in his glorification of the heroes of Israel's past (cf. Joshua, 46:4; Samuel, 46:20;
Elijah; Elisha, 48:13-14). If the *Beispielreihe* serves the purpose of an
encomiastic γένος, then the amplification of the ancestors in such a
manner is to be expected.

Thus far, we have suggested that by his omissions, alterations, and
supplying of new material, Jesus Sirach was engaged in the same general
methods of amplification known from the Greek encomium. But in addition to these methods, I believe it can be sustained that he practiced some
of the specific techniques of amplification which were catalogued earlier.
It is to these that I now wish to turn.

### a. Comparison

In our discussion of the integrity of Sirach 44-50 we noted a series of
parallels which Ben Sira has drawn between the fathers and Simon II. It
would appear to me that these parallels serve as illustrations of amplification by comparison; in each case Simon's person and achievements are

---

[417]Snaith, *Ecclesiasticus*, 240.

seen in the light of the examples offered by the heroes of Israel's past. The comparisons which were identified are in three areas: first, there is the explicit comparison of Simon II with the priests Aaron and Phinehas;[418] second, the comparison implied in Sirach's emphasis on the cultic functions of political leaders (Joshua, Samuel, David, Solomon, Josiah), viz., leaders who, like Simon II, combined cultic and political responsibilities;[419] and third, another explicit comparison of the engineering achievements or public works of Simon with those of Solomon, Hezekiah, Zerubbabel/Joshua, and Nehemiah.[420] All of these fathers—priests, military heroes, kings, governors—are for Sirach types of the high priest.

Alongside this major use of syncrisis, Ben Sira employs what I would call minor forms of comparison as a way of amplifying his narration of particular figures. Thus in his description of Moses at 45:2 he is quick to develop the comparison of Exod 7:1 where Yahweh tells Moses, "See, I make you as God to Pharaoh" (ראה נתתיך אלהים לפרעה). MS B is fragmentary at this point, so we are unclear as to what the Hebrew was for Sirach's use of the Exodus phrase. Although the Greek translator evidently wanted to soften the boldness of the comparison (ὡμοίωσεν αὐτὸν δόξῃ ἁγίων),[421] the sense of comparison remains none-the-less. A proposed restoration of the Hebrew is ויכבדהו כאלהים, "And he honored him as God."[422] Vattioni's text, following Lévi,[423] proposes ויכנהו איש אלהים, a restoration which he does not support nor which is reflected in the Greek. Smend is of the opinion that there is insufficient space in the line for the former proposal of Peters, et al., and suggests ויכנהו באלהים, "And he compared him among the gods," where the Aramaic כון ("to compare") is suggested by the translation ὡμοίωσας of 36:12, and באלהים is seen as behind the δόξῃ ἁγίων of the Greek version.[424] In either case, the idea of comparison in Sirach's portrayal of Moses is retained from Exod 7:1.

---

[418]Above, 12-15.

[419]Above, 15-17.

[420]Above, 18-19.

[421]The Syriac translator chose to eliminate the comparison altogether, cf. ܘܣܓܝ ܠܗ ܒܒܘܪ̈ܟܢ , "And he made him great in blessings."

[422]Cf. Peters, Das Buch, 382-83; Kautzsch, Die Apokryphen, 452; and Segal, Seper ḥokmat, 74. Note that Bmg. adds the comment that the subject of the verb is Yahweh.

[423]Lévi, The Hebrew Text, 60.

[424]Smend, Commentary, 426.

Two elements of comparison are introduced into the account of David
in chap. 47. First, the story of David's selection from the sons of Jesse
(1 Sam 16:1-13) is presented in terms of a comparison: "For as fat is
selected from the offering, so was David from Israel" (כי כחלב מוּרָם מקדש
כן דוד מישראל) (47:2). The image is drawn from the prescriptions for the
sin-offering in Leviticus (cf. Lev 4:8,10,19) where the technical term for
separating the fat from the offering is the hiphil/hophal of רום. The hiphil
is used in Ps 89:20 [MT] (89:19 [EV]) where the context is that of David's
selection and anointing as king. It may be that Psalm 89's הרימותי בחור
מעם suggested to Sirach the מורם מקדש based on Leviticus 4.[425] The
second figure of comparison incorporated into the picture of David is
supplied from the narrative of 1 Sam 17:34-36. Here David argues with
Saul that he is capable of going up against Goliath in that while tending
his father's flock he was able to kill marauding lions and bears. But in Sir
47:3 the lions and bears become figures through which David's bravery is
amplified all the more: "With lions he played (שחק) as (one would) a kid,
and with bears as the herds (lit. 'sons') of Bashan (כבני בשן; cf. Deut
32:14)."[426] Whereas David once killed the beasts who attacked the flock,
now he plays with them as if they were domestic animals. The comparison
drawn here is similar to the commonplace we noted in encomia whereby
the ease with which the subject acts in difficult circumstances is emphasized.

A syncritistic element that Sirach draws from the tradition is the note
in 1 Kgs 10:27 that Solomon made "silver as common in Jerusalem as
stone, and . . . cedar as plentiful as the sycamore of the Shephelah." Ben
Sira, however, modifies the terms of comparison to "you heaped up gold
like iron and like dust you multiplied silver" (47:18b, MS B). The Greek
reads "tin" (χασσίτερον) in place of "iron" (ברזל), which the Syriac understands to be "lead" ( ܐܒܪܐ ), and "lead" (μόλιβον) for "dust" (עפרת =
Syr. ܐܒܪܐ ), but otherwise the comparison is the same. In view of the
law of the king in Deut 17:17 proscribing the accumulation of vast sums of
gold and silver, Smend and Peters take the comparison to be used nega-
tively of Solomon.[427] Yet given the context where v 18 stands at the

---

[425]Cf. Oesterley and Box, "Book of Sirach," 494.

[426]The Greek and Syriac translators seem to have been working from a
text which read כבני צאן or כבני כבשים, instead of כבני בשן. Cf. ἐν
ἄρνασιν προβάτων, ܐܡܪܐ and Smend, Commentary, 449.

[427]Smend, Commentary, 455; and Peters, Das Buch, 407. Although
Peters prefers the negative interpretation, he admits the comparison can
reflect favorably on Solomon.

close of Sirach's narration of Solomon's great deeds and wisdom, I would take the amplification of Solomon's wealth as having a positive purpose. It then is followed at v 19 with a report on the one negative item: how his wives were able to dominate him (cf. Ben Sira's thoughts on wicked women, 25:16-26; 26:5-12). The report here, though, would appear to be introduced with an adversative *waw*, viz.,

> You heaped up gold like iron
> and like dust you multiplied silver.
> But you put (ותתן) a stain on your glory . . .(47:18b-19a)

Thus the comparison describing Solomon's wealth stands as the final element of amplification in the favorable account Sirach gives of his deeds.

In our discussion of the various types of comparison employed in encomia we included the simile in that, as McCall points out, ancient rhetorical theory did not discriminate between it and other forms. Because of this, we need to examine Ben Sira's use of simile under the heading of comparison.

The simile appears to be one of Sirach's favorite literary forms. In addition to his use of similes in Sirach 44-50, they may be found elsewhere in the book (cf. esp. 24:13-17; also 21:2-3,8,16,18-19,21; 22:17; 26:7,16-18) and in other Hebrew wisdom material (cf. e.g., Prov 4:18-19; 11:22; 26:1-2,7-11,18-19). As they are employed in the Praise of the Fathers, they serve to enhance Ben Sira's description of four figures in the *Beispiel-reihe*—Solomon, Elijah, Josiah, and Zerubbabel—as well as to provide a striking picture of Simon II in 50:6-10. Solomon with his abundant wisdom is likened to an overflowing river: תצף כיאר מוסר (47:14), while Elijah "arose like fire" (קם נביא כאש) and "his words burned like a torch" (דבריו כתנור בוער) (48:1). Presumably inspiration for the latter pair of similes came from Mal 4:1 (=3:19 MT). Josiah's name[428] is likened by Sirach to fragrant incense (כקטרת סמים) and his memory to the sweetness of honey on the palate (בחך כדבש ימתיק זכרו) and a song at a banquet (כמזמור על משתה היין) (49:1). The simile regarding Zerubbabel is incorporated directly from Hag 2:23—he is "like a signet ring on the right hand" (כחתם על יד ימין) (49:11).

---

[428]"Name" in MS B and Syriac. The Greek has "memory" (μνημόσυνον) which it has moved up from 49:1c. Cf. Smend, *Commentary*, 468.

The most impressive use of similes by Sirach is the series of eleven he employs to portray the appearance of Simon II when he emerges from the Holy of Holies on the Day of Atonement (50:6-10). His countenance is described as like the morning star, the full moon, the sun shining on the temple, a rainbow, blossoms on the day of the first fruits, lilies, green shoots on Lebanon, fire and incense in the censer, a vessel of gold, an olive tree, and a cypress. And when Simon is depicted offering the daily sacrifices (50:11-16) two additional similes are used: in MS B the priests assisting Simon are compared to young cedars of Lebanon and poplars by a stream (כערבי נחל) (50:12), while the Greek divides the two similes, comparing Simon to the cedars and the other priests to the stems of palm trees (ὡς στελέχη φοινίκων).[429]

### b. The Commonplace of Inadequacy

Among the several commonplaces utilized by encomiasts for the purpose of amplification is the one in which the rhetor or poet protests his sense of inadequacy in view of the magnitude of the task: the subject's deeds and virtues are too numerous to do justice to them. In our discussion of this commonplace we observed that, although it is most appropriate to the prooemium, it can appear elsewhere in the arrangement of the encomium.

Sirach 44-50 appears to contain one example of this commonplace. In the praise of Zerubbabel and the high priest Joshua in chap. 49, Sirach exclaims: "How shall we magnify Zerubbabel?" (מה נגד[ל] [זרובבל]) (49:11a).[430] Set alongside this exclamation of inadequacy, then, is the simile, referred to above, of the signet ring. How is one able to describe one as great as this? For this governor completed the rebuilding of the temple, and in him we see a type of the high priest—one who combines both cultic and political responsibilities as Simon II did.

### c. The Commonplace of Unique or Unprecedented Actions

To attribute unique or unprecedented actions to one's subject was a

---

[429]The Syriac lacks 12de.

[430]Although none of 49:11a in MS B is extant save the lamedh on נגדל, there seems to be no question as to the restoration as given. Cf. Gk. πῶς μεγαλύνωμεν τὸν Ζοροβαβελ; and Syr. ܐܠܘ ܝܕܥܢ ... Cf. Smend, Commentary, 473.

commonplace we observed in the epinicia of the lyric poets, the encomia
of Isocrates and Xenophon, and we saw it enjoined in the handbooks of
Anaximenes, Aristotle, Cicero, and Quintilian. Ben Sira, too, employs
similar forms of amplification in the *Beispielreihe* of 44:16-49:16. In
describing the vestments of Aaron—vestments with which he compares
those of Simon II (cf. 50:9,11)[431]—he concludes by saying: "Before him
there had been none such, and from of old no foreigner ever put them on"
(לפניו לא היה כן מעולם לא לבשם זר) (45:13ab). Due to the fragmentary
condition of MS B, we are uncertain of the restoration of 13b. The Greek
ἕως αἰῶνος suggests עד-עולם, rather than the Lévi-Vattioni proposal of
מעולם. Smend and others, then, would prefer 13b to read ועד-עולם לא,
לבשם זר "And no foreigner will ever put them on."[432] For similar idioms
cf. Exod 10:14, where the locust plague in Egypt was such "as had never
been before, nor ever shall be again," and 1 Kgs 10:12, where the almug
wood used in the temple was of a kind that has not "been seen until this
day." Irregardless of how 13b is read, the uniqueness of Aaron's vestments
is stressed.

In the narration of Elisha, Sirach incorporates three examples of this
commonplace:

> All his days (מימיו) he did not tremble
>     before anyone (לא זע מכל),[433]
> And no one ruled his spirit
>     (ולא משל ברוחו כל בשר).
> Nothing was too hard for him . . .
>     (כל דבר לא נפלא ממנו) (48:12e-13a).

To judge from the Greek translation of Sirach's grandson, the *Rückblick*
of 49:14-16 contains statements regarding the uniqueness of two figures,
Enoch and Joseph.

> No one (οὐδείς) like Enoch has been created on earth, . . .
> Nor (οὐδέ) like Joseph has any man been born, . . . (49:14a,
> 15a).

The first of the two commonplaces is not as definite in the Hebrew of MS

---

[431]Cf. above, 13.

[432]Smend, *Commentary*, 432; Peters, *Das Buch*, 385; and Kautzsch, *Die
Apokryphen*, 454.

[433]On the idiom לא זע מן, "Did not tremble before," cf. Esther 5:9.

B, yet it still expresses something of the incomparability of Enoch: "Few (מעט) have been formed (נוצר) on earth like Enoch" (49:14a).[434] The Hebrew of 15a may be read as a rhetorical question expressing the uniqueness of Joseph, as Peters and Oesterley-Box have done,[435] viz., "Like Joseph (כיוסף) was ever a man born (אם נולד גבר)?" I have, however, a somewhat different reading of 15 b which will be presented in the context of our discussion of 49:14-16 as a part of the γένος of this encomium of Simon II.

Two further instances of where the Greek translator is reading the Hebrew as if it contained commonplaces of incomparability are 48:4, regarding Elijah, and 44:19b in the description of Abraham. The Greek of 48:4 reads:

> How glorious you were, Elijah, in your wondrous deeds!
> And who (τίς) as you (ὅμοιός σοι) can boast of themselves?

The Hebrew, however, seems to require a slightly different interpretation which would weaken the sense that we have here a commonplace of the type we have been discussing:

> How awesome you were, Elijah!
> Whoever (אשר) is like you (כמון),
> let him boast of himself (יתפאר)!

For the Hebrew to have expressed the rhetorical question of the Greek, we would expect the interrogative pronoun מי rather than the relative particle אשר. Yet, although Smend is of the opinion that the אשר is original,[436] this may be questioned. First of all, the Syriac translator of 48:4b employs the interrogative ܡܐ at the opening of the half-verse, and secondly, whenever the Greek renders the relative particle אשר, it regularly uses a Greek relative (e.g., ὅς) or conjunctions (e.g., γάρ, ἵνα); only once is τίς used, and that is here in 4b.[437] The interrogative τίς, rather, is always used to render מי or מה.[438] Thus the Greek and Syriac may very

---

[434]The Syriac ܢܩܦܝ̈ܢ witnesses to the מעט of MS B.
[435]Peters, *Das Buch*, 420; Oesterley and Box, "Book of Sirach," 506.
[436]Smend, *Commentary*, 459.
[437]Barthélemy and Rickenbacher, *Konkordanz*, 43-44.
[438]Ibid., 219; also, cf. R. Smend, *Griechisch-syrisch-hebräischer Index zur Weisheit des Jesus Sirach* (Berlin: Georg Reimer, 1907) 226-27.

well witness to an original מי in 48:4b, such that we would have מי כמוך
יתפאר: "Who will boast of himself as you (are able)?", giving us a rhetorical question to express the unique quality of Elijah.

As the Greek interprets 44:19b, it does so by stressing the incomparability of Abraham:

> Abraham was the great father of a multitude of nations,
> And no one has been found like him in glory
> (καὶ οὐχ εὑρέθη ὅμοιος ἐν τῇ δόξῃ).

The reading ὅμοιος seems to be an error for μῶμος ("blame"), regularly
used in Sirach and in the LXX to translate מום ("blemish").[439] מום does
appear in the Hebrew of MS B, as does the synonymous דופי in B mg. (cf.
Ps 50:20, "stain"), and ܡܘܡ in Syriac. Thus the original of 44:19b is:
לא נתן בכבודו מום, "He did not put a blemish on his honor." μῶμος is
restored to 44:19b in the Greek text of Ziegler which, in turn, is employed
in Vattioni. In the narration of Abraham, then, there does not appear any
use of the commonplace of uniqueness by Ben Sira.

#### d. Actions that Produced Good or Desirable Results

Anaximenes, in his discussion of amplification in epideictic, recommended that the encomiast should show "that the actions of the persons in
question have produced many . . . good results."[440] Certainly this can be
said of the actions of Simon II and the figures with whom he is favorably
compared in Sirach 44-50. Simon is celebrated for his repairs on the
temple, the reservoir (אשיח/מקוה) he had quarried,[441] and his fortification
of Jerusalem (50:1-4). Moreover, the manner in which he discharged his

---

[439]Cf. Barthélemy and Rickenbacher, *Konkordanz*, 211.

[440]Above, 183.

[441]For מקוה, cf. the parallel in Sirach's description of Hezekiah's
water system. The rare term אשיח appears as אשוח in the inscription of
King Mesha of Moab where he recounts how he built Baal-meon and put a
reservoir in it. Cf. H. Dönner and W. Röllig, *KAI, I: Texte*, no. 181, line 9.
אשיח is used to identify four different reservoirs or basins in 3Q15: one at
Qumran, one in Jericho, one in a village whose name is not given, and the
last one that of Bethesda/Beth-zatha. Cf. M. Baillet, et al., *'Les petites
grottes' de Qumran: Texte* (DJD 3; Oxford: Clarendon, 1965) 244.

cultic responsibilities on the Day of Atonement (50:5-10,20-21) and at the daily offerings (50:11-19) is presented in glowing terms. The assessment of his deeds is most positive.

And in the *Beispielreihe* of 44:16-49:16, the only figures about whom a critical word is spoken are Solomon, Rehoboam, and Jeroboam. But as we've seen, Solomon's only fault is that he let himself be controlled by his passions (47:19) which had as its consequence the division of the kingdom (47:20-21). Otherwise Solomon's virtue and achievements are extolled (47:12-18). The actions of Rehoboam and Jeroboam, in accordance with the received tradition (1 Kings 12-14; 2 Chronicles 10-12), are dismissed in vituperative terms: playing on the name Rehoboam (רחבעם), Ben Sira calls him "great of foolishness and deficient of insight" (רחב אולת וחסר בינה) (47:23c). The only other negative elements in the *Beispielreihe* are the judgments sounded on the people of the Northern Kingdom (48:15-16) and the kings of Judah apart from David, Hezekiah, and Josiah (49:4-5). But even these serve the purpose of amplification: the iniquity of the Northern Kingdom is set off over against the piety and deeds of Elijah and Elisha (48:1-14), while the faithfulness of the three great kings of Judah is magnified by comparing them with all the others, for "all of them acted ruinously" (כלם השחיתו) (49:4).

In regard to the fathers whom Ben Sira sets forth as noble examples in 44:16-49:16, a cursory glance will reveal that their actions are all judged to have produced desirable results: Noah guaranteed a remnant, nations were blessed through Abraham, Moses received the commandments, Phinehas made atonement for Israel, Joshua restrained the people from sin, Zerubbabel and Joshua rebuilt the temple, and Nehemiah raised the walls that had fallen, to name but a few. And throughout, the theme which may be traced in the report of each of these heroes, or to put it a different way, the virtue which manifests itself in the actions of each is that of piety or fidelity to the commandments.[442] Consistently the heroes of Israel—from those of the earliest times to Simon II himself—have acted with faithfulness. In a sense this theme is comparable to the commonplace in encomia whereby the actions of the subject reflect the character of the man.[443]

---

[442]Cf. the discussion of this, above, 37-38, 68.
[443]Cf. above, 184-185.

### e. Stylistic Factors in Amplification

As was true of the Greek encomium, it appears to me that Ben Sira practiced amplification through his selection of certain words, phrases, and rhetorical devices. In terms of specific words, an example may be seen in 45:12 where Aaron's headdress is pictured as a "gold crown" (עטרת פז) and "turban" (מצנפת). In Ezek 21:31 (MT; 21:26 [EV]), the two terms are used of the royal headdress of King Zedekiah. While "turban" (מצנפת) may be used of the high priest, as in Exod 28:4, the "crown" is a royal symbol only (cf. the king's עטרת פז, Ps 21:4 [21:3 EV]). By his use of the latter in describing Aaron's vesture Sirach may be amplifying the political authority he attributes to the high priest.[444] Also, it has been suggested that Ben Sira intentionally applied the term נזיר to Samuel (46:13), viz., "A Nazir of Yahweh in prophecy, Samuel, a judge and a priest," interpreting 1 Sam 1:22 as if Samuel had been a Nazirite. Yet the identification of Samuel as such is not unique to Ben Sira—for 4 Q Sam[a] refers to Samuel as a Nazir in its account of Hannah's presentation of Samuel at Shiloh.[445]

The rhetorical or didactic question is a device of which Sirach makes use on numerous occasions in the course of the book;[446] it is a popular form in wisdom materials (e.g., Prov 18:14; 20:6,24; 30:4; Job 9:2,4,12, 19,24; 11:7-8,10; *passim*), and it is employed as a wisdom element in prophetic materials (cf.,e.g., Amos 3:3-6,8; 6:2,12; Isa 40:12-14,18,21-22,25-26). And in the encomium we have seen the rhetorical question utilized as a way of expressing the commonplace of uniqueness or incomparability. We may see the rhetorical question functioning in this manner in Ben Sira. Three instances are in his portrayal of Joshua:

Who was he that could stand firm before him
(מי הוא לפניו יתיצב)?
     For (כי) he fought the battles of Yahweh.
Did not the sun stand still by his hand
(הלא בידו עמד השמש)?

---

[444]Cf. J. G. Snaith, "Biblical Quotations in the Hebrew of Ecclesiasticus," *JTS* N. S. 18 (1967) 7 n. 3.

[445]Cf. M. R. Lehmann, "Ben Sira and the Qumran Literature," *RQ* (1961) 104.

[446]Cf. 2:10; 10:29; 12:13; 13:2,17,18; 17:27; 31:27; 34:23-24 (=31:28-29 Gk.).

And one day become as two
(יום אחד היה לשנים)? (46:3-4).

The Greek reproduces all three rhetorical questions, although under the influence of the narrative in Josh 10:14 it construes לפניו in a temporal sense, viz., πρότερος.[447] The Syriac retains the first of the three ( ܣܘܡ , 46:3a), but under the influence of כי (46:3b), v 4 opens with ܐܠܐ ܘ rather than with an interrogative.[448]

At 49:11 a rhetorical question is used to express the commonplace of inadequacy of which mention was made earlier: "How (מה, πῶς) shall we magnify Zerubbabel?" And there are two verses which the Greek translator interprets to be rhetorical questions, but which are not so, in MS B. the Greek of 47:4 asks regarding David,

In his youth did he not kill a giant,
And take away reproach from the people,
When he lifted his hand with a stone in the sling,
And struck down the boasting of Goliath?

In the Hebrew, however, it is in the form of a declarative statement:

In his youth he struck down a mighty man
(בנעוריו הכה גבור)
And turned aside disgrace forever . . . (47:4ab).

Another rhetorical question that shows up in the Greek, but not in MS B, is one we already noted in the description of Elijah at 48:4b. But there, it will be remembered, we suggested that the τίς and ܡܢ of the Greek and Syriac translations may point to a Hebrew text with מי instead of the אשר of MS B.

Another stylistic device utilized in Sirach 44-50 that appears to serve the purpose of αὔξησις is in a series of exclamations introduced by מה:

How glorious was he (Joshua) when he stretched out his hands
(מה נהדר נטותו יד) . . . (46:2a).
How wise you (Solomon) were in your youth
(מה חכמת בנעריך) . . . (47:14a).
How awesome were you, Elijah,

---

[447]Cf. Smend, *Commentary*, 440.
[448]Ibid.

(48:4a). . . (מה נורא אתה אליהו).
How glorious was he (Simon II) when he looked out from the
tent (מה נהדר בהשגיחו מאהל) . . . (50:5a).

Note especially the verbal correspondence between 46:2a and 50:5a.

A final stylistic device of which frequent use is made in encomia is the
superlative. At 50:1 there is a superlative with which Ben Sira begins the
narration of Simon's achievements. The verse in MS B (to which the Syriac
also witnesses) opens with the phrase    גדול אחיו תפארת עמו (= Gk
49:15b). The adjective גדול, when in construct with a definite noun such
as אחיו here, may be taken as a superlative.[449] Thus Jesus Sirach opens
his praise of Simon with:

> Greatest of his brothers and the glory of his people was Simon
> son of Onias (Johanan) the priest . . . (50:1ab).

## 2. Arrangement or τάξις

In Part I of this study we argued that the Hymn in Praise of the Fathers
extends from 44:1 through 50:24, viz., the verses of chap. 50 which extol
Simon II are an integral part of the poem.[450] Moreover, a case was made
that within the hymn, 44:16-49:16 represent a distinct unit in the form of
a *Beispielreihe*.[451] Thus the Praise of the Fathers would appear to fall
into three sections: 44:1-15; 44:16-49:16; and 50:1-24. The lattermost,
however, may be sub-divided into vv 1-21 and vv 22-24. This division is
suggested by a change in subject-matter. Up through 50:21 Ben Sira has
been celebrating Simon II, a celebration which comes to a climax in vv 20-
21 with a description of Simon's blessing of the congregation on the Day
of Atonement. With v 22 we see Sirach shift to an imperative mood; the
balance of the hymn is a doxology wherein the congregation is called upon
to bless the Lord, after which comes a prayer that Yahweh would continue
his favor toward those of Simon's line (cf. 24ab MS B; omitted in Gk.). We
have already noted that this doxological section parallels the structure of
the doxology/prayer of 45:25ef-26 (MS B; Gk. omits 25ef).[452] Thus 50:22-
24 is to be marked off from the praise of Simon in vv 1-21. Having done

---

[449]Cf. E. Kautzsch and A. E. Cowley, *Gesenius' Hebrew Grammar* (2d
English ed.; Oxford: Clarendon, 1910) secs. 132c, 133g.
[450]Above, 10-21.
[451]Above, 32-48.
[452]Above, 6.

this, the whole of Sirach 44-50 may be divided, then, into four units: an introductory section, 44:1-15, where the subject is the praise of men in general; the *Beispielreihe* of 44:16-49:16; the praise of Simon II in 50:1-21; and the concluding doxology/prayer of 50:22-24. I propose that these four sections are the prooemium, the γένος, the πράξεις, and the epilogue of an encomium by Sirach on Simon II. To support this I would like to comment on the four sections in turn.

### a. The Prooemium: Sir 44:1-15

In our summary of the form of the prooemium attention was called to the freedom permitted the encomiast in developing this particular topic of the τάξις.[453] That freedom is evident in the manner with which Pindar, Isocrates, Xenophon, and Theocritus introduce their prooemia. Isocrates' *Helen* and *Busiris* open with criticisms of the eristic philosophers and the rhetor Polycrates respectively, while his *Evagoras* begins with reference to Nicocles, Evagoras' son, whom Isocrates observed honoring the tomb of his father. There are, however, encomia whose opening lines suggest the summons to praise of Sir 44:1. Pindar's second Olympian commences with:

> Ye hymns which rule the lyre: What God, what hero, aye, and what man shall we loudly praise? . . . Theron must be proclaimed by reason of his victorious chariot . . . (1-2, 5-6) (cf. also Pyth. 2.3-5; Oly. 9.4-9).[454]

And Theocritus introduces his encomium of Ptolemy with:

> From Zeus let us begin, and with Zeus in our poems, Muses, let us make end, for of immortals he is best; but of men let Ptolemy be named, first, last, and in the midst, for of men he is most excellent (Idyll 17.1-4).

The *Agesilaus*, however, would seem to offer a closer parallel in that—in contrast to the above two examples where the note of praise is sounded for the particular individual who is the encomium's subject—Xenophon proclaims that both the subject and his ancestry are worthy of praise: "On one account his fatherland and his family (τὴν τε πατρίδα καὶ τὸ γένος

---

[453]Above, 193.
[454]Quoted above, 111.

αὐτοῦ) are worthy to be praised together (κοινῇ ἄξιον ἐπαινέσαι)"
(Ages. 1.4). In this light compare Sir 44:1:

Let me now praise pious men, our fathers in their generations
(אהללה-נא אנשי חסד את-אבותינו בדורותם).[455]

As Xenophon began his encomium of Agesilaus with the praise of his
fathers, so Ben Sira begins his praise of Simon II by extolling all those
pious men who preceded him in Israel of old.

Within the prooemium we noted that, despite the freedom with respect
to invention, rhetors tended to use certain commonplaces that were
thought to be appropriate. One of these is that of a summary of the
speech to follow. As was noted,[456] Anaximenes recommends it and we
saw an example of one in Plato's Menexenus. Moreover, Plato has Agathon
open his encomium on Eros with a brief summary, viz., the statement seen
earlier that Agathon will divide his speech between what Eros is and what
he does (Symp. 195a).[457]

It appears to me that a summary of those who will be praised is what
Sirach has provided in 44:2-7. In the space of these verses he catalogues
the various types of individuals who are deserving of praise. There have
been questions as to the identity of the particular figures Ben Sira would
see included in each of the several categories: Lévi and Ryssel take them
to be foreign kings and other worthies,[458] while Snaith regards vv 2-7 to
refer to "Jews in general" in contrast to the specific heroes narrated from
44:16 on.[459] Over against both of these suggestions, I would see the
categories listed here as summarizing the individuals whom Sirach will
single out for praise in 44:16 through 50:21, viz., Adam to Simon II.[460]

---

[455]The Greek translator changes the singular cohortative of the
Hebrew (MS B and Masada) to a plural, αἰνέσωμεν. The Syriac translator
evidently failed to understand the enclitic נא and rendered the verb as a
simple imperfect, although he retained the singular form of the Hebrew,
ܢܫܒܚ ܐܢܐ . The Masada scroll provides a witness to the verses of
the prooemium; in v 1 it adds the את, along with Bmg. The sign of the
accusative does not appear in MS B here. Cf. Yadin, Ben Sira Scroll, 34.

[456]Above, 194.

[457]Above, 152.

[458]Cf. the reference to Lévi and Ryssel in Oesterley and Box, "Book of
Sirach," 480.

[459]Snaith, Ecclesiasticus, 216.

[460]Cf. Oesterley and Box, "Book of Sirach," 479.

Thus "rulers of the earth in their kingdoms and men of reknown in their might" (44:3ab)[461] would include David, Solomon, Hezekiah, and Josiah; "counsellors" and "prophets" (44:3cd) would be Moses, Joshua (cf. 46:1 where he is Moses' successor in prophesying), Samuel, Nathan, Elijah, Elisha, etc.; "princes of the nation" (44:4ab) (שרי גוי Masada; cf. Gk. λαοῦ, MS B גוים)[462] may mean Zerubbabel, Nehemiah, and the priests Aaron, Phinehas, and Joshua (49:12), who as types of the high priest of Sirach's day had political responsibilities;[463] the composers of proverbs (44:4cd,5b) would include Solomon (cf. 48:14-17);[464] by the psalmists of 44:5a, Sirach may have meant David and the singers he placed before the altar (cf. 47:8-9); and finally, the men of resources (44:6) would suggest the patriarchs and perhaps Job (cf. 49:9 MS B. "And also he [viz., Ezekiel] remembered Job [איוב]. . .").[465] Oesterley and Box, as well as Peters, would break the six categories I have listed down into twelve.[466] This, however, fails to take into consideration the poetic parallelism of vv 3-7, wherein the bi-cola each refer to one category of Israel's heroes, not two.

In addition to such a summary statement that introduces the subject to the audience, prooemia will often utilize the commonplace through which the encomiast speaks of the sense of duty or obligation he feels toward the subject to sing his praise. When we reviewed the shape of the Greek encomium, we observed that both Aristotle and the *auctor* of the *ad Herennium* commended the use of this theme, and reference was made to how the commonplace was developed in the encomia of Isocrates,

---

[461]41:3ab is omitted in the Masada scroll, but Yadin believes the 3ab of MS B is original and that the Masada copyist inadvertently failed to include it. Cf. Yadin, *Ben Sira Scroll, 35*.

[462]גוי here refers to Israel. Cf. Yadin, *Ben Sira Scroll, 35*, and e.g., Gen 12:3, Exod 19:6, Deut 4:6-8.

[463]For a new interpretation of 4b, the parallel line to "princes of the nation," cf. Skehan, "Staves and Nails," 67-69. Msgr. Skehan interprets the במחקקתם (Mas., במחקרותם of MS B) to refer to "staves." Thus 4b "governors with their staves" parallels 4a "resolute princes of the nation."

[464]Skehan, "Staves and Nails," 67-69, proposes a solution to the reading of במשמרותם in 4d for which he would read "nails" (cf. Eccl 12:11). Thus מושלים במשמרותם, "forgers of epigrams with their nails," with "nails" balancing the "staves" of 44:4b.

[465]The Greek translator read Job (איוב) as "enemy" (אויב), hence the ἐχθρῶν in "He remembered the enemies in a storm" where the Greek understands God to be the subject rather than Ezekiel.

[466]Oesterley and Box, "Book of Sirach," 374; Peters, *Das Buch*, 480.

Xenophon's *Agesilaus,* and the *Menexenus* of Plato.[467] The encomiast believes such praise is necessary so that his subject will be remembered in coming generations. Pindar and Isocrates express this conviction as follows:

> When men are dead and gone, it is only the loud acclaim of praise that surviveth mortals and revealeth their manner of life to chroniclers and bards alike (Pyth. 1.92-94).

> But the spoken words which should adequately recount the deeds of Evagoras would make his virtues never to be forgotten among all mankind (*Evag.* 3).

And that men may find themselves extolled by the encomiast, they

> . . . prefer a glorious death . . . zealously seeking glory . . . doing all that is in their power to leave behind them a name that shall never die (*Evag.* 3).

> They are ready to run all risks . . . to spend money and undergo any sort of toil, and even to die, for the sake of leaving behind them a name that shall be eternal (Plato, *Symp.* 208cd).

But as the heroes of Greece sought to leave a name that could be celebrated by the encomiast, Jesus Sirach saw his purpose in 44-50 to continue the praise of those fathers of Israel whose deeds deserved remembrance. Thus he concludes his summary of the fathers with two bicola which reflect the themes seen in Pindar, Isocrates, and Plato:

> All these were honored in their generations,
> (כל אלה בדרם נכבדו)
> And in their days had glory.
> (ובימיהם תפארתם)
> There are some of them who have left a name,
> (יש מהם הניחו שם)
> To tell of it among their inheritance.
> (לשתענות [Bmg. להשתעות] בנחלתם) (44:7-8)[468]

---

[467]Above, 195-97.

[468]44:7a is as it appears in the Masada scroll; in MS B נכבדו has dropped out. In 44:7b בימיהם is suggested by Bmg., Greek and Syriac as over against the מימיהם of MS B. Either verb is possible in 8b—the hish-

In contrast to these forefathers of Simon whom he will extol in the
course of his hymn, Sirach acknowledges those who failed to do righteous
deeds, who consequently have no encomiast to honor them and who will
leave no remembrance:

And there are some of them who have left no memorial,
(ויש מהם אשר אין לו זכר)[469]
So that they disappeared when they came to an end;
(וישבתו כאשר שבתו)
They became as though they never had been,
(כאשר לא היו היו)
And their sons after them.
(בניהם מאחריהם) (44:9)

Although similar idioms appear in Hebrew and hellenistic Jewish literature,[470] note how Ben Sira's reference to those who perish for want of
noble deeds and an encomiast is paralleled by the passage from Isocrates'
*Antidosis* of which we made mention earlier:

> . . . how many in the generations that are past have left no
> name, although they were far better and worthier men than
> those who are celebrated in song . . . But the latter, you see,
> found their poets and historians, while the others secured no
> one to hymn their praises. (*Antidosis* 136-37).

Both Isocrates and Sirach acknowledge those who have left no name: the
former, because there was no encomiast to sing of their deeds; the latter,
because they had done nothing to warrant the praises of an encomiast like
Ben Sira. Yet there are some in Israel worthy of an encomium, and at this
point Sirach returns to acknowledge those he has already enumerated in
summary fashion in vv 3-7, an acknowledgment which serves as overture
to the two major parts of his hymn, 44:16-49:16 and 50:1-21.

But these were men of mercy,
(אולם אלה אנשי חסד)

---

taphal infinitive of ענה or the hithpael of שעה for which a meaning of "to
tell" is found in Aramaic.

[469]The אשר אין of MS B = the שאין of the Masada text.

[470]Cf. esp. Job 10:19; Obad 16; Wis 2:2,4; CD 2:20; also Isa 26:14;
Ezek 3:20, 18:24.

Their righteous deed(s) will not come to an end.
(וצדקתם לא תשבת)[471] (44:10)

With this verse, then, the final section of the prooemium opens—a section in which Sirach relates that because of their piety the goodness of these men will continue in their sons, their name will be remembered, and the congregation will declare their praise. As the section closes with the declaration that the people will praise the heroes whom Sirach is about to recount, one-by-one, up to Simon himself, I would see 44:15 as forming an inclusion with 44:1

I will now praise (אהללה-נא) men of piety . . . (44:1)
. . . . . . . . . . . . . . . . . . . . . . . . . . .
The assembly recounts their wisdom and the congregation proclaims their praise (תהלתם) (44:15).

Moved by the encomiast's obligation to celebrate those who have done great things, the congregation of Israel is, in effect, invited to join his praise of the fathers. With 44:15 Jesus Sirach is ready to begin his narration of the γένος.

**b. The γένος: Sir 44:16-49:16**

The purpose of the γένος in the encomium was to enumerate the ancestors of the subject, and to mention something to the credit of each (cf. Anaximenes), which would thereby reflect favorably on the subject himself (cf. *ad Herennium*, Quintilian).[472] Both the individual's immediate and remote, i.e., mythical or legendary, ancestors were listed, and together they became a series of examples (*Beispielreihe*) with whom the encomiast would compare the person whom he was extolling in the encomium. Once again, the passage that makes this "comparison with examples" purpose of the γένος most explicit is *Evagoras* 12: ". . . I believe it is fitting that I should recount them (viz., Evagoras' ancestors) . . . that

---

[471]Reading צדקתם with Masada, Gk. and Syr. over against MS B's תקותם; and the restoration of תשבת with Smend, *Commentary*, 420, against תכרת in Yadin, *Ben Sira Scroll*, 36, for which he offers no support. The Greek οὐκ ἐπελήσθησαν "have been forgotten" may have come about, according to Smend, through an error where תשבת became changed to תשכח.

[472]Cf. the discussion, above, 199-201.

all may know that he proved himself not inferior to the noblest and greatest examples (παραδειγμάτων) of excellence which were of his inheritance."

In light of the understanding of the γένος seen above, then, I propose that Sir 44:16-49:16 serves the same purpose within the Hymn in Praise of the Fathers: it is the γένος of an encomium on Simon II. Just as the Greek encomiast would praise his subject's city, the city's eponymous ancestors, and both the immediate and legendary forefathers of the individual himself, so too we find Jesus Sirach extolling all the fathers of Israel from Adam to Nehemiah. And at those points where a syncrisis can be made to highlight the blend of cultic and political functions Sirach believed the high priest of his day ought to exhibit, and which he saw in Simon II, he makes that comparison. The syncrisis, then, which we discussed early in Part I,[473] ought to be understood as a feature of the γένος, rather than that of the general σύγκρισις as a separate topic in the encomium.[474]

From the treatment of Sirach's use of amplification there can be little question that, as he narrates the fathers in 44:16-49:16, he is "mentioning something to their credit" (Anaximenes). In our description of his use of amplification in general, as well as of particular techniques and commonplaces he employed, we repeatedly drew illustrations from the manner in which Ben Sira celebrates these heroes. And even the presence of negative elements in the γένος—e.g., Rehoboam, Jeroboam—has a precedent in the encomiastic γένος. For it was noted that in the Evagoras, Isocrates contrasts his hero with the Phoenician who usurped the throne of Salamis from his fathers (Evag. 19-20).

The principal form-critical difficulty in the γένος of 44:16-49:16, of which mention was made early in this study,[475] is the Rückblick of 49:14-16. It has been suggested that since the recitation of the ancestors began with Enoch at 44:16 and has continued through Nehemiah at 49:13, it is inconceivable that Sirach would interrupt the sequence to return to the figure of Enoch, whom he extolled at the outset, and thence back to Adam.[476] This, coupled with the observation that the second reference to Enoch and the focus on Adam in 49:14-16 seem to represent a view of

---

[473]Above, 12-19.
[474]Cf. the discussion of the two possible uses of "comparison with examples," above, 99-103.
[475]Above, 10-11.
[476]Ibid.

eschatology alien to Ben Sira,[477] has led to the assumption that we have here a later addition to the Praise of the Fathers.

It appears now, however, that the textual evidence offered by the Masada scroll enables the question of 49:14-16 to be answered. For just before the scroll breaks off at 44:17c it is clear that there was a blank line between 44:15, the close of our prooemium, and 44:17ab, the praise of Noah. In other words, 44:16, the first of the two references to Enoch, did not appear at all in the Masada scroll.[478] Moreover, in MS B, where 44:16 does appear, it is much too long: a tri-colon over against the bi-cola of the verses preceding and following. And it seems to duplicate the idiom נמצא תמים found in 44:17:

חנוך נמצא תמים והתהלך עם ייי    v 16
וילקח אות דעת לדור ודור
נח צדיק נמצא תמים    v 17
לעת כלה היה תחליף

Given the problems with 44:16 in MS B, and the fact that it is absent in the Masada scroll, Yadin has proposed that the verse is not original.[479] Rather the only place where Ben Sira recalled the example of Enoch was in 49:14.

> We now may assume that at an early period an attempt had been made to artificially expunge a portion of Ben Sira's observations on Enoch in the concluding verses, and to insert them in their chronological order, i.e., before Noah. Thus we may assume that a part of verse 16 was originally in chapter 49.[480]

Yadin suggests that since the reference to Enoch's being an example of repentance appears in the Greek of 44:16, and that it does not repeat anything said about Enoch in 49:14, it probably is part of the original material in chap. 49 that was transferred to 44:16. Moreover, due to the importance given the theme of Enoch's "walking with God" in Genesis 5, Sirach would have not wanted to omit it in his report. Thus the והתהלך עם ייי of 44:16 is the second original element transferred from 49:14. If we return

---

[477] This is the argument of, e.g., Snaith and Middendorp, cf. above, 11.
[478] Yadin, *Ben Sira Scroll*, 38.
[479] N. B. that 44:16 is omitted in the Syriac translation.
[480] Yadin, *Ben Sira Scroll*, 38.

these two half-lines to their original place in chap. 49, we then come up
with the following arrangement for 49:14-16:

(49:14a) מעט נוצר על הארץ כחנוך
(44:16c) אות דעת לדור ודור
(44:16b) והתהלך עם ייי
(49:14b) וגם הוא נלקח פנים
(49:15) כיוסף אם נולד גבר
וגם גויתו נפקדה
(49:16) שם ושת ואנוש נכבדו
ועל כל-חי תפארת אדם

> Few have been formed on earth like Enoch,
> A sign of knowledge to generation upon generation.
> He walked with Yahweh,
> And also he was bodily taken away.
> If, like Joseph, he had been born a man,
> Then, his corpse also would have been cared for.
> Shem and Seth and Enosh were honored,
> But over all the living is the glory of Adam.

Some comments on the above reconstruction and translation are in
order. First of all, for the translation of 49:15, "If, like Joseph, he had
been born a man, then his corpse also would have been cared for," the
construction גַּם . . . אָם is used of unreal conditions, cf. Gen 13:16: "If
(אָם) a man is able to count the dust of the earth, then also (גַּם) your
descendants can be counted."[481] Thus what we have here is a comparison
of Enoch with Joseph; in amplification of Enoch it is stated that he was
such a remarkable figure that even if he had died as other men, his corpse
would have received the exceptional treatment given to Joseph's bones
(Gen 50:25, Exod 13:19, Josh 24:32).[482] The appearance of Joseph in the
γένος, then, is not for the purpose of including him among the ancestors
of Simon II. The reasons for excluding him have been referred to earlier.
Rather the remembrance of the care given his corpse by ancient Israel

---

[481]Cf. D. R. Meyer, *Hebräische Grammatik, III: Satzlehre* (3d ed.;
Berlin: Walter de Gruyter, 1972) 116.

[482]The sense that Enoch is here being compared to Joseph in some way
was suggested by Smend, *Commentary*, 475. Smend, however, interprets it
to mean that if God evidenced concern for the bones of Joseph, how much
greater concern did he show for Enoch by bodily taking him away.

provided Sirach with the source of a comparison with which he could amplify the person of Enoch. The Greek translator misunderstood this in rendering 49:15 such that Sirach seems to be honoring Joseph by stressing his incomparability: "No man (οὐδὲ . . . ἀνήρ) like Joseph has been born. . . ."

Given the comparison between Enoch and Joseph, פנים in 49:14b ought to be interpreted in opposition to the גויתו ("his corpse") of 49:15. Thus the sense of "bodily" commends itself.[483] In 49:16 MS B employs נפקדו with respect to Shem, Seth, and Enosh. But פקד appears two more times in the immediate context (49:15b, 50:1b), and under that influence, it may be in error. The Greek reads ἐδοξάσθησαν, and thus, with Smend, we would prefer to see נכבדו.[484] Also, it should be noted that what appears as 49:15b in the Greek, ἡγούμενος ἀδελφῶν, στήριγμα λαοῦ, is properly the opening half-line of 50:1, as MS B and Syriac clearly show.[485] Rather than being a part of the reference to Joseph, as the Greek has it, the line serves to open the praise of Simon as we noted above.[486]

With the γένος, then, extending now from Noah (44:17) to Nehemiah (49:13), and then from Enoch back to Adam (49:14-16 as corrected), it appears to me that Ben Sira has provided us with two groupings of the persons who are of Simon's heritage. The first group is that of his "immediate" heritage, Noah to Nehemiah, while the second is that of those heroes who are the most remote. And the juncture of the two is with Noah, whom Sirach remembers as the one who "in a time of destruction became a continuator" (תחליף) (44:17b). The first group becomes those ancestors descended from the "remnant" provided through Noah (44:17c), while the second list is of the remote, antediluvian worthies. And the reason Ben Sira inverts the order of the two may be an intentional move on his part to juxtapose these most ancient figures and Simon II. Immediately after recounting how "over all the living is the תפארת of Adam" (49:16b), Sirach honors Simon as the תפארת of his people (50:1 MS B). Perhaps we have here something comparable to the way in which encomiasts placed the names of their subjects in apposition to the gods from whom the subjects were said to have descended. For example, Isocrates makes mention of Evagoras alongside of Zeus (Evag. 12-23), Xenophon notes that Agesilaus' descent is to be traced from Heracles (Ages. 1.2),

---

[483]Smend, Commentary, 475.
[484]Ibid.
[485]Ibid., 478.
[486]Above, 223.

and Theocritus places Ptolemy side-by-side with Zeus (Id. 17.1-4,13-18).
Thus the enumeration of the antediluvian figures, who became the source
of much apocalyptic speculation in Judaism and early Christianity, is
placed immediately before Ben Sira's celebration of Simon II as a way of
amplifying this great high priest all the more. Peters' description of
49:14-16 as an *Ueberleitung* to the praise of Simon is, then an apt designation.[487]

c. The πράξεις = 50:1-21

In our survey of the πράξεις of the encomium we have noted that it
was regarded as the chief topic in the arrangement—for here were celebrated the virtues and achievements of the subject himself. In organizing
the πράξεις, the encomiast was free to either narrate the deeds chronologically—with the various deeds witnessing to the character or virtues of
the subject—or the material could be categorized in various ways: there
could be a separate catalogue of virtues alongside a narration of achievements, and/or the achievements themselves could be grouped according to
whether they came out of contexts of war or of peace. And as the encomiast described the accomplishments of his hero, he would use all types of
amplification: comparison, as well as commonplaces that his subject was
the first to have performed one action or that his actions had beneficial
consequences, etc.

It is my contention, then, that such a πράξεις is what we have in Sir
50:1-21. First of all, we sense that Sirach has chosen to organize his
presentation of Simon into two categories which, in a sense, parallel the
divisions employed in other encomia. On the one hand, he narrates Simon's
achievements in the "political" realm in vv 1-4 by enumerating his public
works. And on the other hand, vv 5-21 present Simon as a cultic official.
The former set of deeds, it is generally regarded, should be interpreted in
light of the letter of Antiochus III to Ptolemy referred to in Josephus
(*Ant.* 12.139-141).[488] In this letter, written shortly after the battle of
Panium in 198 B.C.E., when Jerusalem passed from Ptolemaic to Seleucid
control, Antiochus gave his permission to the Jews to repair the temple
and the walls. What Antiochus permitted in the letter, Simon II brought to

---

[487] Above, 11; and Peters, *Das Buch,* 422.
[488] Cf. F. M. Abel, *Histoire de la palestine I: de la conquête
d'Alexandre jusqu'a la guerre juive* (Paris: Librairie Lecoffre, 1952) 88-90.

completion.[489] Thus Sirach is recalling those things Simon accomplished as an official who possessed authority and responsibility for the construction of public works in Jerusalem in the eyes of the Seleucid king.

Of the engineering works carried out by Simon, we have had occasion already to call attention to the comparisons Sirach evidently intended between the city walls Nehemiah rebuilt (49:13) and the temple walls built by Simon (50:2),[490] between the construction and reconstruction of the temple under Solomon and Zerubbabel/Joshua (48:13, 49:12) and Simon's temple repair (50:1-2), and between Hezekiah's water-system (48:17) and Simon's reservoir (50:3).[491] In regard to the lattermost comparison we noted the use of the same term מקוה ("reservoir") in both 50:3 and 48:17, in the accounts of Simon and Hezekiah respectively.[492] In the second half of 50:3 Sirach places the term אשיח, mentioned earlier,[493] in apposition to מקוה, and then refers to this reservoir as "like the sea in circumference" (כים בהמונו; λάκκος ὡσεὶ θαλάσσης τὸ περίμετρον) (50:3b).[494] The likening of the dimensions of the reservoir to those of the sea becomes another element of amplification employed by Sirach in his narration of Simon II. To judge from *The Letter of Aristeas*, the reservoir of Simon was one of the cisterns within the temple precinct which were used to provide water to wash away the blood from the sacrifices (*Aristeas* 88-91); compare the ὑποδεχείων (*Aristeas* 89, 91) with the ἀπο-δεχεῖον of Sir 50:3.[495]

In contrast to the above, 50:5-21 represents the other category of Simon's πράξεις: his cultic role as high priest. Here again Sirach has intended a comparison—as we have seen—between Simon and Aaron,

---

[489]Cf. Tcherikover, *Hellenistic Civilization*, 80-81; Middendorp, *Die Stellung*, 168.

[490]Middendorp, *Die Stellung*, 168, believes that the walls repaired by Simon were the walls of the temple enclosure and not the walls of the city.

[491]On the comparisons of Simon's engineering works with those of the fathers, cf. above, 18-19.

[492]Above, 18-19.

[493]Above, 219, n. 441.

[494]Although MS B reads בם בהמונו, it is generally accepted that בם should read כים with the Greek ὡσεὶ θαλάσσης. Cf. Smend, *Commentary*, 480; Peters, *Das Buch*, 427.

[495]Cf. L. Bigot, *Ecclésiastique*, 2048. For *The Letter of Aristeas*, cf. Thackeray's Greek text in H. B. Swete, *An Introduction to the Old Testament in Greek* (rev. R. R. Ottley; reprinted from the ed. of 1902; New York: KTAV, 1968).

Phinehas and those other fathers who are portrayed in cultic terms.[496]
But as he describes Simon's actions in the cultus, Ben Sira does not give us
an enumeration as he did of the engineering achievements. Rather he
depicts how Simon officiated on the Day of Atonement and at the daily
offerings or Tamid.[497] Ben Sira has taken his remembrance of specific
occasions when he had witnessed Simon II presiding in the temple; he has
"photographed" those occasions, "touched them up" through amplification,
and now presents them to us in his encomium. His picture of Simon, then,
is in harmony with the hellenistic characteristic of "idealizing the particular."[498]

In terms of Ben Sira's description of the Day of Atonement and Tamid
rites, we have already commented on the elaborate series of similes
employed to describe Simon's vestments.[499] These vestments were worn
only on the Day of Atonement, were put on only after bathing, and after
the high priest came out of the holy place, they were removed, after
which he would bathe a second time (cf. Lev 16:4, 23-24; and in the Mishnah, *Yoma* 3.3-4,6-7). Alongside of depicting Simon's vesture, Sirach
refers to the high priest's blessing of the congregation on Yom Kippur
with the "Expressed Name":

(50:20) אז ירד ונשא ידיו
על כל קהל ישראל
וברכת ייי בשפתיו
ובשם ייי התפאר
(50:21)[500] וישנו לנפל לשאת
[זכיות א]ל מפניו

Then he came down and lifted his hands
Over the whole congregation of Israel;

---

[496]Cf. above, 12-17.

[497]Snaith, *Ecclesiasticus*, 251-52.

[498]So Prof. George Kustas in a conversation we had while he was Guest
Professor of Rhetoric at the University of California, Berkeley, Nov.
1975.

[499]Above, 216.

[500]The restoration of this verse is by no means certain. I have followed
Smend who reads לשאת in place of MS B's שניה, seeing the infinitive as
behind the Greek's ἐπιδέξασθαι (cf. 51:26 where ἐπιδέχομαι renders נשא).
Some take ברכה to be behind the Greek's εὐλογίαν, but Smend contends
that what remains of the letters in 50:21b point to זכיות, "pardon." Cf.
Smend, *Text*, 59, and *Commentary*, 489.

> And the blessing of Yahweh was on his lips,
>   And in the Name of Yahweh he took glory;
> And they bowed a second time to receive
>   The pardon of God from him.

With this compare *Yoma* 6.2:

> And when the priests and the people which stood in the Temple
> Court heard the Expressed Name come forth from the mouth
> of the High Priest, they used to kneel and bow themselves and
> fall down on their faces and say, 'Blessed be the name of the
> glory of his kingdom for ever and ever'.[501]

In regard to the Tamid or daily offerings, pictured in 50:11-19, Sirach
has already offered the parallel of Aaron's responsibility for them in
45:14. The ritual for the Tamid is outlined in Exod 29:38-42, and again in
the Mishnah, *Tamid* 7.2-3, where the wine libation, the sounding of the
trumpets and the singing of the levitical choir are described. All three of
these elements are mentioned by Ben Sira in 50:15-18.

#### d. The Epilogue: Sir 50:22-24

For the epilogue to an encomium, rhetorical theory permitted a great
deal of freedom with respect to invention. But, as we have observed,
certain basic features tended to recur. Anaximenes recommended a
recapitulation of some kind, while Aristotle emphasized that the epilogue
must appeal to the emotions of the audience: they are to be invited to join
in the praise of the subject and encouraged to emulate his example. Thus
the encomium often ended with hortatory elements and/or a prayer.

The epilogue to the Praise of the Fathers is brief, only three verses,
and brevity in the epilogue was one of the recommendations in the theory
offered by the *auctor* of the *ad Herennium*. The three verses according to
MS B are as follows:

(50:22)   עתה ברכו-נא את ייי אלהי ישראל
המפליא לעשות בארץ
המגדל אדם מרחם
ויעשה כרצונו

---

[501] The translation is that of H. Danby, *The Mishnah* (Oxford: Clarendon, 1933) 169.

(50:23) יתן לכם חכמת לבב
ויהי בשלום ביניכם
(50:24) יאמן עם שמעון חסדו
ויקם לו ברית פינחס
אשר לא יכרת לו
ולזרעו כימי שמים

And now let us bless Yahweh, the God of Israel,
Who does wonderful things on the earth.
Who exalts man from the womb,
And does with him according to his favor.
May he give to you wisdom of heart,
And may there be peace among you.
May his mercy continue with Simon,
And may he raise up for him the covenant of Phinehas,
Which will not be cut off for him,
Nor for his seed according to the days of heaven.

The Greek generally follows the Hebrew except that it drops the specific reference to Simon in 24a and that it omits 24bc altogether. Since the high priesthood was no longer in the hands of those who stood in the covenant of Phinehas by the time of the Greek translator, omission of the priestly themes in his rendition is understandable. Other points where there is some difference are: 22ab, where the Greek translator generalizes MS B's "God of Israel" to "the God of all" and "on earth" to "in all"; in 23a his misreading of חכמת as שמחת which gave him εὐφροσύνην, "gladness";[502] and the error in 23b where he read ביני׳ as בימי׳, hence "our days" instead of "among you." The Greek missed the sense of 24d altogether.

Earlier in our study we called attention to the parallel between the doxology of the epilogue and that of 45:25c-26.[503] The doxology in chap. 45 directly follows Sirach's narration regarding the covenant with Phinehas (vv 24-25ab), and now, in the doxology of chap. 50, that covenant is explicitly recalled, and the wish or prayer is expressed that the lineage of Simon will continue in it. The structure here, then, not only emphasizes the comparison Sirach wishes to make between Simon and Phinehas, but now that comparison is held up before Simon's son—Onias III—in order to challenge him to emulate his father and all those others with whom God

---

[502]The Syriac witnesses to MS B's חכמת with ܚܟܡܬܐ . Peters, *Das Buch*, 433, suggests that the Greek reads שמחת in error.

[503]Above, 6.

had maintained the covenant of Phinehas. Thus, in keeping with the theory laid down for the epilogue of an encomium, we have here the appeal to the emotions: the congregation of Israel is called upon to praise the God to whom all these pious men had been faithful, and the prayer is that Onias III would live up to the example set by Simon II and the fathers, who in ages past served as a *Vorbild* of the high priest. The purpose of Sirach 44-50, with its celebration of Simon and his ancestry providing a picture of the ideal high priest for the benefit of Onias, can be said to be the same as the purpose of Isocrates' *Evagoras:* for the encomium on this ruler of Salamis was written to provide his son Nicocles with an ideal example of kingship to emulate.

# Conclusion

We began Part I of this study with Baumgartner's observation that the Hymn in Praise of the Fathers may be called a "hymn" in only an extremely qualified way: "da hier nicht wie im kultischen Hymnus Gott, sondern Menschen gepriesen werden."[1] In praising men, not God, Sirach 44-50 represents something new in Hebrew literature, and the question was asked as to what source or influence the unique quality of this poem may be attributed. Thus far there have been a number of answers proposed to the question, but no consensus has emerged. The proposals are that Sirach 44-50 is derived from the recitations of Israel's history which may be found within the Hebrew canon (e.g., Ezekiel 20, Nehemiah 9, Psalms 78, 105, 106, etc.) and without (e.g., 1 Maccabees 2:51-60, Wisdom 10, CD 2:17-3:12, etc.). Others have been that Sirach was inspired by certain hellenistic models, specifically the peripatetic type of biographical writing popularized in Alexandria, which in Roman literature became the genre de viris illustribus. In Part I, then, we sought to examine the validity of these proposals. This was done after we first established the formal limits of the poem to be 44:1-50:24. This was necessary since some commentators have linked the Praise of the Fathers with the hymn in honor of God the creator in 42:15-43:33, and/or have sought to separate chap. 50 from 44-49.

From Part I we concluded that the pericopes from the Hebrew canon which have been likened to Sirach 44-50 are either hymns in praise of Yahweh for his acts, or that they are deuteronomistic recitations of Israel's history where the focus is on the obedience/disobedience of the nation as a whole. In neither case do they offer a parallel to Sirach's

---

[1]Baumgartner, "Die literarischen Gattungen," 173.

Praise of the Fathers. The same was found to be true of the intertestamental pericopes cited from the book of Judith. In testing the alleged
hellenistic parallels, we saw that the peripatetic biography/de viris illustribus proposal does not commend itself either. For with respect to
content the Alexandrian biographers took delight in including anecdote,
gossip, and reports of scandal on their subjects. This seems to be quite in
contrast to the reports of piety and fidelity that characterize Ben Sira's
portrayal of Israel's heroes. Moreover, from what little we know about the
form of peripatetic biography, it appears that the biographers may have
structured their works as dialogues. Over against this we have the hymnic
format in which Sirach 44-50 appears.

There was, however, one form that emerged from our discussion that
commended itself as the model employed by Jesus Sirach: that of the
Beispielreihe or series of examples. We noted that most of the intertestamental pericopes which commentators have seen as similar to Sirach
44-50 were of this form (e.g., the pericopes from 1, 3, and 4 Maccabees,
Wisdom 10 and CD 2-3), and although these post-date Sirach, the form had
already been in use in the Greek world prior to Sirach's time. The conclusion to which we came was that the section 44:16-49:16 appears to be that
of a Beispielreihe, a form whose use in Judaism came about under the
influence of hellenism. Yet that raised the question of how we are to
understand the sections of the Praise of the Fathers which frame this
Beispielreihe: viz., 44:1-15 and 50:1-24. Is there a form within which
Beispielreihen are utilized whose purpose it is to praise men?

In Part II, then, we proposed that the answer to the above question is
the encomium. As a rhetorical εἶδος the encomium's purpose was to
praise a man for his achievements and virtues, and in accomplishing this,
the encomium would employ examples, or series of examples, in the form
of the γένος or genealogy of the person being extolled. By including the
examples of other great men, the encomiast sought to amplify the deeds
of his subject through comparing him favorably with these others.

The encomium had its origins in the sixth/fifth-century lyric poets, it
was established as a rhetorical εἶδος in the age of Gorgias and Isocrates,
and it became a common rhetorical exercise in Greek, hellenistic, and
Roman schools. We noted that since rhetoric was marked by conservatism,
the form of the encomium remained basically constant from the time of
Isocrates to the rhetors of the Common Era. The same techniques of
amplification, and the same basic arrangement or τάξις may be seen in
encomia throughout this span of history. The topics in the arrangement
which always seemed to be in evidence, and which, then, could be taken as

basic form—critical marks of the εἶδος, were those of: prooemium, γένος, πράξεις, and epilogue.

Having defined those features of the encomium which are its essential characteristics, the balance of Part II was devoted to analyzing Sirach 44-50 as an encomium. On the basis of this, I suggest that the Hymn in Praise of the Fathers gives evidence of both "proof by amplification" and the basic four-part τάξις of the encomium. Sirach was seen to employ a variety of types of αὔξησις—through omission or suppression of details, by commonplaces through which the unique or unprecedented quality of his subjects' actions was presented, and above all, through comparison. And the four parts of the hymn: 44:1-15, 44:17-49:16, 50:1-21, 50:22-24, were judged to correspond to the prooemium, γένος, πράξεις, and epilogue of an encomium respectively. Thus I suggest that Sirach 44-50 is to be understood as a composition that Sirach consciously patterned after the types of encomia with which he could conceivably have come into contact in his day. His encomium celebrates Simon II, invites the congregation to praise the God who has given them such a faithful high priest, and holds him up as an example for his son, Onias III, to emulate.

The question remains, however, as to whether or not Sirach would have known of and employed a Greek rhetorical form as his model for chaps. 44-50. To this question we are not able to offer any direct, conclusive proof. But we can sketch three lines of development which, when they converge, suggest that the answer to the question is in the affirmative.

The first is in terms of the pervasive character of hellenistic rhetoric. The gymnasium, whose curriculum included the study of rhetoric and the use of the *progymnasmata* or exercises, one of which was the encomium, was an institution known throughout the hellenistic world. There were gymnasia in Ptolemaic Egypt by the third century B.C.E.,[2] and throughout the realm of the Seleucids.[3] Although—to judge from the report given in 2 Macc 4:9-14 and 1 Macc 1:14—the establishment of a gymnasium in Jerusalem did not come about until 175 B.C.E., a few years after Ben Sira's time, it did not appear to be a radical innovation. Rather it found enthusiastic supporters among an aristocracy already influenced by hellenism.[4] Greek language and Greek education had penetrated into

---

[2]Smith, *Art of Rhetoric*, 108, 111.

[3]Cf. M. P. Nilsson, *Die hellenistische Schule* (Munich: C. H. Beck, 1955) 83-84. Also Hengel, *Judaism*, 70-71.

[4]Hengel, *Judaism*, 73-75.

Palestinian Jewish circles as early as the third century,[5] and although I
see no reason to contradict Sirach's assertions that he travelled to foreign
lands as Middendorp does,[6] he could have just as easily come into contact
with Greek literature and rhetoric in Palestine had he not travelled to
Alexandria.

The second line of development is the appearance of Greek rhetorical
forms in rabbinic literature. We already have had occasion to acknowledge
some of the work that has been done in this area by Fischel, Daube,
Liebermann, and Stein.[7] And if Greco-Roman rhetoric is clearly evident
in these later materials, could not it have begun already in the third-early
second centuries B.C.E. at a time when, as was mentioned above, Jerusalem was open to hellenism?

And the third consideration is the presence elsewhere in Ben Sira of
hellenistic influence. The studies of Marböck and Middendorp in recent
years have sought to demonstrate Sirach's familiarity with and use of
Greek literature and ideas.[8] To their studies we could add the opinions of
Lévi and Bigot who both affirm that hellenistic influence may be detected
throughout the book.[9] Even Momigliano, who is among those who are not
inclined to see any clear trace of Greek literary forms in Sirach, still has
to conclude that Ben Sira "had certainly seen something of the Greek
civilization, with its philosophic schools, theatres and gymnasia."[10]

If, then, these three areas are taken in concert, I suggest that they
point toward Sirach's acquaintance with and willingness to use the rhetorical form of the Greek encomium as the model or inspiration for his Hymn
in Praise of the Fathers. And in so doing he employed a hellenistic form as
a means of preserving and honoring traditions of old Israel which he saw
exemplified in Simon II. That hellenistic elements incorporated within
Judaism did not destroy Jewish traditions, but could be compatible with
them, and even be of service in preserving them, has been acknowledged
by Gerhardsson and Hengel.[11] Thus the Praise of the Fathers—inspired by

---

[5]Ibid., 75.
[6]Cf. Middendorp, *Die Stellung*, 170-73, and above, 163.
[7]Cf. above, 53, nn. 179-81.
[8]Cf. above, 2, n. 6.
[9]Ibid.
[10]Momigliano, *Alien Wisdom*, 95.
[11]B. Gerhardsson, *Memory and Manuscript: Oral Tradition and Written
Transmission in Rabbinic Judaism and Early Christianity* (Acta Seminarii
Neotestamentici Upsaliensis, 22; Lund: C. W. K. Gleerup, 1961) 27;
Hengel, *Judaism*, 76.

the form through which Greeks from Pindar to Isocrates and beyond celebrated the great achievements of men—becomes in a Palestinian Jewish setting an apt means for upholding those traditions which Sirach seeks to preserve. In his hands the encomium is as it should be—for ". . . the argumentation in epideictic discourse sets out to <u>increase the intensity of adherence to certain values,</u> . . . The speaker tries to establish a sense of communion centered around particular values recognized by the audience, . . ."[12]

---

[12]C. Perelman and L. Olbrechts-Tyteca, *The New Rhetoric* (Notre Dame, Indiana: University of Notre Dame, 1969) 51. Emphasis mine.

# Bibliography

## I. SIRACH: TEXTS AND TOOLS

Barthélemy, D. and Rickenbacher, O. *Konkordanz zum hebräischen Sirach mit syrisch-hebräischen Index*. Göttingen: Vandenhoeck und Ruprecht, 1973.

*Biblia sacra juxta versionem simplicem quae dicitur Pschitta*. 3 vols. Beirut: Typis Typographiae Catholicae, 1951. (Known as the Mosul edition of the Peshitta.)

*The Book of Ben Sira: Text, Concordance and an Analysis of the Vocabulary*. (Hebrew with an introduction in English.) Jerusalem: The Academy of the Hebrew Language and the Shrine of the Book, 1973.

Cowley, A. E. and Neubauer, Ad. (eds.). *The Original Hebrew of a Portion of Ecclesiasticus (xxxix.15 to xlix.11)*. Oxford: Clarendon, 1897.

Lagarde, Paul A. de. *Libri veteris testamenti apocryphi syriace*. Osnabrück: Otto Zeller, 1972. (Reprinted from the edition of 1861.)

Lévi, Israel (ed.). *The Hebrew Text of the Book of Ecclesiasticus*. Semitic Study Series, III. 3d ed. Leiden: E. J. Brill, 1969.

Schechter, S. and Taylor, C. *The Wisdom of Ben Sira: Portions of the Book Ecclesiasticus from Hebrew Manuscripts in the Cairo Genizah Collection*. Cambridge: The University Press, 1899.

Segal, M. H. *Seper ḥokmat ben-Sira' ha-šalem*. Jerusalem, 1933.

Smend, Rudolf. *Griechisch-Syrisch-Hebräischer Index zur Weisheit des Jesus Sirach*. Berlin: Georg Reimer, 1907.

_____. *Die Weisheit des Jesus Sirach: Hebräisch und Deutsch*. Berlin: Georg Reimer, 1906. (Cited herein as Smend, *Text*.)

Strack, Hermann L. *Die Sprüche Jesus', des Sohnes Sirachs: Der jüngst gefundene hebräische Text*. Leipzig: A. Deichert'sche Verlagsbuchhandlung Nachf. (Georg Böhme), 1903.

Strugnell, John. "Notes and Queries on 'the Ben Sira Scroll from Masada'," *Eretz-Israel* 9 (1969) 109-19.

Vattioni, Francesco. *Ecclesiastico: Testo ebraico con apparato critico e versioni greca, latina e siriaca*. Naples: Instituto Orientale di Napoli, 1968.

Weber, Robert (ed.). *Biblia sacra iuxta vulgatum versionem*. 2 vols. Stuttgart: Württembergische Bibelanstalt, 1969.

Yadin, Yigael. *The Ben Sira Scroll from Masada with Introduction, Emendations and Commentary*. Jerusalem: The Israel Exploration Society, 1965.

Ziegler, Joseph (ed.). *Septuaginta, XII/2: Sapientia, Iesu Filii Sirach*. (Vetus Testamentum Graecum Auctoritate Societatis Litterarum Gottingensis editum.) Göttingen: Vandenhoeck und Ruprecht, 1965.

## II. SIRACH: GENERAL WORKS, COMMENTARIES, AND ARTICLES ON CHAPTERS 44-50

Abel, F. M. *Histoire de la Palestine. Tome I: De la conquête d'Alexandre jusqu'a la guerre juive*. Paris: Librairie Lecoffre, 1952.

Alonso-Schökel, Luis. *Proverbios y Eclesiastico*. Madrid: Ediciones Cristiandad, 1968.

Baumgartner, W. "Die literarischen Gattungen in der Weisheit des Jesus Sirach," *ZAW* 34 (1914) 161-98.

Bigot, L. "Ecclésiastique (Livre de l')," *DTC* 4. Edited by A. Vacant et al. Paris: Librairie Letouzey et Ané, 1939. Cols. 2028-2054.

Box, G. H. and Oesterley, W. O. E. "The Book of Sirach," *The Apocrypha and Pseudepigrapha of the Old Testament in English*. Vol. I: Apocrypha. Edited by R. H. Charles. London: Oxford University, 1971. Pp. 268-517. (Reprinted from the edition of 1913.)

Caquot, André. "Ben Sira et le messianisme," *Semitica* 16 (1966) 43-68.

Carmignac, Jean. "Les rapports entre l'Ecclésiastique et Qumran," *RevQ* 3 (1961) 209-18.

Causse, A. "La Sagesse et la propagande juive à l'époque perse et hellenistique," *Werden und Wesen des Alten Testaments*. BZAW 66. Edited by Johannes Hempel, et al. Berlin: Alfred Töpelmann, 1936. Pp. 148-54.

Crenshaw, James L. "The Problem of Theodicy in Sirach: On Human Bondage," *JBL* 94 (1975) 47-64.

de Boer, P. A. H. "bbrytm ʿmd zrʿm, Sirach xliv 12a," *Hebräische Wortforschung*. VTSup 16. Leiden: E. J. Brill, 1967. Pp. 25-29.

Delekat, L. "Zum hebräischen Wörterbuch," *VT* 14 (1964) 7-66.

Di Lella, Alexander A. "Conservative and Progressive Theology: Sirach and Wisdom," *CBQ* 28 (1966) 139-54.

_____. *The Hebrew Text of Sirach: A Text-Critical and Historical Study*. Studies in Classical Literature 1. The Hague: Mouton and Company, 1966.

Dommershausen, Werner. "Zum Vergeltungsdenken des Ben Sira," *Alter Orient und Altes Testament: Wort und Geschichte*. Festschrift for Karl Elliger. Edited by Harmut Gese and Hans Peter Rüger. Neukirchen-Vluyn: Neukirchener, 1973. Pp. 37-43.

Dubarle, A. M. *Les sages d'Israël*. Lectio Divina 1. Paris: Les éditions du Cerf, 1946.

Duesberg, Hilaire, and Auvray, Paul. *Le livre de l'Ecclésiastique*. "La Sainte Bible." Second edition. Paris: Les éditions du Cerf, 1958.

Duesberg, Hilaire, and Fransen, Irénée. *Ecclesiastico*. La Sacra Bibbia: Antico Testamento. Rome: Marietti, 1966.

Eberharter, Andreas. *Das Buch Jesus Sirach oder Ecclesiasticus*. Die Heilige Schrift des Alten Testaments VI:5. Bonn: Peter Hanstein, 1925.

_____. *Der Kanon des Alten Testaments zur Zeit des Ben Sira*. Alttestamentliche Abhandlungen, III:3. Munster i. W.: Aschendorffsche, 1911.

Fichtner, Johannes. "Zum Problem Glaube und Geschichte in der israelitisch-jüdischen Weisheitsliteratur," *TLZ* 76 (1951) cols. 145-50.

Fransen, Irénée. "Cahier de bible: les oeuvres de Dieu, Siracide 42,1-50,20," *BVC* 79 (1968) 26-35.

Fuss, W. "Tradition und Komposition im Buche Jesus Sirach." Unpublished dissertation, Tübingen University, 1963. (Abstract published in *TLZ* 88 [1963] 948-49.)

Galling, Kurt. *Studien zur Geschichte Israels im persischen Zeitalter*. Tübingen: J. C. B. Mohr (Paul Siebeck), 1964.

Germann, Heinrich. "Jesus Ben Siras Dankgebet und die Hodajoth," *TZ* 19 (1963) 81-87.

Hadot, Jean. *Penchant mauvais et volonté libre dans la sagesse de Ben Sira (L'Ecclésiastique)*. Bruxelles: Universitaires de Bruxelles, 1970.

Hamp, Vinzenz. "Das Buch Sirach oder Ecclesiasticus," *Echter-Bible; Altes Testament: IV*. Würzburg: Echter, 1959.

_____. "Zukunft und Jenseits im Buche Sirach," *Alttestamentliche Studien Friedrich Nötscher*. BBB 1. Edited by Hubert Junker and Johannes Botterweck. Bonn: Peter Hanstein, 1950. Pp. 86-97.

Hart, J. H. A. "Sir.xlviii 17,a,b," *JTS* 4 (1903) 591-92.

Hart, J. H. A. and Taylor, C. "Two Notes on Enoch in Sir. xliv 16," *JTS* 4 (1903) 589-91.

Haspecker, Josef. *Gottesfurcht bei Jesus Sirach*. Analecta Biblica 30. Rome: Biblical Institute, 1967.

Hauer, Christian E. "Water in the Mountain?" *PEQ* 101 (1969) 44-45.

Hengel, Martin. *Judaism and Hellenism*. 2 vols. Translated from the 2nd German edition of 1973 by John Bowden. Philadelphia: Fortress, 1974.

Iwry, Samuel. "A New Designation for the Luminaries in Ben Sira and in the Manual of Discipline (1QS)," *BASOR* 200 (1970) 41-47.

Jacob, Edmond. "L'Histoire d'Israel vue par Ben Sira," *Mélanges bibliques rédigés en l'honneur de André Robert*. Travaux de l'institut catholique de Paris 4. Paris: Bloud and Gay, 1957. Pp. 288-94.

Jansen, H. Ludin. *Die spätjüdische Psalmendichtung: Ihr Entstehungskreis und ihr 'Sitz im Leben.'* SNVAO II: Hist.-filos. klasse, no. 3. Oslo: I kommisjon hos Jacob Dybwad, 1937.

Janssen, Enno. *Das Gottesvolk und seine Geschichte. Geschichtsbild und Selbstverständnis im palästinensischen Schrifttum von Jesus Sirach bis Jehuda ha-Nasi*. Neukirchen-Vluyn: Neukirchener, 1971.

Kellermann, Ulrich. *Nehemia: Quellen, Ueberlieferung und Geschichte*. BZAW 102. Berlin: Alfred Töpelmann, 1967.

Koole, J. L. "Die Bibel des Ben Sira," *OTS* 14. Leiden: E. J. Brill, 1965. Pp. 374-96.

Lamparter, Helmut. *Die Apokryphen I: Das Buch Jesus Sirach*. Die Botschaft des Alten Testaments, 25:1. Stuttgart: Calwer, 1972.

Lang, Bernhard. *Anweisungen gegen die Torheit: Sprichwörter-Jesus Sirach*. Stuttgarter kleiner Kommentar: Altes Testament 19. Stuttgart: KBW, 1973.

Lehmann, M. R. "Ben Sira and the Qumran Literature." *RevQ* (1961) 103-16.

Lévi, Israel. *L'Ecclésiastique ou la Sagesse de Jésus, fils de Sira, texte original hébreu, édité, traduit et commenté.* Vols. I and II. Paris, 1898 and 1901.

_____. "Sirach," *The Jewish Encyclopedia: Vol. XI.* Edited by Isidore Singer. New York: Funk and Wagnalls, 1905. Pp. 388-96.

Maertens, Thierry. *L'Eloge des pères (Ecclésiastique XLIV-L).* Collection lumière et vie 5. Bruges: Editions de l'Abbaye de Saint-André, 1956.

Maier, Gerhard. *Mensch und freier Wille nach den jüdischen Religionsparteien zwischen Ben Sira und Paulus.* (Wiss. Untersuchungen zum NT 12. Tübingen: J. C. B. Mohr, 1971.

Marböck, Johann. "qw—Eine Bezeichnung für das hebräische Metrum?" *VT* 20 (1970) 236-39.

_____. *Weisheit im Wandel: Untersuchungen zur Weisheitstheologie bei Ben Sira.* Bonner Biblische Beiträge 37. Bonn: Peter Hanstein, 1971.

Michaelis, Dieter. "Das Buch Jesus Sirach als typischer Ausdruck für das Gottesverhältnis des nachalttestamentlichen Menschen," *TLZ* 83 (1958) 601-8.

Middendorp, Th. *Die Stellung Jesu Ben Siras zwischen Judentum und Hellenismus.* Leiden: E. J. Brill, 1973.

Moore, George Foot. *Judaism in the First Centuries of the Christian Era: The Age of the Tannaim: Vol. I.* Cambridge: Harvard University, 1950.

_____. "Simeon the Righteous," *Jewish Studies in Memory of Israel Abrahams.* Edited by G. A. Kohut. New York: Jewish Institute of Religion, 1927. Pp. 348-64.

Morawe, Günter. "Vergleich des Aufbaus der Danklieder und Hymnischen Bekenntnislieder (1QH) von Qumran mit dem Aufbau der Psalmen in Alten Testament und in Spätjudentum," *RevQ* 4 (1963) 323-56.

Mowinckel, Sigmund. "Die Metrik bei Jesus Sirach," *Studia Theologica 9* (1955) 137-65.

_____. "Psalms and Wisdom," *Wisdom in Israel and in the Ancient Near East.* VTSup 3. Edited by M. Noth and D. Winton Thomas. Leiden: E. J. Brill, 1955. Pp. 205-24.

Müller, Karlheinz. "Geschichte, Heilsgeschichte und Gesetz," *Literatur und Religion des Frühjudentums: Eine Einführung.* Edited by Johann Maier and Josef Schreiner. Würzburg: Echter, 1973. Pp. 73-105.

Noack, Bent. *Spätjudentum und Heilsgeschichte.* Stuttgart: W. Kohlhammer, 1971.

Pautrel, Raymond. "Ben Sira et le stoïcisme," *RSR* 51 (1963) 535-49.

Penar, Tadeusz. *Northwest Semitic Philology and the Hebrew Fragments of Ben Sira.* Biblica et Orientalia 28. Rome: Biblical Institute, 1975.

_____. "Three Philological Notes on the Hebrew Fragments of Ben Sira," *Bib* 57 (1976) 112-13.

Peters, Norbert. *Das Buch Jesus Sirach oder Ecclesiasticus.* Exegetisches Handbuch zum Alten Testament 25. Münster i. W.: Aschendorffsche, 1913.

Pfeiffer, R. H. *A History of New Testament Times with an Introduction to the Apocrypha.* New York: Harper and Row, 1949.

Priest, John. "Ben Sira 45,25 in the Light of the Qumran Literature," *RevQ* 5 (1964) 111-18.

Purvis, James D. "Ben Sira and the Foolish People of Shechem," *The Samaritan Pentateuch and the Origin of the Samaritan Sect.* HSM 2. Cambridge: Harvard University, 1968. Pp. 119-29.

Rickenbacher, Otto. *Weisheits Perikopen bei Ben Sira.* OBO 1. Freiburg: Universitätsverlag, 1973.

Rüger, Hans Peter. *Text und Textform im Hebräischen Sirach.* BZAW 112. Berlin: Walter de Gruyter and Company, 1970.

Rundgren, Frithiof. "Zum Lexicon des Alten Testaments," *AcOr* (Copenhagen) 21 (1953) 301-45.

Ryssel, V. "Die Sprüche Jesus', des Sohnes Sirachs," *Die Apokryphen und Pseudepigraphen des Alten Testaments: I.* Edited by Emil Kautzsch. Darmstadt: Wissenschaftliche, 1962. Pp. 230-475. (Reprinted from the edition of 1921.)

Sauermann, Otto. "Auch des Job gedachte er! (Sir 49:9)," *Dienst an der Lehre: Studien zur heutigen Philosophie und Theologie.* Wiener Beiträge zur Theologie, X. Edited by the Catholic Theological Faculty, University of Vienna. Vienna: Herder, 1965. Pp. 119-26.

Schildenberger, Johannes. "Die Bedeutung von Sir 48:24f. für die Verfasserfrage von Is 40-66," *Alttestamentliche Studien Friedrich Nötscher.* BBB 1. Edited by Hubert Junker and Johannes Botterweck. Bonn: Peter Hanstein, 1950. Pp. 188-204.

Schilling, Othmar. *Das Buch Jesus Sirach.* Herders Bibelkommentar, VII/2. Freiburg: Herder, 1956.

Schlatter, Adolf. *Geschichte Israels von Alexander dem Grossen bis Hadrian*. Mit einer Vorbemerkung zum Neudruck von Leonhard Goppelt. Stuttgart: Calwer, 1972.

Siebeneck, Robert T. "May Their Bones Return to Life!—Sirach's Praise of the Fathers," *CBQ* 21 (1959) 411-28.

Skehan, Patrick W. "Staves, and Nails, and Scribal Slips (Ben Sira 44:2-5)," *BASOR* 200 (1970) 66-71.

Smend, Rudolf. *Die Weisheit des Jesus Sirach*. Berlin: Georg Reimer, 1906. (Cited herein as Smend, *Commentary*.)

Snaith, John G. "Ben Sira's Supposed Love of Liturgy," *VT* 25 (1975) 167-74.

_____. "Biblical Quotations in the Hebrew of Ecclesiasticus," *JTS* N. S. 18 (1967) 1-12.

_____. *Ecclesiasticus or the Wisdom of Jesus, Son of Sirach*. The Cambridge Bible Commentary: New English Bible. New York: Cambridge University, 1974.

Stewart, R. A. "The Sinless High-Priest," *NTS* 14 (1967-68) 126-35.

Täubler, E. "Jerusalem 201-199 BCE: On the History of the Messianic Movement," *JQR* 37 (1946-47) 1-30, 125-37, 249-63.

Tcherikover, V. *Hellenistic Civilization and the Jews*. Translated by S. Applebaum. Philadelphia: Jewish Publication Society, 1966.

te Stroete, G. "Van Henoch tot Simon: Israels geschiedenis in de 'Lof der vaderen' van Sirach 44,1-50,24," *Vruchten van de uithof*. Festschrift H. A. Brongers. Edited by A. R. Hulst. Utrecht: Theologisch Instituut, 1974. Pp. 120-33.

Trinquet, J. "Les liens 'sadocites' de l'Ecrit de Damas, des manuscrits de la Mer Morte et de l'Ecclésiastique," *VT* 1 (1951) 287-92.

van den Born, A. *Wijsheid van Jesus Sirach (Ecclesiasticus)*. De Boeken van het Oude Testament. Roermond: J. J. Romen and Zonen, Uitgevers, 1968.

Vawter, Bruce. "Levitical Messianism and the NT," *The Bible in Current Catholic Thought*. Edited by John L. McKenzie. New York: Herder and Herder, 1962. Pp. 83-99.

von Rad, Gerhard. "The Wisdom of Jesus Sirach." *Wisdom in Israel*. New York: Abingdon, 1972. Pp. 240-62.

## III. CLASSICAL TEXTS

Aristotle. *Volume XVI: Problems, Books xxii-xxxviii; Rhetorica ad Alexandrum.* Translated by W. S. Hett and H. Rackham. Loeb Classical Library. Cambridge: Harvard University, 1957.

Aristotle. *Volume XXII: The "Art" of Rhetoric.* Translated by J. H. Freese. Loeb Classical Library. New York: G. P. Putnam's Sons, 1926.

Athenaeus. *The Deipnosophists: I-VII.* Translated by C. B. Gulick. Loeb Classical Library. Cambridge: Harvard University, 1928-51.

Bacchylides. *Lyra Graeca: III.* Translated by J. M. Edmonds. Loeb Classical Library. New York: G. P. Putnam's Sons, 1927.

Callimachus. *Callimachus and Lycophron; Aratus.* Translated by A. W. Mair and G. R. Mair. Loeb Classical Library. New York: G. P. Putnam's Sons, 1921.

[Cicero.] *Ad C. Herennium de Ratione Dicendi* (Rhetorica ad Herennium). Translated by Harry Caplan. Loeb Classical Library. Cambridge: Harvard University, 1954.

Cicero. *De Inventione; de Optimo Genere Oratorum; Topica.* Translated by H. M. Hubbell. Loeb Classical Library. Cambridge: Harvard University, 1949.

Cicero. *De Oratore, I: Books I-II.* Translated by E. W. Sutton and H. Rackham. Loeb Classical Library. Cambridge: Harvard University, 1959.

Cornelius Nepos. *Lucius Annaeus Florus: Epitome of Roman History; Cornelius Nepos.* Translated by E. S. Forster. Loeb Classical Library. New York: G. P. Putnam's Sons, 1929.

Diogenes Laertius. *Lives of Eminent Philosophers: I-II.* Translated by R. D. Hicks. Loeb Classical Library. Cambridge: Harvard University, 1970-72.

Hermogenes. *Hermogenes Opera* (Rhetores Graeci, VI). Edited by Hugo Rabe. Leipzig: B. G. Teubner, 1913.

Hunt, A. S. *The Oxyrhynchus Papyri: IX.* London: Oxford University Press for the Egypt Exploration Society, 1912.

Isocrates. *Volumes I-III.* Translated by George Norlin (Vol. I-II) and Larue Van Hook (Vol. III). Loeb Classical Library. Cambridge: Harvard University, 1954.

Jacoby, Felix. *Die Fragmente der Griechischen Historiker: IIB, Nr. 106-261.* Leiden: E. J. Brill, 1962.

Jacoby, Felix. *Die Fragmente der Griechischen Historiker: IIIC, Nr. 709-856.* Leiden: E. J. Brill, 1958.

Lycurgus. *The Minor Attic Orators: II.* Translated by J. O. Burtt. Loeb Classical Library. Cambridge: Harvard University, 1962.

Müller, Karl. *Fragmenta Historicorum Graecorum: II-III.* Paris: Editore Ambrosio Firmin Didot, 1928.

Philo. *Volume VIII: On the Special Laws, Book IV; On the Virtues; On Rewards and Punishments.* Translated by F. H. Colson. Loeb Classical Library. Cambridge: Harvard University, 1960.

Philo. *Volume IX: Every Good Man is Free; On the Contemplative Life; On the Eternity of the World; Against Flaccus; Apology for the Jews; On Providence.* Translated by F. H. Colson. Loeb Classical Library. Cambridge: Harvard University, 1967.

Philodemus. *Philodemus Volumina Rhetorica: I-II.* Edited by Siegfried Sudhaus. Leipzig: B. G. Teubner, 1892, 1896.

Pindar. *The Odes of Pindar.* Translated by J. E. Sandys. Loeb Classical Library. New York: G. P. Putnam's Sons, 1930.

Plato. *Platonis Opera, II: Symposium; Phaedrus.* Edited by J. Burnet. Scriptorum Classicorum Bibliotheca Oxoniensis. Oxford: Clarendon, 1901.

Plato. *Volume I: Euthyphro; Apology; Crito; Phaedo; Phaedrus.* Translated by H. N. Fowler. Loeb Classical Library. Cambridge: Harvard University, 1960.

Plato. *Volume III: Lysis; Symposium; Gorgias.* Translated by W. R. M. Lamb. Loeb Classical Library. Cambridge: Harvard University, 1946.

Plato. *Volume IX: Timaeus; Critias; Cleitophon; Menexenus; Epistles.* Translated by R. G. Bury. Loeb Classical Library. New York: G. P. Putnam's Sons, 1929.

Quintilian. *Institutio Oratoria: Volumes I-IV.* Translated by H. E. Butler. Loeb Classical Library. Cambridge: Harvard University, 1953.

Simonides. *Lyra Graeca: II.* Translated by J. M. Edmonds. Loeb Classical Library. New York: G. P. Putnam's Sons, 1924.

Suetonius. *Volume II: The Lives of Illustrious Men.* Translated by J. C. Rolfe. Loeb Classical Library. Cambridge: Harvard University, 1959.

Tacitus. *Dialogus; Agricola; Germania.* Translated by William Peterson. Loeb Classical Library. New York: G. P. Putnam's Sons, 1932.

Theocritus. *Theocritus Edited with a Translation and Commentary: I-II.* Edited by A. S. F. Gow. Cambridge: Cambridge University, 1952.

Xenophon. *Scripta Minora.* Translated by E. C. Marchant. Loeb Classical Library. New York: G. P. Putnam's Sons, 1925.

## IV. LITERATURE RELATIVE TO
## THE FORM OF SIRACH 44-50

Ackroyd, P. R. and Evans, C. F. (eds.) *The Cambridge History of the Bible, I: From the Beginnings to Jerome.* Cambridge: Cambridge University, 1970.

Baldwin, Charles Sears. *Ancient Rhetoric and Poetic.* Reprinted from the 1924 edition. Westport, CT: Greenwood, 1971.

_____. *Medieval Rhetoric and Poetic.* Reprinted from the 1928 edition. Gloucester, MA: Peter Smith, 1959.

Bloch, Renée. "Midrash," *DBSup* 5. Edited by L. Pirot, A. Robert, and H. Cazelles. Paris: Librairie Letouzey et Ané, 1957. Cols. 1263-1281.

_____. "Note methodologique pour l'étude de la littérature rabbinique," *RSR* 43 (1955) 194-227.

Bowra, C. M. "Simonides on the Fallen of Thermopylae," *Classical Philology* 28 (1933) 277-81.

Bruns, Ivo. *Das literarische Porträt der Griechen im fünften und vierten Jahrhundert vor Christi Geburt.* Berlin: Wilhelm Hertz, 1896.

Bryant, Donald C. *Ancient Greek and Roman Rhetoricians: A Biographical Dictionary.* Compiled for the Speech Association of America. Columbia, MO: Artcraft, 1968.

Buchheit, Vinzenz. *Untersuchungen zur Theorie des Genos Epideiktikon von Gorgias bis Aristoteles.* Munich: Max Hueber, 1960.

Burgess, Theodore C. "Epideictic Literature," *University of Chicago Studies in Classical Philology: III.* Chicago: The University of Chicago, 1902. Pp. 89-261.

Bursian, Conrad. *Der Rhetor Menandros und seine Schriften.* Abhandlungen der K. Bayer. Akademie der Wissenschaft I., Cl. XVI:3. Munich: Verlag der K. Akademie, 1882.

Childs, Brevard S. "Midrash and the Old Testament," *Understanding the Sacred Text.* Edited by John Reumann. Valley Forge: Judson, 1972. Pp. 47-59.

Clark, Donald Lemen. *Rhetoric in Greco-Roman Education*. New York: Columbia University, 1957.

Clarke, Ernest G. *The Wisdom of Solomon*. The Cambridge Bible Commentary: New English Bible. Cambridge: Cambridge University, 1973.

Crusius. "Enkomion," *PW: V,2*. Cols. 2581-83.

Daube, David. "Rabbinic Methods of Interpretation and Hellenistic Literature," *HUCA* 22 (1949) 239-64.

Delcourt, M. "Les biographies anciennes d'Euripide," *L'Antiquite Classique* 2 (1933) 271-90.

de Romilly, Jacqueline. *Magic and Rhetoric in Ancient Greece*. Cambridge: Harvard University, 1975.

de Vries, G. J. *A Commentary on the Phaedrus of Plato*. Amsterdam: Adolf M. Hakkert, 1969.

Dihle, Albrecht. *Studien zur Griechischen Biographie*. Abhandlungen der Akademie der Wissenschaften in Göttingen philologisch-historische Klasse: III, 37. Göttingen: Vandenhoeck und Ruprecht, 1956.

Eisenhut, Werner. *Einführung in die antike Rhetorik und ihre Geschichte*. Darmstadt: Wissenschaftliche Buchgesellschaft, 1974.

Fischel, Henry A. *Rabbinic Literature and Greco-Roman Philosophy: A Study of Epicurea and Rhetorica in Early Midrashic Writings*. SPB 21. Leiden: E. J. Brill, 1973.

_____. "Story and History: Observations on Greco-Roman Rhetoric and Pharisaism," *American Oriental Society, Middle West Branch: Semi-Centennial Volume*. Edited by Denis Sinor. Bloomington: Indiana University, 1969. Pp. 59-88.

_____. "The Transformation of Wisdom in the World of Midrash," *Aspects of Wisdom in Judaism and Early Christianity*. Edited by Robert L. Wilken. Notre Dame: University of Notre Dame, 1975. Pp. 67-101.

Focke, Friedrich. "Synkrisis," *Hermes* 58 (1923) 327-68.

Fraustadt, Georgius. *Encomiorum in Litteris Graecis usque ad Romanam Aetatem Historia*. Leipzig: Typis Roberti Noske Bornensis, 1909.

Freeman, Kathleen. *Ancilla to the Pre-Socratic Philosophers: A Complete Translation of the Fragments in Diels, Fragmente der Vorsokratiker*. Cambridge: Harvard University, 1957.

_____. *The Pre-Socratic Philosophers: A Companion to Diels, Fragmente der Vorsokratiker.* 3rd edition. Oxford: Basil Blackwell, 1953.

Frey, Hermann. *Der βίος Εὐριπίδου des Satyros und seine literaturgeschichtliche Bedeutung.* Zürich: Druck von Friedrich Andreas Perthes A. G. Gotha, 1919.

Funailoi. "Suetonius," *PW: Band IV A, 1.* Cols. 593-641.

Gerhardsson, Birger. *Memory and Manuscript: Oral and Written Transmission in Rabbinic Judaism and Early Christianity.* ASNU 22. Lund: C. W. K. Gleerup, 1961.

Gerstinger, H. "Biographie," *RAC 2.* Edited by Theodor Klausner. Stuttgart: Anton Hiersemann, 1954. Cols. 386-91.

_____. "Satyros, Bios Euripidou," *Wiener Studien* 38 (1916) 54-71.

Goldin, Judah. "A Philosophical Session in a Tannaite Academy," *Traditio* 12 (1965) 1-21.

Goodenough, Erwin R. *An Introduction to Philo Judaeus.* 2nd edition revised. New York: Barnes and Noble, 1962.

Gudeman, Alfred. *Tacitus: Agricola and Germania.* Boston: Allyn and Bacon, 1900.

Gueraud, O. and Jouquet, T. (eds.). "Un livre d'écolier," *Publications de la société Royale Egyptienne de Papyrologie, Textes et documents II.* Cairo, 1938.

Gunkel, H. *The Psalms: A Form-Critical Introduction.* Facet Books: Biblical Series, No. 19. Philadelphia: Fortress, 1967.

Gunkel, H. and Begrich, J. *Einleitung in die Psalmen.* Göttingen: Vandenhoeck und Ruprecht, 1933.

Hadas, Moses. *Hellenistic Culture: Fusion and Diffusion.* Morningside Heights, NY: Columbia University, 1959.

Hadas, Moses. *A History of Greek Literature.* New York: Columbia University, 1950.

Hadas, Moses and Smith, Morton. *Heroes and Gods: Spiritual Biographies in Antiquity.* Religious Perspectives, Vol. 13. London: Routledge and Kegan Paul, 1965.

Hayes, John H. (ed.) *Old Testament Form Criticism.* San Antonio: Trinity University, 1974.

Heinemann, Isaak. *Philons Griechische und Jüdische Bildung.* Hildesheim: Georg Olms, 1962. (Reprinted from the original edition of 1929-32.)

Jaeger, Werner. *Paideia: The Ideals of Greek Culture: I-III.* Translated by Gilbert Highet. New York: Oxford University, 1939, 1944.

Jebb, R. C. *The Attic Orators from Antiphon to Isaeus: Vol II.* New York: Macmillan and Co., 1893.

Kennedy, George. *The Art of Persuasion in Greece.* Princeton: Princeton University, 1963.

_____. *The Art of Rhetoric in the Roman World: 300 BC-AD 300.* Princeton: Princeton University, 1972.

_____. "The Earliest Rhetorical Handbooks," *American Journal of Philology* 80 (1959) 167-78.

Kind. "Satyros," *PW: Band II A, 1.* Cols. 224-35.

Knox, Wilfred L. *Some Hellenistic Elements in Early Christianity.* The 1942 Schweich Lectures of the British Academy. London: Oxford University, 1944.

Kornhardt, Hildegard. *Exemplum: Eine bedeutungsgeschichte Studie.* Göttingen: Robert Noske, 1936.

Kraus, H. J. *Psalmen: I-II.* BKAT 15/1-2. Neukirchen: Neukirchener, 1960.

Launey, Marcel. *Recherches sur les armées hellénistiques.* Bibliothèque des écoles Françaises d'Athènes et de Rome, 169:2. Paris: E. de Bocard, 1950.

Lausberg, Heinrich. *Elemente der literarischen Rhetorik.* 3rd edition. Munich: Max Hueber, 1967.

le Déaut, Roger. "Apropos a Definition of Midrash," *Int* 25 (1971) 259-82.

Leo, Friedrich. *Die griechisch-römische Biographie nach ihrer Literarischen Form.* Leipzig: B. G. Teubner, 1901.

_____. "Satyros ΒΙΟΣ ΕΥΡΙΠΙΔΟΥ," *Ausgewählte kleine Schriften: II.* Edited by Eduaro Fraenkel. Rome: Edizioni di Storia e Letteratura, 1960. Pp. 365-83.

Lesky, Albin. *A History of Greek Literature.* New York: Thomas Y. Crowell, 1966.

Lieberman, Saul. *Greek in Jewish Palestine.* New York: The Jewish Theological Seminary of America, 1942.

_____. *Hellenism in Jewish Palestine*. Texts and Studies of the Jewish Theological Seminary of America, Vol. 18. New York: The Jewish Theological Seminary of America, 1950.

Lietzmann, H. "Hieronymos," *PW: Band VIII, 2*. Cols. 1565-81.

Lohse, Eduard (ed.). *Die Texte aus Qumran: Hebräisch und Deutsch*. 2nd edition. Munich: Kösel, 1971.

Lumpe, A. "Exemplum," *RAC* 6. Edited by Theodor Klausner. Stuttgart: Anton Hiersemann, 1966. Cols. 1229-57.

Maass, F. "Von den Ursprüngen der rabbinischen Schriftauslegung," *ZTK* 52 (1955) 129-61.

McCall, Marsh H., Jr. *Ancient Rhetorical Theories of Simile and Comparison*. Cambridge: Harvard University, 1969.

Maier, Johann. *Die Texte vom Toten Meer, II: Anmerkungen*. Munich/ Basel: Ernst Reinhardt, 1960.

Marrou, H. I. *A History of Education in Antiquity*. Translated by George Lamb. New York: Sheed and Ward, 1956.

Miller, Merril P. "Targum, Midrash and the Use of the Old Testament in the New Testament," *JSJ* 2 (1971) 29-82.

Misch, Georg. *A History of Autobiography in Antiquity: Volume I*. International Library of Sociology and Social Reconstruction, Karl Mannheim, ed. Translated from the 3rd German edition of 1949-50 by E. W. Dickes. Westport: CT: Greenwood, 1973.

Momigliano, Arnaldo. *Alien Wisdom: The Limits of Hellenization*. New York: Cambridge University, 1975.

_____. *The Development of Greek Biography*. Cambridge: Harvard University, 1971.

Mowinckel, Sigmund. *Psalmenstudien: I-VI*. Amsterdam: Schippers, 1961.

_____. "Psalms and Wisdom," *Wisdom in Israel and in the Ancient Near East*. VTSup 3. Edited by M. Noth and D. Winton Thomas. Leiden: E. J. Brill, 1955. Pp. 205-24.

_____. *The Psalms in Israel's Worship: Vols. I-II*. Oxford: Basil Blackwell, 1962.

Münzer. "Sotion," *PW: Band III A, 1*. Cols. 1235-39.

Murphy, James J. (ed.) *A Synoptic History of Classical Rhetoric*. New York: Random House, 1972.

Murphy, Roland E. "Yeşer in the Qumran literature," *Bib* 39 (1958) 334-44.

Neusner, Jacob. "'Pharisaic-Rabbinic' Judaism: A Clarification," *HR* 12 (1972-73) 250-70.

Norden, Eduard. *Die Antike Kunstprosa: Vols. I-II.* Reprint of the 5th edition. Stuttgart: B. G. Teubner, 1958.

Nilsson, Martin P. *Die Hellenistische Schule.* Munich: C. H. Beck, 1955.

Perelman, Ch. and Olbrechts-Tyteca, L. *The New Rhetoric: A Treatise on Argumentation.* Translated by John Wilkinson and Purcell Weaver. Notre Dame: University of Notre Dame, 1969.

Perlman, S. "The Historical Example, Its Use and Importance as Political Propaganda in the Attic Orators," *Scripta Hierosolymitana: VII.* Edited by A. Fuks and I. Halpern. Jerusalem: Magnes, 1961.

Pfuhl. "Hermippos," *PW: Band VIII, 1.* Cols. 844-57.

Rabin, Chaim. *The Zadokite Documents.* 2nd edition revised. New York: Oxford University, 1958.

Reese, James M. *Hellenistic Influence on the Book of Wisdom and Its Consequences.* AnBib 41. Rome: Biblical Institute, 1970.

Roberts, W. Rhys. *Greek Rhetoric and Literary Criticism.* New York: Longmans, Green and Co., 1928.

Ronconi, A. "Exitus Illustrium Virorum," *RAC* 6. Edited by Theodor Klausner. Stuttgart: Anton Hiersemann, 1966. Cols. 1258-67.

Rose, H. J. *A Handbook of Greek Literature.* 4th edition revised. London: Methuen and Co., Ltd., 1951.

Rost, Leonhard. *Judaism Outside the Hebrew Canon: An Introduction to the Documents.* Translated by David E. Green. Nashville: Abingdon, 1976.

Russell, D. A. and Winterbottom, M. (eds.). *Ancient Literary Criticism: The Principal Texts in New Translations.* London: Oxford University, 1972.

Sanders, James A. *The Dead Sea Psalms Scroll.* Ithaca: Cornell University, 1967.

Sandmel, Samuel. "The Ancient Mind and Ours," *Understanding the Sacred Text.* Edited by John Reumann. Valley Forge: Judson, 1972. Pp. 29-43.

_____. "The Haggada within Scripture," *JBL* 80 (1961) 105-22.

Schmid, W. "'Επιδειξις," *PW: Band VI, 1.* Cols. 53-56.

Schwarz, Ottilie J. R. *Der erste Teil der Damaskusschrift und das Alte Testament.* Lichtland: Diest, 1965.

Smith, Morton. "Prolegomena to a Discussion of Aretalogies, Divine Men, the Gospels and Jesus," *JBL* 90 (1971) 174-99.

Smith, Robert W. *The Art of Rhetoric in Alexandria: Its Theory and Practice in the Ancient World.* The Hague: Martinus Nijhoff, 1974.

Spicq, C. *L'Epitre aux hébreux: Vol. I, Introduction; Vol. II, Commentaire.* Paris: J. Gabalda, 1952-53.

Stein, S. "The Influence of Symposia Literature on the Literary Form of the Pesah Haggadah," *JJS* 8 (1957) 13-44.

Stuart, Duane Reed. *Epochs of Greek and Roman Biography.* Berkeley: University of California, 1928.

Susemihl, Franz. *Geschichte der griechischen Literatur in der Alexandrinerzeit: I-II.* Leipzig: B. G. Teubner, 1891, 1892.

Tarn, Wm. and Griffith, G. T. *Hellenistic Civilization.* 3rd edition. London: Edward Arnold, Ltd., 1952.

Thyen, Hartwig. *Der Stil der Jüdisch-Hellenistischen Homilie.* Göttingen: Vandenhoeck und Ruprecht, 1955.

Tiede, David Lenz. *The Charismatic Figure as Miracle Worker.* SBLDS 1. Missoula: Scholars Press, 1972.

Vermes, Geza. "Bible and Midrash: Early Old Testament Exegesis," *The Cambridge History of the Bible, Vol. I: From the Beginnings to Jerome.* Edited by P. R. Ackroyd and C. F. Evans. Cambridge: The University Press, 1970. Pp. 199-231.

_____. *The Dead Sea Scrolls in English.* Baltimore: Penguin Books, 1962.

Volkmann, Richard. *Die Rhetorik der Griechen und Römer in systematischer Uebersicht.* 2nd edition. Leipzig: B. G. Teubner, 1885.

von Kienle, Walter. *Die Berichte über die Sukzessionen der Philosophen in der hellenistischen und spätantiken Literatur.* Berlin: Philosophischen Fakultät der Freien Universität, 1961.

Wacholder, Ben Zion. *Eupolemus: A Study of Judaeo-Greek Literature.* Monographs of the Hebrew Union College, No. 3. Cincinnati: Hebrew Union College, 1974.

_____. *Nicolaus of Damascus.* University of California Publications in History: Vol. 75. Berkeley: University of California, 1962.

Wifstrand, Albert. *Die alte Kirche und die griechische Bildung.* Bern: A. Francke, 1967.

Wissowa, G. "Cornelius Nepos," *PW: Band IV, 1.* Cols. 1408-17.

Wright, Addison G. *The Literary Genre Midrash.* Staten Island, NY: Alba House, 1967.

Ziegler, K. "Panegyrikos," *PW: Band XVIII, 3.* Cols. 559-71.

# Index

## SIRACH PASSAGES

## BIBLICAL PASSAGES

## QUMRAN AND RABBINIC MATERIALS